The
Foster Care
Crisis

Child, Youth, and Family Services

The Foster Care Crisis

Translating Research into Policy and Practice

Edited by Patrick A. Curtis,
Grady Dale Jr., and
Joshua C. Kendall

Foreword by
Senator John D. Rockefeller IV

Published by the University of
Nebraska Press, Lincoln and London,
in association with the
Child Welfare League of America

Portions of chapter 6 were previously published
in "Welfare reform and child welfare services"
in A. J. Kahn and Sheila B. Kamerman, eds.,
Child Welfare in the Context of Welfare Reform (pp. 1–35),
Confronting the New Politics of Child and Family Policy in the
United States, vol. 5, 1997, New York: Columbia
University School of Social Work.

Library of Congress Cataloging-in-Publication Data
The foster care crisis: translating research into policy and practice /
edited by Patrick A. Curtis, Grady Dale Jr., and Joshua C. Kendall;
foreword by John D. Rockefeller IV.
p.   cm.—(Child, youth, and family services)
"In association with the Child Welfare League of America."
Includes bibliographical references and index.
ISBN 0-8032-1483-9 (cl: alk. paper).—ISBN 0-8032-6399-6 (pa: alk. paper)
1. Foster children—United States.
2. Foster children—Services for—United States.
3. Foster home care—United States.
4. Child welfare—United States.
5. Child care services—United States.
I. Curtis, Patrick A. (Patrick Almond), 1944–
II. Dale, Grady.   III. Kendall, Joshua C., 1960–
IV. Series.
HV881.F636   1999
332.73′3′0973—dc21
99-13225   CIP
Published by the University of Nebraska Press
in association with the
Child Welfare League of America

For Adam Simon Super Curtis

Contents

vii

Foreword

On 19 November 1997, President Clinton signed into law the Adoption and Safe Families Act. The most significant overhaul of the American foster care system since 1980, the new law is the result of an unprecedented bipartisan effort on behalf of America's abused and neglected children. For the first time, this law makes it clear that the health and safety of a child are paramount. This simple but compelling statement will refocus our efforts to help abused and neglected children. In this landmark legislation, we have preserved and enhanced the range of choices available to promote the health and safety of children in foster care. Where appropriate, the law helps to speed a child's adoption into a loving family. At the same time, the Adoption and Safe Families Act preserves vital funding and services to reunify children with their families when it is safe to do so.

What makes the events of this year most exciting is that federal policy has begun to find the balance that the National Commission on Children and organizations like the Child Welfare League of America have sought for years. The Adoption and Safe Families Act has finally embraced the principle that each child is unique. There should be a range of services to respond to the special needs of each child and each family. My colleagues and I have worked hard to make sure that the foster care system now has the federal policy foundations to adequately serve all of these purposes.

Permanency has a new priority. For those children who have had to wait too long in a foster care system, the best option for permanency is often adoption into a safe and loving home. For some families, reunification is still the appropriate option. For those caring relatives and friends who are

ix

raising abused and neglected children, we must make certain that kinship care has the recognition and understanding it deserves. The Adoption and Safe Families Act endorses a range of choices, all of which allow foster parents, social workers, lawyers, and judges in the field to make the best, safest, and most efficient decisions about children in their care.

As exciting as it is, this new law is only the beginning of the story. Finding effective solutions to the troubling issues of abuse and neglect remains a challenge for our country and our communities. The dedicated people working on the front lines need the proper support and training to make good decisions for children and families. Together with those workers who experience the problems firsthand, we must do more to prevent abuse and neglect, not just cope with its tragic consequences.

This book will play a vital role in sharing the policy solutions that have been found to be most effective in daily child welfare practice. Let me emphasize that throughout our work on the Adoption and Safe Families Act, we relied again and again on success stories from the field. We took a thorough look at dozens of individual state and local programs. We asked questions: Which court systems were most effective at training their judges and attorneys? Which states were most effective in forging public agency and private nonprofit partnerships? How can we encourage states to replicate other local programs that have really worked?

The answers to these important questions helped chart the course for this legislation. They should also guide us toward the next steps in designing a comprehensive federal policy for child welfare. I hope that the content of this book, the product of careful research and analysis from child welfare experts in the field, will encourage the same kinds of creative processes among child welfare experts across the country.

A significant accomplishment, the Adoption and Safe Families Act of 1997 is only the first step in a series of necessary reforms. No federal law will prevent abuse and neglect of vulnerable children on its own. That is why I look forward to using much of the research in this publication to continue our efforts to ensure that every abused and neglected child is able to find a safe, stable, and permanent home. In the process of making sure every child's needs are appropriately addressed, we must be careful not to ignore the interests of the family, the foster parents, and the kinship caregivers who step forward to care for these children. We also cannot forget the frontline social workers and researchers who work so hard with so few resources.

I want to extend my thanks to the University of Nebraska Press, the Child Welfare League of America, and the dedicated participants in this project for their ongoing contributions to improve the child welfare system. It is my sincere hope that *The Foster Care Crisis: Translating Research into Policy and Practice* will continue to bring focus and energy to the work still left to be done on behalf of America's most vulnerable children.

Senator John D. Rockefeller IV
West Virginia

Acknowledgments

The editors would like to thank all the individuals who helped make this project possible. Thanks to Nancy Rosen, former acquisitions editor for the University of Nebraska Press, who has to take some credit and responsibility for the end result because it was her idea, and also to Douglas Clayton, our original editor at the University of Nebraska Press. Thanks to the program staff at the Child Welfare League of America, particularly Kathy Barbell, director of Family Foster Care Services, for her comments and insights, and to Amy Gordon, CWLA research associate, who helped us pull together the final manuscript. In addition, Dr. Curtis would like to thank his wife, Stacia Iona Super, and Dr. Dale would like to thank his wife, Helen, for their undaunted courage and support.

Introduction: The Chronic Nature of the Foster Care Crisis

Patrick A. Curtis

The term *foster care crisis* does not refer to the institution of foster care but to the reality that too many children are staying in foster care for too long a time. The crisis is not too many children living away from home for their own protection and safety but the existence of a number of complex and chronic social problems that generate at-risk children, families who cannot protect their children from harm, and the need for foster care services. The real crises are, among other factors, how child welfare is funded by the federal government, poverty, the growing number of single-mother households, the misuse of alcohol and other drugs, homelessness, and the ever increasing number of children reported as victims of child abuse and neglect.

Although most children enter foster care as the result of child maltreatment, many enter care as status offenders or delinquent minors. The intent is to shelter them in a family-like environment while parents are assisted in correcting whatever led to the need for foster care services. Most children return home, but many do not. For those unable to return home, a permanent solution to their dependency, such as adoption, is sought. The reasons many children do not return home in a timely fashion, are not adopted, or do not find permanent living arrangements are examined in this book from the perspective of research and its potential contributions to child welfare policies and practices.

This volume has its origins in a symposium presented at the 103rd annual meeting of the American Psychological Association in New York City in August 1995. Organized by Grady Dale Jr. and Joshua Kendall of the

Health Clinic at the Baltimore City Department of Social Services, this panel is believed to have been the first formal discussion of foster care research and policy conducted under the auspices of the APA. The excitement generated by the presentations gave impetus to further attempts to disseminate the scholarship on foster care.

The book has three primary objectives that correspond roughly to its main sections: to provide an overview of the foster care crisis, to describe the special needs of children living in foster care, and to identify policies and practices that address the foster care crisis. Thus, in chapters 1 and 2, we provide an overview of recent advances in describing and measuring the foster care crisis. In chapters 3 through 5, various contributors focus on the special needs of children living in foster care. In chapters 6 through 10, the emphasis shifts to particular policies and practices that will help alleviate the foster care crisis. The book concludes with a vision of what foster care will look like in the 21st century. The book's target audience includes direct service practitioners, pediatricians, psychologists, social workers, child protective service workers, program managers, policy analysts, and legislators.

In the present political climate, public discussion of many social problems has often been reduced to sound bites and simplistic solutions. This troubling phenomenon is particularly in evidence in current debates over welfare reform, crime and delinquency, and the plight of children in the child welfare system. Instead of addressing the complex issues, some national leaders have steered the public's attention toward such alleged quick fixes as orphanages for indigent children, boot camps for antisocial youth, and the prosecution of increasingly younger juvenile offenders as adults. This book aims to elevate the level of public discourse on these at-risk children by carefully delineating their problems and needs and by proposing a series of policy and practice options designed to effect long-term changes.

Foster Care in the United States

Foster care, often misunderstood by professionals, policymakers, and the general public, is a generic term for children living in out-of-home care. Most foster children are wards of the state with histories of child abuse or neglect. Historically, foster care was referred to as "boarding-out." The term implied that foster parents, almost always nonrelatives, were reimbursed for the expenses of caring for dependent children in private households under the assumption that the arrangement was temporary. (In adoptive homes, once referred to as "placing-out," parents were not reimbursed for expenses, and the arrangement was expected to result in adoption.)

There are four basic types of foster care: family (nonrelative) foster care, kinship (relative) care, therapeutic foster care, and residential (congregate) group care. (Although not foster care per se, children in residential group care are represented in national statistics as living in foster care.) Therapeutic foster care is also referred to as treatment foster care or specialized foster care. In some jurisdictions, terms such as therapeutic as opposed to treatment foster care have special meanings, but there is much overlap in meaning from place to place. Although these distinctions are generally not important to the public, they have many implications for practice and policy, including the funding of child welfare services and research. For the sake of discussion, the terms *out-of-home care* and *foster care* are used interchangeably in this book. The terms *family foster care, kinship care, therapeutic foster care*, and *residential group care* are used to refer to specific types of out-of-home care.

Family foster care typically includes 24-hour supervision by nonrelative laypersons in private homes that are licensed or approved and then monitored by either private or public child welfare agencies. Although many foster parents are recruited as potential adoptive parents, most children are placed temporarily. Kinship care typically includes 24-hour supervision by relatives, overwhelmingly by grandparents, in private homes that are normally licensed or approved and then monitored by private or public child welfare agencies.

Hawkins (1990) identified nine characteristics typical of many, but not all, therapeutic foster care programs: (a) foster parents are considered professionals; (b) foster parents take care of only one or two children; (c) case managers have small caseloads; (d) foster parents are given special training; (e) foster parents implement the child's treatment plan; (f) foster parents are provided with professional and emotional support; (g) crisis intervention services are available 24 hours each day; (h) assessment and fulfillment of each child's educational needs are emphasized; and (i) each child's system of care is coordinated. In addition, parents may be required to have a special background, such as teaching or health care, and one parent may be required not to work out of the home. A higher board rate is normally provided to therapeutic foster care parents than is provided to family foster care parents. Residential group care typically includes 24-hour supervision by nonrelative professional staff in dormitory or cottage-like facilities. Like psychiatric hospitals, these facilities emphasize the treatment of emotionally and behaviorally disturbed children, but they usually provide less restrictive care and employ fewer medical professionals. However, wide program variation makes generalization difficult. According to the Child Welfare League of America, out of a total of approximately 483,000 children living in out-of-home care at the end of 1995, 49% were living in family foster care, 23% in kinship care, 15% in residential group care, 1.7% in therapeutic foster care, and 11.3% in other facilities such as emergency shelters and psychiatric hospitals (Petit & Curtis, 1997).

Examining the Foster Care Crisis

If we refer to the foster care crisis as too many children staying in out-of-home care for too long a time, the crisis is not new. In 1909 one of the concerns addressed by the first White House Conference on Children was the estimated 170,000 children living in out-of-home care (approximately 95,000 in orphanages and institutions for the developmentally disabled, 50,000 in foster care, and 25,000 in juvenile correctional facilities) (Bremner, 1983). In a companion piece to the Pittsburgh survey of poverty conducted in the early 1910s (Kellogg, 1914), Florence Lattimore compiled statistics and case histories of children living in institutions in Allegheny County and concluded that the great majority of children she observed were self-maintaining and never should have been removed from their homes in the first place. Her criticisms sound very modern and probably represent the first published evidence of longstanding problems in child welfare, such as the failure to preserve family connections, the separation of siblings from one another, the restricting of family visiting in institutions, the failure to prosecute men who desert their families, and the failure to utilize less restrictive alternatives to institutional care.

A few studies of child abuse and neglect appeared in the professional literature during the first half of the 20th century, but it was not until the publication of "The Battered Child Syndrome" by C. Henry Kempe and his colleagues in 1962 that the general public began to become aware of child abuse and neglect as a significant social problem (Kempe, Silverman, Steele, Droegemueller, & Silver, 1962). In 1974 Congress passed the Child

Abuse Prevention and Treatment Act (CAPTA), which provided for the collection of national statistics, the conduct of national household surveys, and funding for research and demonstration projects, as well as funding to the states for the prevention and treatment of child abuse and neglect. In order to be eligible for the funds, states had to pass surveillance laws that required professionals, usually physicians and teachers, to report child abuse and neglect to local child welfare agencies, resulting in a dramatic impact on the out-of-home care system. By 1977 the number of children living in out-of-home care had reached approximately 502,000, almost 8 children out of every 1,000 in the U.S. population (Westat, 1978).

Partly in response to this phenomenon, Congress passed Public Law 96-272, the Adoption Assistance and Child Welfare Act in 1980. The law required that states make reasonable efforts in preventing the unnecessary placement of children into foster care. If placement prevention was not possible and children were unable to be returned home safely, states were required to seek permanent solutions to the children's dependency, preferably through adoption. As a result, from 1980 to 1982 the number of children in out-of-home care decreased, but this figure has since grown dramatically every year (American Public Welfare Association [APWA], 1993). Several factors led to the increase in the number of children entering care, including how child welfare is funded by the federal government, population and poverty, the number of minorities in the child population, single-mother households, misuse of alcohol and other drugs, homelessness, and the ever increasing number of children reported as victims of child abuse and neglect. Because fairly reliable approximations of the out-of-home care are available in the end-of-year census for each year from 1980 to 1995, most analyses in this chapter employ that 16-year time frame whenever possible.

THE NUMBERS

From 1980 to 1995 the number of children living in out-of-home care increased 59.9%, from approximately 302,000 to approximately 483,000 (Petit & Curtis, 1997; APWA, 1997). See Figure 1. Most analyses of the foster care population employ the end-of-year census as the primary measure. This is a useful measure as it also approximates the number of children living in out-of-home care on any given day, but the end-of-year census does not account for the full scope of the foster care crisis. If all the children who enter foster care in any given year are added to the end-of-year census for

Figure 1. Children in out-of-home care, end-of-year census, 1980–1995.

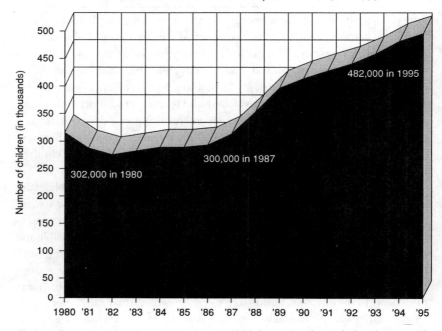

Sources: Petit, M. R., & Curtis, P. A. (1997). *Child abuse and neglect: A look at the states: The* CWLA *stat book*. Washington DC: Child Welfare League of America. American Public Welfare Association. (1997, February). *Voluntary Cooperative Information System*. Washington DC: Author.

the previous year (making the assumption they are still there on 1 January), the total for each year is much larger. From 1982 (the first year the number of children entering out-of-home care was available) to 1995, the total number of children in foster care increased 63.2%, from 435,000 to 710,000. See Figure 2.

POPULATION AND POVERTY

The growing number of children living in foster care paralleled increases in the number of children in the U.S. population, the number of children living in poverty, the ethnic populations, and the number of single-parent households. Poverty is sometimes overlooked in the analysis of foster care, yet about half of all children living in out-of-home care come from families eligible for AFDC (U.S. House, 1996). From 1980 to 1995 the number of individuals in the United States under 18 years of age increased a modest

Figure 2. Total number of children in out-of-home care, 1982–1995.

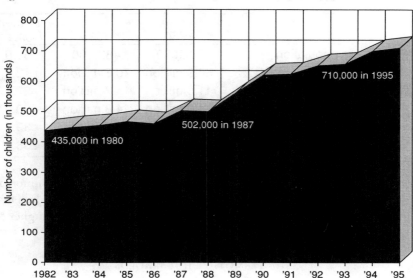

Sources: Petit, M. R., & Curtis, P. A. (1997). *Child abuse and neglect: A look at the states: The CWLA stat book.* Washington DC: Child Welfare League of America. American Public Welfare Association. (1997, February). *Voluntary Cooperative Information System.* Washington DC: Author.

12.2%, from 62.9 million to 70.6 million, but the number of children living in poverty increased 27.8%, from 11.5 million to 14.7 million (Baugher & Lamison-White, 1995). See Table 1.

MINORITY CHILDREN

A disproportionate number of children living in the out-of-home care system are minorities, with the greatest disparity between the number of African-American children in the U.S. population compared to the out-of-home care population. The results of a 50-state survey conducted by the Child Welfare League of America found that in 1995 African-American children made up approximately 16% of the U.S. child population compared to approximately 44% of the out-of-home care population (Petit & Curtis, 1997). Although an excellent review of the literature by Courtney, Barth, Berrick, Brooks, Needell, and Park (1996) found no empirical evidence to support discriminatory practices influencing the number of children entering foster care, disturbing discrepancies were found in the

Table 1. Selected Risk Factors

	1980	1995	Percent increase
Foster care population	302,000	483,000	59.9
Child population	62.9 million	70.6 million	12.2
Child poverty	11.5 million	14.7 million	27.8
African-American child poverty	4.0 million	4.8 million	20.0
Single mother households	6.3 million	8.8 million	39.7
Child abuse and neglect	1.2 million	3.1 million	258.3

amount of social services provided to white children compared to minority children. From 1980 to 1995 the number of African-American children living in poverty increased 20%, from 4.0 million to 4.8 million (Baugher & Lamison-White, 1995).

SINGLE-MOTHER HOUSEHOLDS

Although it is not known how many children in foster care come from single-parent families, it is well known that single parenthood is strongly linked to poverty and other risk factors. From 1980 to 1995 the number of single-mother households increased 39.7%, from 6.3 million to 8.8 million. In 1995 there were also 1.9 million single-father households with children, but single-mother households were twice as likely to be living in poverty. Approximately 16.3% of all households are living below federal poverty guidelines, compared to 41.5% of single-mother households and 19.7% for single-father households (Baugher & Lamison-White, 1995).

ALCOHOL AND OTHER DRUGS

The misuse of alcohol and other drugs (AOD) has had a devastating effect on the child welfare system and has exacerbated longstanding problems such as lengthy stays in foster care, frustrating family preservation and re-unification efforts and taxing already limited treatment resources in the community (Curtis & McCullough, 1993). Surprisingly, the number of users of illicit drugs in the United States has been decreasing steadily since 1979, although there were slight upturns in 1993 and 1994 (the latest year for which data are available). Results from the National Household Survey on Drug Abuse found that 12.2 million individuals used an illicit drug at least once in the month preceding the survey compared to 24.8 million in

1979 (Substance Abuse and Mental Health Services Administration [SAM-HSA], 1995). However, the number of hard-core drug users has remained fairly constant since 1988. According to the Office of National Drug Control Policy (ONDCP), in 1993 there were 2.7 million hard-core drug users in the United States, defined as individuals who used cocaine or heroin at least weekly (ONDCP, 1995). In chapter 3 Susan Zuravin and Diane DePanfilis provide an in-depth analysis of AOD as a risk factor in predicting entry into foster care.

HOMELESSNESS

Despite the prohibition by state policies against placing children into foster care solely because of homelessness, homelessness does, in fact, lead to placement. Only recently have researchers attempted to count the number of homeless children in the United States, so no trend data are yet available. The Stewart B. McKinney Homeless Assistance Act of 1987 (amended in 1990) required the states to provide estimates of the number and location of homeless children within their jurisdictions. In 1993, 18 states had identified 86,534 homeless preschool children, whereas the total number of homeless school-age children identified by all the states plus the District of Columbia, Puerto Rico, and the Bureau of Indian Affairs was 744,266 (U.S. Department of Education [USDE], 1995). No data are available as to the percentage of these children who entered foster care. Experts estimate that up to 80,000 healthy children will be orphaned by AIDS by the year 2000, with approximately one-third entering the out-of-home care system (Brown, Wilcyzinski, Moore, & Cullen, 1993).

CHILD ABUSE AND NEGLECT

All 50 states require professionals who work directly with children and, in 18 states, all citizens to report their suspicions about child abuse and neglect to the police or to a state or local child welfare agency (National Center on Child Abuse and Neglect [NCCAN], 1996). Following an investigation, the police and, in most states, child protective services (CPS) workers have the authority to remove children from their homes when they are found to be in imminent danger. Parents then have the right to a court hearing, usually within 48 hours. Contrary to a popular misconception, only judges, not CPS workers, are empowered to remove children permanently from their homes.

Figure 3. Children reported as victims of child abuse and neglect, 1980–1995.

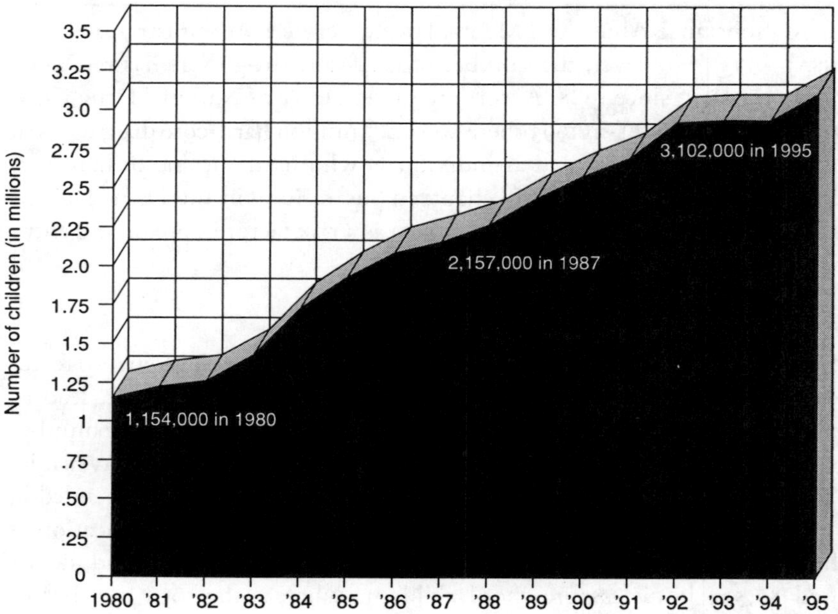

Chart. Y-axis: Number of children (in millions), 0 to 3.5. X-axis: years 1980 to '95.
Labels: 1,154,000 in 1980; 2,157,000 in 1987; 3,102,000 in 1995.

Sources: Petit, M. R., & Curtis, P. A. (1997). *Child abuse and neglect: A look at the states: The CWLA stat book.* Washington DC: Child Welfare League of America. National Center on Child Abuse and Neglect. (1997). *Child maltreatment 1995: Reports from the states to the National Child Abuse and Neglect Data System.* Washington DC: U.S. Department of Health and Human Services.

Because of greater public awareness of child maltreatment as well as the societal risk factors described earlier in this chapter, there have been astounding increases in the number of children reported as victims of child abuse and neglect, from 1.2 million in 1980 to 3.1 million in 1995, a 258.3% increase (Petit & Curtis, 1997; NCCAN, 1997) (see Figure 3). There were also substantial increases in the number of children reported as victims of abuse and neglect per 1,000 children in the population, from 18.3 per 1,000 children in 1980 to 44.0 in 1995, a 240.4% increase, or approximately 1 out of every 25 children in the United States. Although the identification of exact causes may remain elusive, the numbers support what we already know, that the ever increasing number of children reported to child welfare because of child abuse and neglect as well as other important risk factors is highly related to the growing number of children in the out-of-home care system, and until those problems are reversed, there will be no end to the foster care crisis.

THE FEDERAL FUNDING OF FOSTER CARE

The federal funding of out-of-home care services, although crucial to the protection of children, tends to discourage prevention and family preservation efforts. Under Title IV-E of the Social Security Act, funds are made available to the states for sheltering in foster care those children whose families of origin meet AFDC eligibility guidelines. Title IV-B of the act provides funds to the states for child welfare services in the home as well as in foster care. Services may include case management, counseling, or specialized services such as treatment for alcohol and other drugs (AOD). Historically, Title IV-E funds have existed as an open-ended entitlement, but for the most part, Title IV-E funds may not be used for other child welfare services. Title IV-B funding is dependent on annual appropriations.

From 1986 to 1995 Title IV-E federal foster care expenditures grew from $605 million to $3.05 billion, a hefty 504% increase. During that same 10-year period, Title IV-B funding for other child welfare services grew from $198 million to $292 million, a 47.5% increase. Separate allocations for family preservation services, funds allocated specifically for the purpose of preventing foster care and supporting families, did not exist until 1994; in 1995 funding was set at $150 million, or approximately 5% of the total cost of Title IV-E foster care (U.S. House, 1996).

family presv.-
federal

Addressing the Foster Care Crisis

There should be a concerted effort in child welfare to reduce the number of children living in out-of-home care. If we waited for society to address all the ramifications of teen pregnancy, single motherhood, and child maltreatment in a meaningful way, many children who could be worked with now, returned home, or adopted would not be. There should be a focused attempt to achieve this single goal of reducing foster care caseloads for the sake of achieving permanency on behalf of those children who are the most likely candidates. Actual reductions in the numbers of children already living in out-of-home care can be achieved by implementing the following strategies.

REUNIFICATION

The first strategy entails identifying those children least at risk for subsequent child abuse and neglect and sending them home to parents or relatives with whatever community-based services are needed to assure their safety and to support their families. Unfortunately, despite the number of maltreated children, the number entering foster care, and concerns about the costs of social dependency, there are few concerted efforts currently under way for the specific purpose of reducing the number of children living in out-of-home care through the use of wraparound or intensive reunification services. For a review of the strategies to be used in such an effort as well as the empirical evidence to support their efficacy, refer to the work of Anthony Maluccio in chapter 10.

ADOPTION

The second strategy for reducing the number of children in out-of-home care entails identifying those children most likely to be adopted and to provide whatever casework or legal services are required to facilitate their adoption. Late in 1996 President Clinton signed a directive to the Department of Health and Human Services (HHS) for the purpose of working with the states to move children more quickly from foster care to adoption. The goal of the initiative was to double the number of adoptions and placements with legal guardians by the public child welfare system, from approximately 27,000 to 54,000 annually, by the year 2002 (White House, 1996). HHS was directed to work with the states in setting specific goals for increasing the number of adoptive placements. Progress in meeting the goals was to be monitored and published, with successful states being recognized for their efforts. In return, the federal government agreed to provide financial incentives to the states. It was hoped that the initiative would pay for itself by reducing state and federal foster care expenditures. States were directed to prohibit adoption agencies from delaying the placement of children waiting for adoption because of race, color, or national origin. Both Congress and the states were also directed to propose changes to the "reasonable efforts" requirements of PL 96-272 in order to expedite reductions in the time children stay in foster care. Whether the initiative is fully implemented remains to be seen, but it is the kind of effort that is needed and should be supported.

There is precedent for such a strategy. In 1977, when approximately 502,000 children were living in out-of-home care (Westat, 1978), the U.S. Children's Bureau estimated that up to 102,000 children, many of them Af-

12

rican Americans, sibling groups, and children with disabilities, were legally free and awaiting adoptive families. Spurred on by the passage of PL
96-272, along with a major shift of resources into adoption and reunification services, the number of children in out-of-home care fell precipi-
tously. Unfortunately, by the mid-1980s, for the reasons stated above, the
system was inundated by the number of children reported as victims of
child abuse and neglect.

The problems described in this book did not develop overnight, and
even with a concerted, coordinated, and systematic effort, they will not
suddenly disappear. The scholarship presented in this volume will bring to
the foster care crisis both a thoughtful and informed analysis and recommendations for a variety of concrete initiatives. As a society, we cannot afford to ignore this crisis.

References

American Public Welfare Association. (1993). *Characteristics of children in substitute and adoptive care: A statistical summary of the VCIS National Child Welfare Data Base* (Based on FY 82 through FY 90 data). Washington DC: Author.

American Public Welfare Association. (1997). *Voluntary Cooperative Information System*. Washington DC: Author.

Baugher, E., & Lamison-White, L. (1995). *Poverty in the United States: 1995* (Current Population Reports, Series P60-194). Washington DC: Bureau of the Census.

Bremner, R. H. (1983). Other people's children. *Journal of Social History, 16,* 83–103.

Brown, S. T., Wilcyzinski, C., Moore, E., & Cullen, F. (1993). Perinatal AIDS: Permanence planning for the African-American community. *Journal of Multicultural Social Work, 2*(3), 85–105.

Courtney, M. E., Barth, R. P., Berrick, J. D., Brooks, D., Needell, B., & Park, L. (1996). Race and child welfare services: Past research and future directions. *Child Welfare, 75,* 99–137.

Curtis, P. A., & McCullough, C. (1993). The impact of alcohol and other drugs on the child welfare system. *Child Welfare, 72,* 533–542.

Hawkins, R. P. (1990). The nature and potential of therapeutic foster care programs. In R. P. Hawkins and J. Breiling (Eds.), *Therapeutic foster care: Critical issues.* Washington DC: Child Welfare League of America.

Kellogg, P. U. (Ed.). (1914). *Pittsburgh district: Civic frontage.* New York: Russell Sage Foundation.

Kempe, C. H., Silverman, F. N., Steele, B., Droegemueller, W., & Silver, H. R. (1962). The battered child syndrome. *Journal of the American Medical Association, 181,* 17–24.

National Center on Child Abuse and Neglect. (1996). *Child abuse and neglect state statute series: Vol. 1, Reporting laws.* Washington DC: U.S. Department of Health and Human Services.

National Center on Child Abuse and Neglect. (1997). *Child maltreatment 1995: Reports from the states to the National Child Abuse and Neglect Data System.* Washington DC: U.S. Department of Health and Human Services.

Office of National Drug Control Policy. (1995). *What America's users spend on illegal drugs, 1988–1993.* Washington DC: Author.

Petit, M. R., & Curtis, P. A. (1997). *Child abuse and neglect: A look at the states: The CWLA stat book.* Washington DC: Child Welfare League of America.

Substance Abuse and Mental Health Services Administration. (1995). *Preliminary estimates from the 1994 National Household Survey* (Advance Report No. 10). Washington DC: Author.

U.S. Department of Education. (1995). *Report to Congress: A compilation and analysis of reports submitted by the states in accordance with Section 722(d)(3) of the Education for Homeless Children and Youth Program.* Washington DC: Author.

U.S. House of Representatives, Committee on Ways and Means (1996). *1996 green book.* Washington DC: Author.

Westat. (1978). *National study of social services to children and their families.* Rockville MD: Author.

White House, Office of the Press Secretary. (1996). *Steps to increase adoptions and alternate permanent placement for waiting children in the public child welfare system.* Washington DC: Author.

Overview

Foster Care Dynamics

Robert M. Goerge, Fred Wulczyn, and Allen Harden

The fact that foster care populations *are* dynamic has long been a stumbling block to policymakers, administrators, researchers, and others concerned with the fate of this vulnerable population. Aggregate statistics compiled and published by the U.S. Department of Health and Human Services and the Voluntary Cooperative Information System of the American Public Welfare Association have documented steadily rising foster care populations since the 1980s.[1] Although all child welfare professionals are conscious of the increasing pressure on foster care, relatively little is known with certainty about the conditions that cause or accompany caseload increases, about how service needs may be shifting as a result, or about the types of children who make up this large and growing population. Without such knowledge, child welfare professionals will be hard-pressed to allocate their energies and resources effectively in the face of intensifying and sometimes conflicting demands.

Detailed statistical information about foster care trends can help remedy this situation, and this chapter aims to advance this cause in several ways. First, it presents a series of statistical measures that together offer a detailed and sophisticated view of change in the foster care population. It not only employs such familiar measurements as caseload counts but also examines a variety of longitudinal trends that can influence caseload size: factors such as the duration of children's stays in care, the relation of admissions to discharges, and the prevalence of foster care in relation to the general child population. In short, the chapter showcases types of statistical reporting on foster care that might more commonly and fruitfully be employed.

Second, this chapter identifies a number of specific conditions that have coexisted with, and help to explain, increases in the size of the foster care population. The following pages document a large influx of first-time entrants into foster care in the late 1980s, a development that strained agencies to the utmost at the time, and that has continued to affect the foster care system profoundly to the present day. During this period, entry into foster care not only increased in raw numbers, but use of foster care also became more common when considered in relation to the size of the total child population. Also dating from this period were increases in the entry of specific subpopulations of children—such as very young children, children in cities, and children living in kinship placements—who are prone to particularly long foster care stays. Although in the late 1980s and the 1990s foster care systems often came close to discharging as many children as they admitted, overall the high rates of entry and continuing reentry into care have contributed to record-high populations.

Finally, this chapter calls attention to how widely foster care dynamics vary from state to state, underscoring the importance of comparative and state-level statistical analysis. Although a primary goal in child welfare has been to develop better national data—a goal that we wholeheartedly support—our findings suggest the danger of valuing such statistics exclusively. The data presented here on five states—California, Illinois, Michigan, New York, and Texas—are fully comparable, lending themselves to both aggregations and cross-state comparisons that are statistically valid. Because these five states comprise nearly half of the nation's foster care population, trends occurring within them illuminate foster care trends nationally. At the same time, these states often differ surprisingly from one another in terms of placement rates, the prevalence of foster care, caseload composition, and foster care duration. Such dramatic differences among the states not only imply that the implementation and effect of federal principles and mandates are profoundly affected by local conditions; they also suggest that an adequate system of statistical reporting on foster care must combine an analysis of national trends with detailed analysis and comparison of individual states.

History and Rationale

The figures presented in this analysis represent a new generation of statistical reporting on foster care. Drawing on data from a powerful research repository known as the Multistate Foster Care Data Archive, this report analyzes longitudinal change in the entire foster care populations of the five study states for periods ranging from 7 to 12 years. The Multistate Foster Care Data Archive is a collaborative effort that is funded by the U.S. Department of Health and Human Services, sustained by contributions of data and policy information from state child welfare agencies, and maintained at the Chapin Hall Center for Children at the University of Chicago.

The archive is a permanent research database built from the computerized data records that state agencies use to track children living in child welfare settings. Although foster care records have been accumulating in state tracking systems for over a decade, several conditions account for the scant use that has been made of them. First, child-tracking data require the passage of time before analysis of trends and patterns is meaningful. Second, these service agencies, designed to protect and care for children, have often lacked sufficient technical and human resources to exploit the research potential of their data. Third, the event–history research techniques that are best suited to the analysis of dynamic processes have only recently gained currency in the study of foster care populations. Finally, many agencies have information policies that result in historical information being modified or destroyed over time.

Several attributes of the archive derive from its use of administrative data and result in an unusually nuanced, full, and reliable view of the foster care population. First, because the data sets contributed to the archive are comprehensive for each state, the archive produces findings that are highly accurate and free of the limitations associated with sample studies. Second, data in the archive are historical in nature. Although recently contributed data offer a timely view of recent trends, older data in the archive stretch back into the 1980s. This long and growing time span is invaluable for documenting long-term developments in foster care and for providing the retrospective context needed if recent developments are to be interpreted accurately. Third, and perhaps most important, the data in the archive are longitudinal at the level of the child. That is, data received at the archive are linked so that all records of events pertaining to an individual child are identified and related to form a complete current history of each child's foster care experience. The longitudinal structure of the data means that the crucial temporal aspects of foster care—such as duration of care and reentry into foster care—can be studied.

Altogether, the archive represents a distinct advance in the tools available to monitor changes in the national and state foster care populations. For many years, an array of formidable practical and conceptual obstacles has stymied the monitoring of foster care trends. For example, limits on time and expense have made feasible the study of only relatively small foster care cohorts, and even then outcomes could be analyzed only after all the children's experiences of foster care had been completed, a process often requiring a decade or longer.

Given the difficulties formerly associated with the study of longitudinal trends, it is not surprising that statistical reporting on foster care has relied mainly on point-in-time measures. Comparing a series of cross-sectional counts, each describing a foster care caseload at a given time, is valuable for documenting the extent to which the size and composition of a foster care population have changed over time. However, because caseload counts do not provide any information about the temporal dynamics of foster care, they cannot tell us why foster care caseloads have changed and so constitute an incomplete aid to informed caseload management.

Despite these difficulties, obtaining a clearer understanding of foster care dynamics remains a compelling and urgent cause for bureaucratic and humanitarian reasons. Child welfare agencies have been facing increased demands for their services at a time when their budgets are being cut or are stagnating. Agencies need information about their foster care populations in order to efficiently allocate scarce resources in a manner most likely to help them fulfill their mandates. A deeper knowledge of the realities of foster care is also necessary to gauge the feasibility of existing federal policies and, in some instances, to identify why particular policies are or are not working. At a time when the goals of many social welfare programs are being questioned, it is necessary to understand the effects and implications of those services in order to be able to determine whether they are worthwhile. Finally, the children in foster care, who are among the nation's neediest, merit the improved care that may result from a more complete understanding of their characteristics, needs, and experience in foster care.

Fortunately, advances in data collection and computer technology, along with the creation of new analytic methods for studying population dynamics, have dramatically increased our ability to describe foster care populations with a high degree of sophistication and accuracy. These conditions make it possible to use administrative data to explore a wide variety of trends in foster care, to compile timely statistics on state foster care populations, to compare foster care trends among states, and to extend analyses of trends over long periods of time.

Characteristics and Use of Data

A major challenge in creating this data archive was to incorporate and organize data that each state had created and defined based on its own specific foster care policies and its internal system of coding information. Although state child welfare databases largely contain the same types of information, the actual data elements are defined in a wide variety of ways. The task was not only to extract comparable data from this diversity but also to retain the original characteristics of state data in order to preserve the data's integrity and long-term research utility.

A first principle of the project was, therefore, to accept administrative data from the states without alteration. This principle encouraged the states to participate because it relieved them of the difficult task of preparing special data summaries that would conform to an external standard. Instead, all data sent to the archive are preserved in their original form. Archive staff carefully study the codes and classifications of each state's database in order to identify and convert the key variables into a format that is as comparable as possible with the data of other states. By retaining all the original local data on hand, the archive preserves researchers' future capacity to revise notions of how "comparable" data items should be defined. Archive data may be reframed entirely in order to address new research questions.

Although agencies differ in the number and type of variables they define, certain basic data elements are available that describe the characteristics of each child in state custody, including the child's date of birth, gender, ethnicity, and place of residence. These elements form the "core" child data that the archive can collect and compare in every state. Similarly, certain important foster care events that define a child's foster care experience are identifiable in each state's record system, notably any entrance to or changes in out-of-home placement and any exit from the foster care system. The child's ID, event date, and type of event compose the core event data that the archive can collect and compare in each state.[2] These core elements are configured in a relational database structure that contains two parts: a *child table*, with a unique record that identifies each child who has been a foster care client and describes his or her demographic and service characteristics; and an *event table* that separately identifies every foster care placement or discharge that the state has ever recorded. The child and event tables are "related" to each other, and can be joined, by the unique child identifier field. This versatile data storage model allows for both cross-sectional and longitudinal analysis, supports descriptive analyses of the service population and of system activity, and supports research on foster care "careers" and service use patterns.

Linked child–event data can be used to form new data elements that express the sequence, duration, and consequence of a child's foster care experience. For example, placement event and discharge data are used to construct *spells* in placement. The placement spell, defined as a continuous episode in out-of-home care, is the principal analytic unit that has been used in the archive project to document and compare children's foster care experiences. This construct is used to get beyond the often confusing array of separate placements in a child's foster care experience by creating a simpler entity that represents the discrete span of time in substitute care. Spells are also more directly comparable between states than are specific placement-type definitions. A spell begins with any new foster care placement and ends only with a return home or with some other legal movement out of foster care (e.g., adoption or reaching the age of majority). Within a placement spell, a child might experience one or more substitute care living arrangements. Because a placement spell has a specific beginning and end, a duration may be computed. If a spell has not ended by the time of the most recent data collection, the full duration of the spell cannot be observed and the spell is referred to as *censored*. Spell data express children's experiences in a unit that is at once conceptually meaningful and statistically versatile.

Although the archive is capable of supporting a wide variety of specialized studies, in this chapter archive data are used to supply an overview of major changes occurring in five states' foster care populations. The five states discussed not only comprise a significant portion of the national foster care population, as mentioned above, but also embrace a wide variety of regional, economic, and social characteristics and give ample evidence of state-to-state variation. Here we are concerned with such questions as how many children have been foster children, how their demographic composi-

Data sources	California	Illinois	Michigan	New York	Texas	
Child welfare agency	Dept. of Social Services (DSS)	Dept. of Children and Family Services (DCFS)	Family Independence Agency (FIA)	Dept. of Social Services (DSS)	Dept. of Protect. Regulatory Services (DPRS)	
State information system	Foster Care Information System (FCIS)	Child and Youth Centered Information System (CYCIS)	Children's Services Mgmt. Information System (CSMIS)	Child Care Review Service (CCRS)	Foster Care, Adoption & Conservatorship Tracking System (FACTS)	
Years of full coverage	1988–94	1975–94	1981–94	1982–94	1985–94	
	Five-state comparable data (1988 – 94 entrants)					*Total*
Total children	182,095	64,062	34,390	127,388	37,434	445,369
Total spells	218,878	83,188	44,137	153,394	46,055	545,652
	Three-state comparable data (1983 – 94 entrants)					*Total*
Total children	–	93,090	56,047	197,423	–	346,560
Total spells	–	123,061	71,510	236,490	–	431,011

tion has changed, the rates at which they have entered and left care, how long they have stayed, and who has experienced long stays. An overview of the archive data and populations for each state is profiled in Table 1. Although this analysis begins, like so many others, with caseload counts, it soon introduces other measures that make it possible to distinguish and gauge several striking developments that have shaped foster care in the past decade.

Caseload Counts

Analysis of archive data confirms a continuous and substantial rise in the number of children in foster care since the mid-1980s. Between 1983 and 1994, the combined foster care population of the five states increased 147% (Figure 1).[3] The number of children in care in the five states rose from under 90,000 in 1983 to over 218,000 in 1994. The pattern of growth mirrors national trends as estimated by the American Public Welfare Association. California and New York registered the greatest numerical increases: by the end of the period, California's system was caring for 52,000 more children than it had at the beginning (Figure 2 and Table 2). California, Illinois,

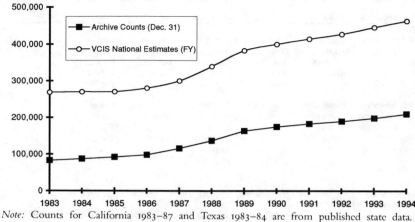

Figure 1. Foster care census by year: Five-state archive counts and vics national estimates.

Note: Counts for California 1983–87 and Texas 1983–84 are from published state data. vcis=Voluntary Cooperative Information System of the American Public Welfare Association.

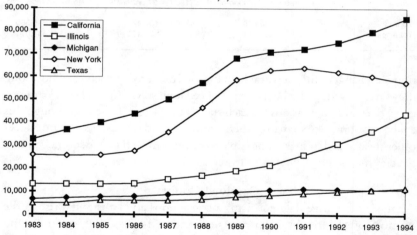

Figure 2. Foster care census for five states by year.

Note: Counts for California 1983–87 and Texas 1983–84 are from published state data.

New York, and Texas experienced increases in their foster care populations ranging from 124 to 232%. Michigan's relative growth was the smallest, but its caseload increased by 65%.

The foster care population grew exceptionally fast in the late 1980s (Table 3). From 1987 through 1989, the combined five-state caseload increased

Table 2. Foster Care Census for Five States by Year

Year	Cal.*	Ill.	Mich.	N.Y.	Tex.*	Total
1983	32,520	13,170	6,733	25,709	4,992	88,343
1984	36,540	13,145	7,249	25,480	4,996	92,539
1985	39,666	13,091	7,685	25,644	6,152	97,456
1986	43,599	13,363	7,913	27,472	6,058	103,629
1987	49,990	15,310	8,722	35,566	6,195	121,150
1988	57,150	16,982	9,206	46,318	6,704	141,949
1989	68,120	19,048	10,035	58,550	7,834	169,878
1990	70,826	21,484	10,794	62,787	8,560	181,208
1991	72,087	26,010	11,271	63,853	9,388	189,888
1992	74,875	30,801	11,154	62,000	10,211	196,822
1993	79,448	36,097	10,955	60,160	10,958	206,005
1994	85,367	43,711	11,126	57,474	11,781	218,332

*Counts for California 1983–87 and Texas 1983–84 are from published state data.

by roughly 64%. Whereas in previous years the combined caseload had grown at a rate that hovered between 4 and 7% annually, between 1986 and 1989 the annual growth rate ranged from 16.9% to nearly 20%. Hypergrowth was most evident in California and New York. The New York foster care population grew 113% during these 3 years.

After 1989, the rate of caseload growth in all states except Illinois tapered off. In California, New York, and Michigan, caseload growth slowed to pre-1987 rates, and Michigan and New York even registered slight caseload decreases in the 1990s. Illinois's growth rate, by contrast, accelerated further in the 1990s, averaging an annual growth of 18% between 1990 and 1994. At the end of 1994, the state's caseload was twice as large as it had been in 1990.

URBAN CASELOAD GROWTH

Geographic analysis shows that caseload growth has been concentrated in cities. This phenomenon manifests when the primary urban region of each state is compared with the balance of the state. Areas designated "urban" for the purposes of this analysis are California's Los Angeles County, Illinois's Cook County (Chicago), Michigan's Wayne County (Detroit), New York City, and Texas's Dallas and Harris Counties (Dallas and Houston).

Table 3. Percentage Change in Foster Care Census for Five States by Year

Year	Cal.*	Ill.	Mich.	N.Y.	Tex.*	Total
1983	–	–	–	–	–	–
1984	12.4	-0.2	7.7	-0.9	0.1	4.7
1985	8.6	-0.4	6.0	0.6	23.1	5.3
1986	9.9	2.1	3.0	7.1	-1.5	6.3
1987	14.7	14.6	10.2	29.5	2.3	16.9
1988	14.3	10.9	5.5	30.2	8.2	17.2
1989	19.2	12.2	9.0	26.4	16.9	19.7
1990	4.0	12.8	7.6	7.2	9.3	6.7
1991	1.8	21.1	4.4	1.7	9.7	4.8
1992	3.9	18.4	-1.0	-2.9	8.8	3.7
1993	6.1	17.2	-1.8	-3.0	7.3	4.7
1994	7.5	21.1	1.6	-4.5	7.5	6.0

*Counts for California 1983–87 and Texas 1983–84 are from published state data.

These urban regions accounted for over two-thirds of the total caseload growth from 1988 to 1994 (Figure 3).[4] Concentrated urban caseload growth was most evident in New York and Illinois, where virtually all growth occurred in New York City and Cook County, respectively. During the 12-year period from 1983 through 1994, caseloads in New York City and Cook County increased threefold and sixfold, respectively, while caseloads in the balance of the state increased by one-fourth in New York and by less than one-half in Illinois.

Caseloads in Los Angeles, Detroit, Houston, and Dallas also grew, but they did so in the context of a variety of statewide patterns. Unlike Chicago and New York City, these cities did not dominate the caseloads in their respective states, and their rates of growth were matched or exceeded by those of the states' other geographic regions. In Michigan, where the foster care population was almost equally divided between Detroit and the remainder of the state, caseloads in both regions increased equally. In California, the Los Angeles caseload often grew faster than that of the balance of the state, but it did not exceed the size of the latter (also growing) population. In Texas, the caseload of the balance of the state was larger and grew more rapidly than the combined caseload of Dallas and Houston. Thus,

Figure 3. Foster care census for five states: Primary urban region vs. balance of state.

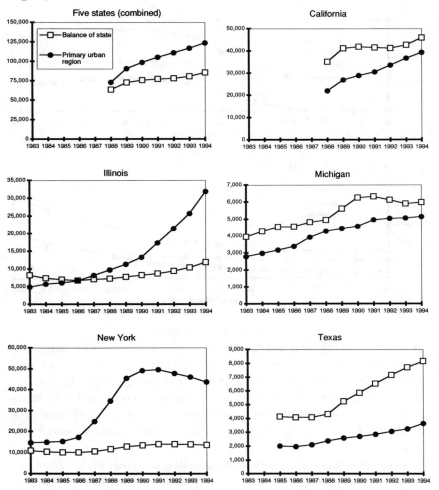

while the growth of urban foster care populations is a highly significant aggregate trend, within each state the geographic distribution of caseload growth has varied substantially. Although nationally it might make sense to concentrate on developing strategies for containing urban caseload growth, such strategies would not entirely suffice for states also experiencing significant caseload growth outside their principal urban regions.

27

Figure 4. Illinois: Kinship vs. other placements.

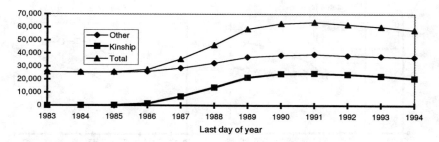

Figure 5. New York: Kinship vs. other placements.

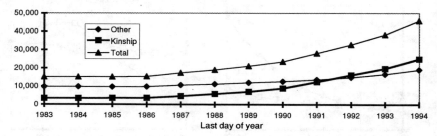

KINSHIP PLACEMENTS

A second phenomenon associated with caseload growth is kinship placements; that is, the formal placement of children with relatives. It is not possible to discuss this phenomenon for all five archive states because recordkeeping procedures in Michigan and Texas do not allow for the study of kinship placements.[5] In two of the three states where the phenomenon can be studied, however, kinship placements dramatically increased relative to other placements.

The phenomenon was most apparent in Illinois, where in the early 1980s roughly one-quarter of the foster care population was living in kinship placements (Figure 4). Between 1986 and 1991, however, the number of children living in kinship care tripled and then doubled again in the 3 years following. By 1994, kinship care composed well over half of the state's foster care population, and its growth showed no sign of slowing.

Kinship care in New York (Figure 5) also grew dramatically, although the magnitude of the change is harder to pin down because of changes in the way New York tracks kinship placements. Before 1985, New York did not track kinship care as a feature of the child welfare system. In 1985, the

Figure 6. California: Kinship vs. other placements.

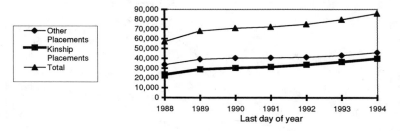

year such tracking began, it recorded only 200 such placements. However, as in Illinois, kinship placements then escalated dramatically.[6] By 1990, children living in kinship care accounted for 39% of the state's total caseload. In both New York and Illinois, growth in kinship placement far outstripped growth in other forms of placement.

California presented a more stable pattern (Figure 6). There, kinship placement was a well-established aspect of foster care before 1988, with 41% of children in state custody living in such arrangements. Over the next 5 years, both kinship and non-kinship placements grew in roughly equal degrees, such that by the end of 1994, children in kinship care accounted for 46% of the foster care population.

Although these figures suggest the importance of studying kinship care as an aspect of the foster care system, the causal relation, if any, between growing levels of kinship care and growth in the caseload overall is unknown. Only further statistical and policy analysis can determine whether an increase in kinship placements is driving such growth, or whether kinship placements are a concomitant of burgeoning foster care intake.

Prevalence

Caseload counts, which represent raw numbers of children in care, are of limited utility because they do not take into account differences or changes in the size of each state's general child population. The calculation of prevalence rates controls for such differences. Prevalence rates express how many children are in foster care per 1,000 children in a state's population.

Prevalence varies considerably by state, and differences among the states' prevalence rates increased in the late 1980s (Figure 7). Before 1986, prevalence rates for the states under study clustered within a definite range: between 1 and 6 children per 1,000 in each state were in some form of foster placement. New York's prevalence rate stood at around 6 foster children

29

Figure 7. Foster care prevalence rates for five states.

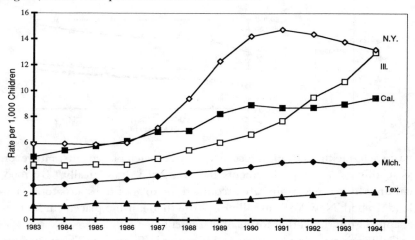

Note: Rates for California 1983–84 are based on published state data. Rates for all years are based on Census Bureau population estimates for 1 July, except 1990, which is based on counts for 1 April.

per 1,000, while Texas's rate, the lowest of the group, stood at 1 foster child per 1,000 children in the early 1980s.

Since 1986, prevalence rates in all five states have increased. The change has been modest in Michigan and Texas and more considerable in California, Illinois, and New York. California's rate climbed from around 5 per 1,000 in 1983 to over 9 per 1,000 in 1994. New York's prevalence rate reached a high of nearly 15 foster children per 1,000 children in 1991. Although that rate subsequently declined, it stood at no less than 13 children per 1,000 in the final year studied. Although in most states the rapid rise in prevalence abated in the 1990s, the prevalence of foster care among Illinois children continued to escalate dramatically. Whereas only 4 Illinois children per 1,000 were in foster care in 1983, by 1994 the number of foster children per 1,000 had risen to 13. Even the modest increase in Texas represented a doubling of the prevalence of foster care within that state's child population.

By the end of the period studied, the states exhibited widely varying prevalence rates, ranging from 2 to 13 foster children per 1,000 children in the state population. Despite some modest declines in recent years, in general, prevalence rates stood at much higher levels than they had a decade

Figure 8. Incidence rates of first entry to foster care in five states.

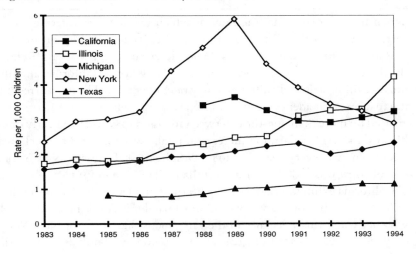

earlier. Overall, these trends indicate that a larger proportion of children in each state are foster children.

Incidence (Rates of Entry)

From the steady upward slope of caseload curves, one might suppose that more and more children have been entering foster care every year. Caseload counts and prevalence measures can be somewhat deceptive in this regard. As relatively inelastic and undifferentiated measures, they tend to mask the underlying volatility of foster care dynamics and do not supply the information necessary to understand why caseloads have been rising. Developing such an explanation involves examining a variety of trends, including the rates at which children enter care, the types of children entering care, the lengths of time they stay in care, the numerical relation between admissions and discharges, and the rates at which children who have been discharged from the system are reentering. Each of these subjects is taken up in the remainder of this chapter.

Considering only the population of children who enter care each year brings to light several dynamics that have reshaped foster care profoundly. Figure 8 depicts the numbers of children who entered foster care for the first time in a given year relative to the total child population in each state.

When tracked over time, the rates at which children are entering foster care, known as *incidence*, represent the children's changing risk of entry.

Rates of entry in the five states do not describe a single pattern. In fact, the three states with the largest caseloads—New York, California, and Illinois—exhibit strikingly different entry rates over time. The most arresting fluctuation of incidence occurred in New York, where rates of entry increased by more than one-third between 1986 and 1987 and had nearly doubled by 1989. This alarming increase in intake was followed by declining rates of entry in every year after 1989. Despite these decreases, New York's rate of entry was 23% higher in 1994 than it had been in 1983.

California exhibits a fluctuating pattern of incidence similar to, but less radical than, that of New York. Unfortunately, it is not possible to tell whether California's declines in the early 1990s, like those of New York, only succeeded a period of great increase. Moreover, unlike New York, California once again began to experience slowly rising rates of entry after 1992.

Illinois's rates of entry grew more gradually between 1986 and 1989, only to increase significantly after 1990, while incidence rates in the other states remained relatively steady or declined. In 1994, Illinois's placement rate was the highest of the five states, having increased 145% during the period studied.

VERY YOUNG ADMISSIONS

Incidence rates broken down by age indicate that children under the age of 5 years are twice as likely as older children to enter foster care and that large increases in the placement of young children have had much to do with rising rates of entry. Entry rates for young children were more volatile and registered greater increases than those of older children (Figure 9). In New York, the fluctuating rate of entry for children under age five was clearly responsible for the pronounced spike in admission levels that occurred during the late 1980s.

A general downward shift in the age of children entering care becomes more evident by pooling the five-state age data for children entering care for the first time. Figure 10 shows the age distribution of new entrants for three separate time periods—1983–1986, 1987–1989, and 1990–1994—which were characterized by different patterns in rates of placement, as described above.

The most notable feature of the age distribution is the large and in-

Figure 9. Incidence rates of first entry to foster care in five states by age group.

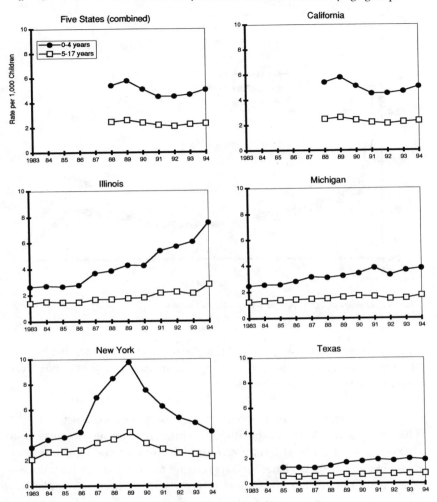

creased number of infant placements. Whereas in 1983–1986, infants made up 16% of all children entering care, by 1987–1989 that figure had increased to 23%. Moreover, although overall rates of entry declined in some states after 1989, the proportion attributed to infants continued to increase, constituting 24% of all first admissions. In the early 1990s, children under the age of 1 year were three times more likely to enter foster care than children in the next year of life. A high rate of infant placement is among the most

Figure 10. Distribution of age at first admission to foster care in five states.

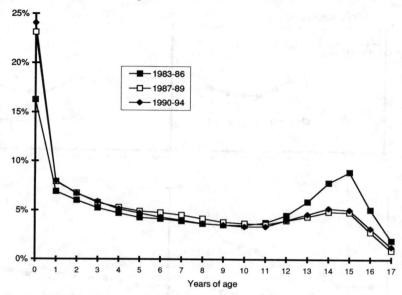

Note: Single years of age appear as a percentage of total for the time period; data for the five states are combined.

disturbing trends in foster care and is made more so by the fact that infants placed in care tend to remain there longer than other children (a point established in the section on duration, below).

RACIAL AND ETHNIC COMPOSITION OF ENTRY COHORTS

The racial and ethnic composition of children entering care has also changed considerably, although it is difficult to gauge the significance or consequences of these changes. Data relating to race and ethnicity underscore again the diversity of state trends, for state foster care populations vary strikingly not only in their composition but also in directions in which these populations are shifting (Figure 11). Analysis of race and ethnicity is complicated by the use in all states of an "other" category, which includes small numbers of Native Americans and Asian Americans as well as children of mixed or unknown race or ethnicity.

In Texas, African-American and Hispanic children made up relatively stable portions of the foster care population, while the white presence in the population declined and the number of children categorized as "other"

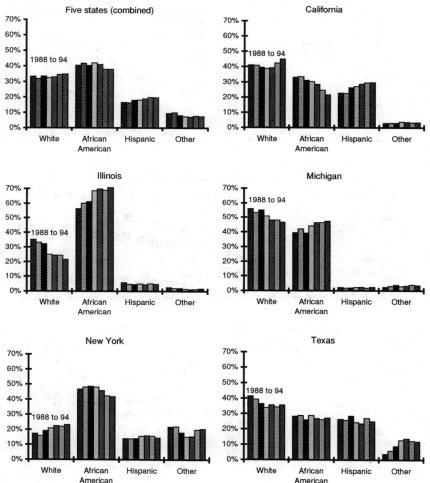

Figure 11. Racial/ethnic distribution of first admissions to foster care for five states (as a percentage).

increased substantially. In California, the proportion of Hispanic children increased from 23% in 1988 to 30% in 1994, while the proportion of African-American children declined. In Illinois, the percentage of white children placed in foster care decreased by over one-third between 1988 and 1993, while the percentage of African-American children increased by one-quarter. In New York, white children increased as a proportion of first admissions, but this may partly reflect improved data recording. Among all

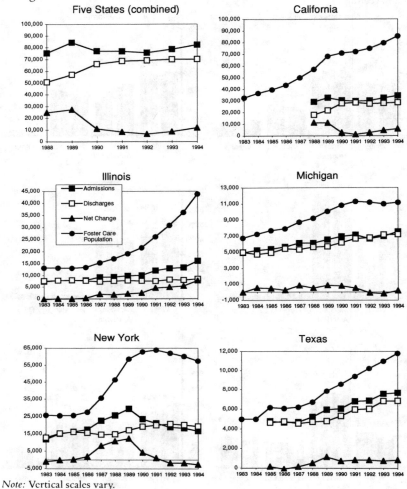

Figure 12. Foster care census for five states: Admission, discharge, and net caseload change.

Note: Vertical scales vary.

five states, roughly 33% of first admissions in 1994 were white, 38% were African American, and 20% were Hispanic.

Admissions and Discharges

Although the intake population has a strong impact on the child welfare system, other dynamics also affect the nature of demands placed on the

36

child welfare system and overall caseload size. Among these is the relation between the number of children being admitted to the system and the number of children the system is discharging. Caseloads will rise as long as admissions outnumber discharges, regardless of whether discharges are rising, or admissions falling. The numerical relation between admissions and discharges determines whether caseloads grow quickly or slowly (Figure 12). The growth of California's caseload between 1988 and 1994 offers an illustration. Between 1988 and 1990, discharges from the foster care system increased 55 percent and after that time nearly kept pace with admissions, which were relatively stable. Nonetheless, because admissions continued to exceed discharges throughout this period, the state's caseload still increased a full 50 percent by 1994. Likewise, although increases in both admissions and discharges nearly kept pace with one another in Texas, between 1985 and 1994 its caseload increased 91 percent.

Between 1988 and 1994, the five-state caseload grew continuously, but at a slowing rate. Admissions remained stable or declined, but they were at a level higher than discharges, even while discharges increased. This combination of conditions produced annual net increases in the combined caseload ranging from 9,000 to 27,000 cases annually. In Illinois, increases in admissions were not offset by increases in discharges, so that growth in the caseload accelerated. After 1991, discharges outnumbered admissions in New York, helping to bring about a decrease in that recently swollen population. In Michigan, increases in admissions were nearly matched and, at one time, even exceeded by increases in discharges, so that between 1991 and 1993 its caseload shrank. Nonetheless, because admissions between 1983 and 1994 outnumbered discharges by an average of 399 children per year, Michigan experienced a caseload increase over the whole period. The task of reducing caseloads appears the more daunting because, relative to discharges, admissions tend to exhibit greater volatility.

Duration

Another dynamic of concern in child welfare is duration, or the length of time children stay in foster care. This important feature of foster care not only affects caseload size but also represents the length of time that children are separated from their parents and that the state is responsible for them. Duration varies for different groups of foster children. Knowing which groups of children have tended to stay in care for long periods of time helps

Table 4. Median Duration of First Spells in Foster Care in Five States, 1988–1993 (in Months)

	Cal.	Ill.	Mich.	N.Y.	Tex.
All new entrants	17.2	32.7	11.4	23.0	8.4
Region					
Primary urban*	20.9	58.4	17.6	31.7	7.2
Rest of state	15.4	14.4	9.1	13.4	9.1
Race/ethnicity					
African-American	28.3	51.8	13.8	31.6	8.7
Hispanic	14.2	20.9	7.8	21.6	8.1
Other	12.5	16.8	10.4	25.0	9.7
White	14.1	12.8	9.9	12.6	8.0
Age at entry (years)					
<1 year	24.4	41.4	18.1	42.0	10.9
1–2 years	17.9	45.2	12.0	27.8	7.2
3–5 years	17.2	47.6	11.6	27.4	7.0
6–8 years	17.3	47.2	12.5	27.6	8.1
9–11 years	17.0	39.6	12.0	24.2	9.4
12–14 years	11.9	19.6	8.2	13.2	9.8
15–17 years	8.6	10.3	6.0	10.3	7.0
Year of entry					
1988	20.7	15.7	9.9	30.6	7.4
1989	18.1	18.2	11.6	27.3	9.4
1990	15.9	23.1	11.5	20.4	8.5
1991	14.9	37.1	11.7	19.9	8.2
1992	16.5	no est. **	11.2	18.7	8.5
1993	16.2	no est.	12.1	18.8	8.6
1994	no est.	no est.	no est.	no est.	7.7
*Exit type***					
Reunification	5.6	5.1	5.8	8.6	4.1
Adoption	32.0	34.3	25.9	44.7	29.0
Age out	24.6	24.2	21.8	28.3	25.1
Runaway	7.6	7.1	7.5	4.9	6.3

*Primary urban places are defined as Los Angeles County, Cook County (Ill.), Wayne County (Mich.), New York City, and Harris and Dallas Counties (Tex.).
**No value for the median duration can be estimated for cells noted "no est." because an insufficient proportion of these spells had been completed by the time of most recent observation in December 1994.
***Unlike other categories, median durations by exit type are computed from completed spells only.

account for why caseloads have remained high and enables child welfare agencies to identify children who are at risk of particularly long stays.

The duration figures presented in Table 4 were calculated using the methods of event-history analysis, which produces reliable estimates of the length of time children who have recently entered foster care are likely to stay, based on data relating to both complete and incomplete (censored) cases.[7] Although duration can be measured in many ways, the calculations presented here all express *median duration*: the time by which precisely 50% of the children in a particular group will have left foster care. Table 4 gives estimated median durations (in months) for all first spells that began between 1988 and 1994, by state, region, race or ethnicity, age, and the child's destination on being discharged from foster care.

The length of time a child is likely to remain in care varied widely across the five states and among different subgroups of their populations. The overall state medians differed widely, ranging from just over 8 months in Texas to more than 32 months in Illinois. These figures signify that, for a typical group of children entering foster care for the first time in Illinois, it would take almost four times longer for half the children to exit care than it would for a group of children in Texas. In California and New York, which have the two largest foster care populations, the median duration of stay was 17.2 months and 23 months, respectively.

In all states except Texas, urban foster children were likely to stay in care substantially longer than children in other areas. The most striking contrast in this regard was furnished by Illinois, where the median duration for Cook County children was just under 5 years, roughly three-and-a-half times longer than that of children in the rest of the state.

Duration in care also varied by race or ethnicity. African-American children tended to experience substantially longer first placement spells than children of other races in California, Illinois, and, to a lesser extent, New York. White children had durations shorter than other children in all states except Michigan, where Hispanic children had the briefest median duration. Median durations for Hispanic children were relatively long compared with those of white children in Illinois and New York.

Age is likewise an important factor affecting the length of time children have remained in placement. Children entering foster care as infants in California, Michigan, New York, and Texas remained in care longer than those in any other entering age group. In New York, the median duration for infants was 42 months, more than 1 year longer than for any other group of children. In Illinois, the median duration for infants was also relatively high, although not the highest in the state. Multivariate analysis conducted using archive data for the combined five-state caseload and for most of the states analyzed separately shows that urban region, infant age, African–American ethnicity, and kinship care (in the states where it could be identified) were each independently and positively related to duration.[8]

The length of time that individual children spend in foster care apparently has much to do with the permanency goals set for them. Children with a foster care outcome of adoption stayed in care for a much longer time than children who were discharged to be reunited with their families. Among the five states, children who were discharged to their families had an average median duration in care of less than 6 months, whereas children adopted from the system experienced median durations of 2 to nearly 4 years. The disparity in median durations for the two groups probably reflects both the protracted nature of the formal adoptive process and the severity of family problems that often results in adoption as the planned outcome.

Reentry

The extent to which children reenter foster care at some time after discharge from a prior child welfare experience is an extremely important component of foster care dynamics. Much of the discussion of length of stay implied that short durations are preferable, but clearly earlier discharge is not beneficial if it is to a setting from which the child must be removed once again. A more comprehensive study on reentry, which necessarily requires a substantial time series of data, is currently being developed. Our preliminary findings, however, indicate that the rate of reentry among children who had left care typically ranged from 17 to 29% in the five states (Table 5). There is some tendency for children who leave foster care sooner to reenter at higher rates. For all five states combined, about 29% of children who left foster care after an initial stay of less than 3 months returned to foster care again, whereas fewer than 20% of those discharged after 1 year returned to care (Table 6). Reentry is an important outcome to be considered, and it is clear that reentering children constitute a significant portion of the states' foster care caseloads.

Summary and Implications

A complex set of trends and conditions coexists with and helps to explain the gross increase in state foster care populations. As the foregoing paragraphs suggest, caseloads are the product of both cumulative and current conditions. Historical and longitudinal developments shape caseloads as powerfully as events of the present day. On closer inspection, the single

Table 5. Reentry to Foster Care in Five States: Experience of Children Who First Entered Foster Care in 1988–1990

State	Risk population % of first entries from 1988 – 90 ever discharged	Reentries as % of ever discharged (risk) population	Reentries as % of 1988 – 90 cohort	Number of reentries observed
California	80.7	19.3	15.6	12,248
Illinois	75.1	28.5	21.4	4,339
Michigan	93.6	20.4	19.1	2,885
New York	77.7	16.9	13.1	8,775
Texas	91.8	19.8	18.2	2,581
Five-state total	80.9	19.6	15.8	30,828

Note: Both discharges and reentries were observed prior to 31 December 1994.

Table 6. Reentry to Foster Care by Length of Time in Care in Five States: Children Who Entered Care in 1988–1990 and Were Discharged Before December 1994

Length of completed first spell in care	Completed spells	Reentries to second spell	% discharges resulting in a reentry spell
< 1 month	21,060	6,026	28.6
1–2 months	19,055	5,519	29.0
3–5 months	15,138	3,961	26.2
6–11 months	22,465	4,970	22.1
12–17 months	18,086	3,582	19.8
18–35 months	33,592	4,828	14.4
≥ 36 months	28,343	1,942	6.9
Total: all first spells	157,739	30,828	19.5

Note: Both discharges and reentries were observed prior to 31 December 1994.

population represented statistically as "a caseload" dissolves into more distinct subpopulations of children, some of whom may be entering foster care at unprecedented rates, may exit or reenter care quickly, or may remain in care for long periods of time, for plainly identifiable reasons. Recognizing the existence and needs of such groups of children may be a key to serving foster care populations more effectively.

Many of the findings presented above document profound trends that began to reshape foster care in the late 1980s. That period was notable not only for high incidence rates but for shifts in the types of children coming into care, especially for the entry of children who were likely to experience long foster care stays. Increases in infant placements, urban placements, and kinship placements—each associated with stays of long duration—all date from this period. The period's most astronomical growth was concentrated in specific geographic areas—in some major cities and several of the largest states—but it was not entirely confined to them, and such growth was, in any event, of sufficient magnitude to affect the profile of the national foster care population.

Even states relatively unaffected by the more dramatic trends of the late 1980s experienced a gradual increase in foster care use dating from the early 1980s, confirming a steady underlying pressure on foster care systems relative to the general population. We have not studied the extent to which such increases in prevalence and incidence are attributable to worsening social conditions, changes in popular culture regarding the use of social services, or changes in child welfare practice and policy. However, in light of such trends, it makes sense to view child welfare in the 1990s as struggling with developments originating in the previous decade. Although some indicators have returned to their pre-1987 levels or appear to have peaked, others continue at elevated marks and, in some instances, are even skyrocketing.

Given the influx of children into foster care systems, states would need to perform well in several areas if their goal were to contain or reduce their caseloads. On a year-to-year basis, some caseloads would almost have stabilized if all that mattered were a balance between their admission and discharge figures. But in order for states to reduce the size of their caseloads, several conditions must exist: discharges must consistently outnumber admissions, stays in care must be briefer, and there must be lower rates of reentry. This combination of conditions was seldom met. In general, consistently high rates of placement, foster care stays of long duration, and significant rates of reentry all combined to keep caseloads high.

The complexity of foster care dynamics makes it all the more necessary that administrators and policymakers have broad and up-to-date views of the populations they are serving. Programmatic efforts to control one dimension of foster care will fall short if not considered in relation to other factors. Discharging children more rapidly may be of little benefit if it results in higher rates of reentry; long stays in foster care may be necessary if the goal of permanency is being met increasingly through adoption. For these reasons, a prerequisite of effective service management is timely and sophisticated statistical reporting.

Fortunately, producing such statistics is increasingly feasible. Exploiting the research potential of administrative data offers child welfare agencies and policymakers the means to draw a detailed picture of the foster care population. A number of issues that state and federal agencies confront can be elucidated through the analysis of administrative data. For example, administrative data contain valuable information on the effect of kinship care on children, on their continuity of care and protection from harm, and on the financial implications of the more general use of kinship care in the context of the existing system of foster care subsidies. Likewise, such data can be used to study the services used by distinct populations, such as substance-exposed infants or the children of teen parents. The prospect of such knowledge offers an incentive to states to exploit administrative data more fully as an aid to managing services and formulating policy.

At a time when the federal government's role in promoting social welfare is being reexamined, the degree of state-level diversity documented here is worth pondering. Since the mid-1980s, state child welfare systems have operated in a manner delimited by a relatively stable set of federal goals, reimbursements, and mandates. Yet states exhibit a rather stunning degree of diversity, whether gauged in terms of rates of placement, the prevalence of foster care, or foster care duration. Although such diversity underscores the difficulty of attaining even the simplest national child welfare goals—or determining when they have been attained—it also prefigures the variations in state performance that are likely to emerge all the more strongly in an era of greater state flexibility.

In any event, comparative analyses of the type presented here represent the beginnings of a typology of foster care in states that can be profoundly useful to both the federal government and the states. Understanding the dynamics of foster care in states, and seeing how these dynamics resemble and differ from one another, may be the cornerstone of effective state-level management and workable federal policy.

Notes

1. For example, see Toshio Tatara, U.S. Child Substitute Care Flow Data for FY 1994 and Trends in the State Child Substitute Care Populations, *VCIS Research Notes* 12 (Washington DC: American Public Welfare Association, June 1996), and Office of the Assistant Secretary for Planning and Evaluation, *Trends in the Well-Being of America's Children and Youth: 1996* (Washington DC: U.S. Department of Health and Human Services, 1996), pp. 26–27.

2. In addition to containing these core data that are available for every state, the archive contains "extended" modules of additional salient data for each state. The extended modules provide a way of retaining data that should not be discarded on the grounds that they are not comparable or available in other places. Although such data are not cited in the following analysis, they constitute a latent resource for exploring further topics and special issues.

3. This paragraph and its accompanying tables and figures draw on some non-archive data in order to provide a complete analysis of the entire 12-year period for the five states under study. For the most part, the census figures presented are derived from archive data and represent the number of children in care on 31 December of each year. The archive does not contain data on Texas and California for the whole period 1983–1994, however. Our Texas data span the years 1985–1994, and our California data cover 1988–1994. Therefore, the year-end census counts for these two states, presented in Table 2, include internal agency tallies for the years that predate available archive data. All subsequent tables and figures in the chapter present archive data exclusively.

4. This analysis probably understates the total effect of urban caseload growth because some urbanized areas, such as San Antonio, Texas, and the San Francisco Bay area in California, are classified in the balance of the state.

5. In Michigan, kinship placements arranged through private agencies are indistinguishable from non-kin placements. In Texas, paid kinship placements are coded in the same manner as other licensed foster home placements and thus cannot be distinguished.

6. The increase is partly attributable to the large number of children who were already living with relatives as foster children but who were not counted as part of New York City's foster care population. As the result of a legal challenge, this "pre-existing" kinship caseload was formally recognized in 1987.

7. See R. M. Goerge, "The Reunification Process in Substitute Care," *Social Service Review* 64(3, 1990), pp. 422–457, and Paul D. Allison, *Event History Analysis: Regression for Longitudinal Event Data* (Beverly Hills: Sage, 1984).

8. See R. M. Goerge, F. H. Wulczyn, and A. W. Harden, *Foster Care Dynamics, 1983–1992: A Report from the Multistate Foster Care Data Archive* (pp. 39–41) (Chicago: University of Chicago, Chapin Hall Center for Children, 1994), for the results of an analysis using proportional hazards models.

2

The Adoption and Foster Care Analysis and Reporting System: Implications for Foster Care Policy

Raymond Collins

Mandated by the Congress and implemented by the Children's Bureau of the U.S. Department of Health and Human Services (HHS), the Adoption and Foster Care Analysis and Reporting System (AFCARS) is an ambitious attempt to collect comprehensive, uniform, case-level information on all children in the foster care system nationwide. AFCARS was designed to shed light on what happens to children who enter foster care, their characteristics, their living arrangements and the services provided, and, finally, the case outcomes. This chapter assesses this systematic effort to compile comparative information over time and across political jurisdictions on foster children.

Reliable and in-depth longitudinal information about foster care may help to illuminate the interrelationships of social policies and programs, such as the relationship between child abuse and neglect, on the one hand, and social interventions, such as welfare reform, family preservation, and foster care, on the other hand. The propensity for child welfare research to highlight "micro-events," at the expense of examining trends that affect large numbers of children and families, often precludes a balanced assessment of the costs and benefits associated with a social program.

For example, while child abuse and neglect account for approximately half of the children who enter the foster care system (Tatara, 1993), this awareness appears to have had comparatively little impact on the thinking and behavior of judges in relation to either child protective services (CPS) or foster care. Perhaps better information on the risks of reunifying children with abusing parents might alter court decisions. Welfare reform, passed by the Congress and signed by President Clinton in August 1996, offers another case in point. Proponents and opponents of this landmark social experiment differ markedly in their predictions about its potential impact on children and families. One relatively unambiguous social indicator is the extent to which welfare reform may result, directly or indirectly, in large numbers of children entering the foster care system. Some researchers (see Patrick Curtis's introduction to this book) have raised the concern that earlier state experiments with welfare reform have led to increases in the foster care population. State AFDC caseloads have been declining in recent years, accompanied by a disturbing parallel increase in foster care caseloads.[1] The Center for Law and Social Policy (1995) reported that 44 states reduced their AFDC caseloads by almost 324,000 families from the end of FY 1994 to mid-1995. During this period, the available evidence suggests that the number of children in foster care rose to nearly an all-time high. Over the next few years, more rigorous data collection and analysis should enable us to measure the effect of changes in the structure of welfare benefits on the child welfare system.

In addition to broader policy issues, the availability of AFCARS data, together with other child welfare information that is being collected on a larger scale and more systematically than heretofore, makes it possible to address fundamental questions about the functioning and effectiveness of the foster care system. In particular, basic information about case outcomes has been lacking at the state and national level (Courtney & Collins, 1994). As a result of the development of AFCARS and the related automated management information system (MIS) and monitoring initiatives, these data gaps are beginning to be addressed by the federal government and the states.

This chapter begins by outlining the major features of the emerging child welfare MIS that is likely to be in operation as we transition into the 21st century. After summarizing the new data on foster children made available by AFCARS and other large-scale initiatives, I delineate the benefits and limitations of foster care case-level data collection. Lastly, I analyze the implications of the evolving child welfare MIS for social policy and practice at federal, state, and community levels.

The Emerging Child Welfare MIS

The use of administrative data for child welfare research and evaluation purposes has been summarized elsewhere (Courtney & Collins, 1994).

Two key developments are of continuing significance for foster care policy and practice. The first is the development of the Voluntary Cooperative Information System (VCIS) by the American Public Welfare Association (APWS), with encouragement and funding support provided by HHS. VCIS was launched in 1982 in response to a shift of "program responsibilities from the federal to the state level" and efforts "to eliminate or reduce federal reporting requirements" (Tatara, 1993, p. 2), themes that echo in the present. Since its inception, aggregate VCIS data have been collected annually from state child welfare agencies about children in out-of-home care and special needs adoptions.

The second key development is the Multistate Foster Care Data Archive by the Chapin Hall Center for Children at the University of Chicago under a series of grants from the Children's Bureau combined with foundation support (Goerge, Wulczyn, & Harden, 1994). As discussed in chapter 1 of this book, the archive contains foster care data from California, Illinois, Michigan, New York, and Texas. This landmark research project includes the five states that represent approximately half the foster care caseload nationwide and aims to add five additional states. The availability of case-level longitudinal comparative data across states supports in-depth analyses of children in out-of-home care that would be impossible using VCIS aggregate point-in-time estimates. Data and reports generated by VCIS and the Multistate Foster Care Data Archive provide important insights into the functioning of the foster care system. However, neither represents an operational database with case-level data based upon uniform definitions at the state levels and nationwide.

In order to develop authoritative profiles of children in the foster care system, Congress enacted key legislation over the past decade. As part of the Omnibus Budget Reconciliation Act of 1986, Title IV-E of the Social Security Act was amended by adding Section 479, which launched a process that led to the development of AFCARS. Section 479 called for creation of the Advisory Committee on Adoption and Foster Care Information and set forth a timetable and a series of steps to develop an adoption and foster care data collection system. The committee report endorsed the collection of uniform foster care and adoption data. At the core of their proposal was the following recommendation (1987, p. 4), which became central to the genesis of the AFCARS system, particularly for foster care: "Individual child case information at the State and local level would be the foundation and

47

nucleus of the proposed data collection system. These are data used by State and local agencies in managing adoption and foster care programs on a day to day basis. A critical subset of data types and elements has been identified by the Committee that States would be mandated to submit for the national data collection system." The committee also recommended that VCIS data continue to be collected until uniform data become available so there would be no gap in the availability of adoption and foster care information.

The second step called for by Section 479 was that the secretary of HHS shall submit a report to the Congress that proposes a system for the collection of data relating to adoption and foster care. The following points in the secretary's report (HHS, 1989, p. 1) provided the framework for subsequent development of AFCARS: "The system must be mandatory throughout the nation, be able to provide reliable, consistent and uniform data over time and among jurisdictions using uniform definitions. The foster care data should encompass the population of all children under the responsibility of the State child welfare agency, including all children placed by private agencies under contract with the State agency. This population of children is the same as that covered by the requirements of Section 427 of the Act."

Regulations development was the third step in the implementation of Section 479. On 27 September 1990, HHS published a Notice of Proposed Rulemaking (NPRM), which reflected the original legislative requirement to begin full implementation of the data collection and reporting by 1 October 1991. However, HHS later sent the states an Information Memorandum stipulating that the final rule would specify the actual implementation date. During the interim, Congress passed and President Clinton signed into law in August 1993 the Human Resources Amendments of the Omnibus Budget Reconciliation Act (PL 103-66), which provided funding for family preservation and support and authorized enhanced funding for the development of automated child welfare systems, provided they incorporated the mandatory foster care and adoption reporting required by Section 479.

The availability of enhanced funding for child welfare systems development within the states had a galvanizing effect on the HHS regulatory process. Only 4 months after PL 103-66 became law, the AFCARS final rule was promulgated, together with an interim final rule providing for enhanced funding of the Statewide Automated Child Welfare Information Systems

(SACWIS) (*Federal Register*, 1993a and 1993b). Enhanced federal funding for SACWIS at the 75% matching rate, originally provided through 1996, was extended through 1997 by the welfare reform legislation, PL 104-193.

Under the AFCARS and SACWIS rules, states were faced with a choice. They could opt for a stand-alone AFCARS system, in which case the costs of systems development and implementation would be eligible for federal funding support at a 50% matching rate. Or they could opt for enhanced funding at the 75% match for a comprehensive SACWIS, including the full costs of AFCARS computer hardware and software development, but only to the extent that AFCARS is an integral part of a system that meets both sets of rules. The majority of states, not surprisingly, have chosen the latter option.

States are required to collect AFCARS data and report every 6 months on all children for whom the state Title IV-B/IV-E agency has responsibility for placement, care, or supervision, including Native American children. The final rule allows states a start-up transition before penalties phase in, with no penalties in effect for the reporting periods 1 October 1994 to 31 March 1995 through the period 1 April 1997 to 30 September 1997. AFCARS data to be submitted include:

general information—relating to the state agency reporting
child's demographic information
removal/placement setting indicators
circumstances of removal
current placement setting
most recent case plan goal
principal caretaker(s) information
parental rights termination (if applicable)
foster family parent(s) data
outcome information
source(s) of federal financial support/assistance for child

In order to receive enhanced funding under SACWIS, states must comply with all of the AFCARS requirements. In addition, they must design a comprehensive child welfare information system that, at a minimum, includes the following state systems:

systems operated under Title IV-A (AFDC)

National Child Abuse and Neglect Data Systems (NCANDS) (National
Center on Child Abuse and Neglect, 1996)
systems operated under Title XIX (Medicaid)
systems operated under Title IV-D (Child Support Enforcement)

The broad outlines of the 21st-century child welfare MIS are now clear, and
they are in the process of being implemented in states that are in the forefront of these developments. Apart from a handful of states that may
choose to forego enhanced funding, an overwhelming number of states
can be expected to implement AFCARS within the context of SACWIS. Thus,
in most states caseworkers and supervisors will be using computers for
their day-to-day recordkeeping. Information collection will be consistent
with AFCARS and capable of being mapped onto uniform definitions for
state and federal reporting purposes. Electronic interface will be possible
across foster care and adoption, child abuse and neglect, AFDC (or TANF),
Medicaid, and Child Support Enforcement.

With caseworkers, supervisors, administrators, and policymakers utilizing the same data systems, the reliability of the child welfare MIS, heretofore suspect, should be improved by an order of magnitude. Frontline
workers, for the first time, should receive regular reports from the MIS that
will help them to do their jobs, giving them a stake in ensuring that the data
in the system are accurate. Often they will be able to access the data directly
through a computer on their desk or to carry a laptop with them as they
move about the community. As these systems are fully phased in over the
next few years, the energies of policymakers, administrators, and practitioners can focus on identifying meaningful outcomes and learning how to
use the data wisely, rather than on the complexities of launching new
mechanisms for data collection and reporting.

What We Are Learning From AFCARS

At present, the only AFCARS data available are preliminary foster care data
from the first reporting period. These data cover the period 1 October 1994
to 31 March 1995 and reflect the status of children as of the last day of the
reporting period. AFCARS data are to be transmitted electronically within 45
days after the close of the reporting period, and these data were due at the
Administration for Children and Families (ACF) no later than 15 May 1995.
Since AFCARS was in a start-up phase, ACF allowed the states additional time
in order to improve the coverage and quality of the reporting and to

Table 1. Children in Substitute Care on 31 December, 1980–1994, Trend Rates, and Comparative AFCARS Data for 31 March 1995

Year	No. of children in substitute care (estimated)	Trend rate (%)	No. of states reporting	Data source
1980	303,443	NA	52	Office for Civil Rights 1980 census of the substitute care population
1981	NA	NA	NA	Not available
1982	262,000	NA	43	Voluntary Cooperative Information System (VCIS)
1983	269,000	2.7	51	VCIS
1984	270,000	0.4	52	VCIS
1985	270,000	0.0	52	VCIS
1986	280,000	3.7	32	VCIS
1987	300,000	7.1	36	VCIS
1988	340,000	13.3	32	VCIS
1989	383,000	12.6	34	VCIS
1990	400,000	4.4	52	VCIS
1991	414,000	3.5	45	VCIS
1992	427,000	3.1	47	VCIS
1993	445,000	4.2	50	VCIS
1994	462,000	3.8	33	VCIS (national total extrapolated from states reporting as of Aug. 1995)
March 1995 (6 mos.)	257,620	11.2	24	AFCARS data are actual no. of children reported by the 24 reporting states who reported on all population flow data elements.

Note: AFCARS=Adoption and Foster Care Analysis and Reporting System; VCIS=Voluntary Cooperative Information System of the American Public Welfare Association.

streamline data transmission. Twenty-five states had submitted AFCARS foster care data at the time of the analyses summarized here, although some submissions did not include all of the data elements. These analyses were prepared using AFCARS foster care data available as of January 1996.

The most striking AFCARS findings relate to the population flow data, which tend to confirm other information presented in this book about the continued growth of foster care caseloads. Table 1 shows the number of children in foster care over the past decade and a half, largely based upon VCIS data, compared with the most recent AFCARS data. The point-in-time estimate of the number of children in foster care ("substitute care" as defined by VCIS) increased from 262,000 children in 1982 to an estimated 462,000 children in 1994, or a growth of 76%. The annual trend rate began

51

the period at 2.7%, peaked at 13.3%, and ended the period at 3.8%.[2] Comparative vcis data are taken from vcis Research Notes (Tatara, 1995).

AFCARS data for the 6 months of the reporting period suggest that the mushrooming expansion of foster care is not over. AFCARS population flow data are available from 24 states (including the District of Columbia and Puerto Rico and excluding Indiana, which submitted AFCARS data but not sufficient information to calculate population flow indicators). The total foster care population in those 24 states as of the end of the reporting period was 257,620, nearly as many children as were in foster care in the entire country on the last day of 1982. Moreover, the trend rate for the 6-month period was a robust 11.2%. If this pace of percentage change in the number of children in care were sustained for the 12-month period ending 30 September 1995, it would lead to a trend rate greater than that reflected by vcis data for any previous year (see Table 1).

In an attempt to assess the validity of these AFCARS foster care data, we compared them with data from the Multistate Foster Care Data Archive for the period 1983–1993. Comparisons are possible only in the case of California and Illinois (AFCARS data were not available from Michigan, New York, and Texas). Table 2 reports the number of children in foster care in the two states from 1983, including year-by-year trend rates. Both states have experienced increases greater than the national average. California's year-end foster care population increased from 32,520 to 82,647 during 1983–1993, a 154% rise. California's annual trend rate varied from a low of 3% to a high of 20.4%. California's AFCARS 6-month trend rate of 5.5% is well within the parameters of the state's experience in recent years. As of 31 March 1995, California reported serving 89,347 children in foster care. Illinois's year-end foster care population increased during the same period from 15,285 to 39,408, a 158% rise. That state's trend rate ranged from a low of minus 1.5% to a high of 19.7%. Illinois's AFCARS 6-month trend rate of 7.8% is in the ballpark based upon these longitudinal data on trend rates. At the end of the AFCARS reporting period, Illinois reported serving 47,172 children in foster care.

Although the growth in the foster care population over time is important, so is the pattern of changes during the reporting period as a reflection of children entering and exiting care. AFCARS reports of caseload dynamics indicate that the net growth of 25,891 children over a 6-month period is accounted for by a high level of admissions coupled with a relatively low

Table 2. Children in Foster care in California and Illinois on 31 December, 1982–1993, Trend Rates, and Comparative AFCARS Data for 1 October 1994–31 March 1995

Year	No. of children in foster care California	Trend rate (%)	No. of children in foster care Illinois	Trend rate (%)	Data source
1983	32,520	NA	15,285	NA	*An Update from the Multistate Foster Care Data Archive: Foster Care Dynamics 1983-1993*, The Chapin Hall Center for Children
1984	36,540	12.4	15,240	-0.3	Chapin Hall
1985	39,666	8.6	15,017	-1.5	Chapin Hall
1986	43,599	9.9	15,081	0.4	Chapin Hall
1987	49,990	14.7	17,121	13.5	Chapin Hall
1988	55,393	10.8	19,005	11.0	Chapin Hall
1989	66,670	20.4	21,242	11.8	Chapin Hall
1990	70,630	5.9	23,876	12.4	Chapin Hall
1991	72,743	3.0	28,584	19.7	Chapin Hall
1992	77,087	6.0	33,749	18.1	Chapin Hall
1993	82,647	7.2	39,408	16.8	Chapin Hall
March 1995 (6 months)	89,347	5.5	47,172	7.8	AFCARS data are actual no. of children reported by Cal. & Ill.

Note: AFCARS = Adoption and Foster Care Analysis and Reporting System.

level of children being discharged from foster care. There were 231,729 children reported in AFCARS at the start of the reporting period, with 53,395 children entering care during the 6 months and 27,504 children exiting care, to leave 257,620 children in care on the last day of the reporting period. The AFCARS entry rate of 18.7% contrasts with an exit rate of 9.7%.[3]

The number of children in foster care is in part a function of the size of a state's child population. Prevalence rates measure the number of children in foster care at a particular time compared with the population of children under age 21.[4] On average, 65 children out of 10,000 children aged 21 and under were in foster care as of 31 March 1995 in the 24 states submitting AFCARS population flow data. The highest ratio was 203 children in the District of Columbia. Other states with high ratios of children in foster care included Illinois, 133; Rhode Island, 129; Vermont, 104; Massachusetts, 96; and California, 90.

Comparisons with VCIS suggest that the proportion of the national population of children in foster care has increased over time. In 1982, the prevalence rate was 32 children in substitute care. In 1990, 50 children out of

53

10,000 were in substitute care. The likelihood that a child would be in foster care on 31 March 1995 was more than double what it was on 31 December 1982, at least for those states submitting AFCARS data.

The average age of children at the time of removal from home for the purpose of being placed in foster care most recently was 6.8 years in reporting states, with a low of 5.6 years in Colorado and a high of 11.2 years in Vermont.

Approximately equal numbers of males (51.4%) and females (48.6%) were in foster care averaged across the reporting states. There were a total of 330,838 children reported on this data element, with 262 children reported as missing.

The national percentages for races reported for children in foster care were as follows: white, 41.6%; black, 42.4%; American Indian or Alaskan native, 1.9%; and Asian or Pacific Islander, 0.9%. Race and ethnicity posed difficulties for many states in reporting AFCARS data. Race and Hispanic origin are reported separately. Of the 330,838 children reported on the race data element, 13,126 were reported as undetermined and 30,338 were reported as missing this data element.

The states reported Hispanic origin information on a total of 314,778 children, including 53,536 children for whom they were unable to determine origin. Hispanic children accounted for 12.9% of those reported on this data element.

The most common placement setting was foster family home (nonrelative), which accounted for 38.6% of the children, followed by relative foster family home, 28%, and group home, 10%. A total of 330,838 child records were reported for current placement setting; however, 32,686 were recorded as missing this data element.

Children, including some who were discharged, had spent an average of 10.1 months in their latest placement setting, with a high of 17.4 months in Indiana. Other states reporting lengthy periods in the latest placement were California, 13.1 months; New Jersey, 12.7 months; and Massachusetts, 10.6 months.

The most recent case plan goal was one of the most universally available data elements, with 330,838 AFCARS records reported. However, 29,018 records were missing this data element, and for 11,500 children the case plan goal was not yet established. The most common goal was reunification, which accounted for half the children in foster care (49.6%). Adoption was the case plan goal for 11% of the children. Long-term foster care was similarly reported as the goal for 11% of the children.

Fifteen states provided some information about children discharged from foster care, indicating that a total of 39,092 children were discharged during the reporting period. The average length of time in the last foster care episode was 20.1 months, with a high of 33.3 months in Illinois. Other states reporting a long period of time in the last foster care episode were Massachusetts, 25.8 months; New Jersey, 23.1; and California, 21.2.

The average age of children at the time of discharge was 10.2 years. This ranged to a high of 13.1 years in Vermont.

Twenty-one states reported on the reason for discharge. The most common reason was the child's return to his or her family, which occurred in 67.7% of the reported cases. The next most common reason was adoption, which was the outcome for 9.2% of the children.

Benefits and Limitations of Case-Level Foster Care Data

After a decade of development, AFCARS is finally off the drawing board and becoming a reality in state after state. The lengthy delays in launching the system may, in fact, have helped build a consensus around the need for mandatory adoption and foster care data collection. It also enabled the technology to catch up with the demands posed by large-scale case-level data systems. Perhaps most important, AFCARS arrived on the scene together with the enhanced funding of SACWIS to make the development of a comprehensive child welfare MIS feasible.

Preliminary analyses of AFCARS data, like those presented in this chapter, should be used with caution. Until all states are submitting data and pending improvements in AFCARS data collection and reporting, the data will continue to pose pitfalls for the unwary. States are making good-faith efforts to come into compliance with the AFCARS requirements as rapidly as possible. This means that initial reports will be submitted at the same time that the states are modifying their systems to incorporate the uniform definitions called for in the AFCARS final rule. The problems that states experienced in reporting on race and Hispanic origin, with numerous cases recorded as unable to be determined or missing, illustrate the complexities of introducing new systems of case-level information.

These data incongruities lurk beneath the surface in systems of aggregate reporting like VCIS. With case-level reporting in AFCARS, they become obvious. States that have been in the forefront of AFCARS reporting should be commended for taking the risks inherent in making their data public. Experience with early data collection and reporting will ultimately prove to be the fast track to valid and reliable data.

The AFCARS regulations set forth careful safeguards to protect confidentiality, a critical consideration in case-level reporting systems. This is particularly true of AFCARS, where the ultimate intent is to allow public access to the database with appropriate safeguards. In the effort to preserve confidentiality, a state is not allowed to submit AFCARS reports that contain case record identifiers as they appear in the state's information system. States were given the option of either assigning sequential numbers or encrypting record numbers. Encryption is encouraged since it facilitates analysis of the data, as an encrypted record number can be used to follow a particular case over time across a sequence of AFCARS 6-month reporting periods. This allows for longitudinal analysis while protecting the particular child's identity. Procedures for analyzing data across reporting periods will differ from state to state, depending on whether the state has elected to use a common encrypted child identifier or has assigned a unique case number for each reporting period. It remains to be seen to what extent this issue will restrict the longitudinal analyses of AFCARS data.

Policy and Program Implications

The AFCARS final rule spelled out the purposes of establishing the data collection and reporting system and the expectations for uses of the data. Broadly, AFCARS was designed to serve the dual ends of policy development and program management at both state and federal levels. The data were crafted to meet the policy needs of the Congress, the Office of Management and Budget (OMB), and HHS to conduct strategic planning, formulate budget projections, and develop legislative proposals. It was assumed that similar purposes would be served within state legislatures and child welfare agencies. AFCARS data were expected to shed light on why children are in foster care and to help develop ways to keep children out of the child welfare system.

Some important issues can be addressed by AFCARS alone, including many related to the functioning of the foster care system, child demographic characteristics, and some outcome information. As can be seen from the preliminary analysis of the first wave of AFCARS reports presented

Table 3: Child Welfare Outcome Indicators and Principal Data Sources

Outcome indicators	Data source(s)
Rate of reported/substantiated child abuse and neglect in the overall child population.	SACWIS
Rate of reported/substantiated child abuse or neglect in active protective services cases.	SACWIS, AFCARS
Rate of reported/substantiated child abuse or neglect in formerly active protective services cases.	SACWIS, AFCARS
Out-of-home placement rate for children with families who received family preservation services.	AFCARS, special research
Rate of reunification of children in care with their families over time.	AFCARS
Rate of children in care receiving other permanent placements (e.g., long-term foster care with relative, guardianship, adoption) over time.	AFCARS
Rate of substantiated repeat abuse and neglect over time for children returned home or in other permanent placement.	AFCARS, SACWIS
Rate of out-of-home care recidivism over time for children returned home or in other permanent placement.	AFCARS
Measures of permanent stability for children in care (e.g., number of placement changes per each year in care).	AFCARS
Rates of abuse, neglect, injury, and death of children in permanent placement.	SACWIS, AFCARS
Rates of unsuccessful discharge from permanent placement (e.g., runaway from placement with refusal to return, incarceration).	AFCARS, special research
Truancy rate of children in care.	AFCARS, special research
Arrest and conviction rates of children in care.	AFCARS, special research
Pregnancy rates of adolescents in care.	AFCARS, special research
Housing, employment, financial, and educational achievement status of youths in care at exit from long-term out-of-home care.	AFCARS, special research

Note: AFCARS = Adoption and Foster Care Analysis and Reporting System; SACWIS = Statewide Automated Child Welfare Information Systems.

above, however, the data take on greater significance in addressing major policy and program strategy questions when combined with other information.

Answering many critical questions requires that AFCARS data be combined with data from other elements of a comprehensive child welfare MIS, such as is hoped will result from SACWIS. Since there is no national system of SACWIS reporting (the separate strands of AFCARS, NCANDS, AFDC/TANF,

Medicaid, and Child Support Enforcement are required to be woven together at the state level, but not nationally), these issues can be studied only by individual states or through special multistate research initiatives, such as that undertaken by the Chapin Hall Center for Children.

Analyzing other questions may call for combining AFCARS data with ad hoc, in-depth research studies to explore particular topics. The relationship of family preservation and support and foster care would be an example of the latter type of study, since SACWIS may not encompass essential data necessary to identify outcomes of children served by family preservation programs who are at risk of foster care.

Table 3 spells out a list of outcome indicators that have been identified as the essential minimum for a child welfare MIS, including foster care (Courtney & Collins, 1994), and indicates, on the basis of current information, whether the critical data are likely to be contained in AFCARS or SACWIS, or if obtaining the data would involve special research studies. Out of the 15 indicators, AFCARS is the principal data source for 4; the primary source, coupled with other information, for an additional 7; a supplemental source to SACWIS for 3 outcomes; and not necessary to address 1 of the outcomes. Therefore, AFCARS data will no doubt contribute to important policy and program management goals at federal and state levels.

Notes

1. AFDC (Aid to Families with Dependent Children) was replaced by TANF (Temporary Assistance to Needy Families) in the welfare reform legislation, the Personal Responsibility and Work Opportunity Reconciliation Act of 1996 (Public Law 104–193).

2. Trend rate is the percentage change in the number of children in care (the number of children in care on the last day of the reporting period less the number of children in care on the first day) out of the total number of children in care on the first day of the reporting period.

3. Entry rate is the percentage of children entering care out of the total number of children served. Exit rate is the percentage of children exiting care out of the total number of children served.

4. Prevalence rate is the percentage of total number of children served out of the U.S. census estimate of the number of children under age 21. The rate is presented as per 10,000 children.

References

Administration for Children and Families. (1987). *Report of the Advisory Committee on Adoption and Foster Care Information.* Washington DC: Author.

Center for Law and Social Policy. (1995). *AFDC caseloads, FY 1994 and July 1995.* Washington DC: Author.

Courtney, M. E., & Collins, R. C. (1994). New challenges and opportunities in child welfare outcomes and information technologies. *Child Welfare, 73,* 359–378.

Federal Register. (1993a, 22 December). Adoption and foster care analysis and reporting system (AFCARS). Final Rule (45 Code of Federal Regulations, Parts 1355 and 1356).

Federal Register. (1993b, 22 December). Statewide automated child welfare information systems (SACWIS) Interim Final Rule (45 Code of Federal Regulations, Parts 1355 and 1356).

Goerge, R. M., Wulczyn, F. H., & Harden, A. (1994). *Foster care dynamics: California, Illinois, Michigan, New York and Texas—A first-year report from the Multistate Foster Care Data Archive.* Chicago: University of Chicago, Chapin Hall Center for Children.

National Center on Child Abuse and Neglect. (1996, April). *Child maltreatment 1994: Reports from states to the National Center on Child Abuse and Neglect.* Washington DC: U.S. Department of Health and Human Services.

Tatara, T. (1993). *Characteristics of children in substitute and adoptive care: A statistical summary of the VCIS National Child Welfare Data Base.* Based on FY 1982 through FY 1990 data. Washington DC: American Public Welfare Association (APWA).

Tatara, T. (1995, August). *U.S. child substitute care flow data for FY 1993 and trends in the state child substitute care populations* (VCIS Research Notes No. 11). Washington DC: American Public Welfare Association.

U.S. Department of Health and Human Services. (1989). *Adoption and foster care data collection: Report of the secretary of the Department of Health and Human Services to the Congress of the United States.* Washington DC: Author.

Children in Foster Care

3

Predictors of Child Protective Service Intake Decisions: Case Closure, Referral to Continuing Services, or Foster Care Placement

Susan Zuravin and Diane DePanfilis

The primary objective of child protective services (CPS) is to protect the child from recurrences of child maltreatment. With the advent of risk assessment in a majority of CPS programs (English & Pecora, 1994), the investigative caseworker is faced with the necessity of making one of three possible decisions: (a) to close the case at the end of intake because the child(ren) is(are) at low risk for re-maltreatment; (b) to refer the family for continuing CPS; or (c) to institute placement of the child(ren) in foster care. While there is a large clinical and empirical literature on decision-making factors, studies have yet to examine if the predictors of the three decisions are similar or different (Zuravin & DePanfilis, in press). The purpose of the study reported in this chapter is to begin to fill this gap in the empirical knowledge base.

Researchers have paid considerable clinical and empirical attention to decision-making factors (Zuravin & DePanfilis, in press). Studies have examined demographic, maternal, child, and family characteristics. Despite the plethora of studies conducted (DePanfilis & Scannapieco, 1994; Kadushin & Martin, 1988) and variables examined, conclusions regarding those factors that influence decision making are not forthcoming for two possible reasons. First, study designs differ enormously with regard to factors selected for exploration, operationalization of the same potential pre-

The research reported in this chapter was funded by grants from the Lois and Samuel Silberman Foundation and the National Center on Child Abuse and Neglect (Grant no. 90-CA-1376). The authors are grateful to the Baltimore City Department of Social Services for their willingness to share data and helpful assistance with the study.

dictors, unit of analysis (child vs. family), type of maltreatment studied, and analytic strategy. With regard to the latter, few investigators have used multiple regression approaches to identify predictors (e.g., Lindsey, 1991, 1992; Runyan, Gould, Trost, & Loda, 1981). Consequently, it is impossible to identify factors that have unique effects on caseworker decision making. Second, and equally important, studies differ with regard to jurisdiction. Some employ cases from multiple locations, whereas others examine cases from a single program. Given differences among jurisdictions with regard to predictors of the substantiation decision (Zuravin, Orme, & Hegar, 1995) and the apparent powerful effect of jurisdiction on foster care decision making (e.g., Jeter, 1963; Runyan et al., 1981), it is not surprising to find that results conflict across studies.

Notwithstanding clinical decision-making models (for a review, see De-Panfilis & Scannapieco, 1994) that emphasize the importance of maternal and family characteristics as important decision-making factors as well as research findings suggesting that parent alcohol and drug problems (AOD) increase the likelihood of CPS intervention in general (Zuravin, Orme, & Hegar, 1995) and foster care placement in particular (Zuravin & DePanfilis, in press), few studies have examined AOD problems in the context of a multiple regression analytic approach. The same is true for other maternal and family problems, including domestic violence, maternal developmental limitations, and emotional health difficulties. Studies that have focused on multiple types of maltreatment (Lindsey, 1991, 1992; Runyan et al., 1981) as opposed to sexual abuse only (Hunter, Coulter, Runyan, & Everson, 1990; Leifer, Shapiro, & Kassem, 1993; Pellegrin & Wagner, 1990) have focused mainly on demographic factors. Another deficit characteristic of the literature is the failure to examine interactions between potentially important predictors. Consequently, it is not possible to determine whether predictors are dependent on such factors as maltreatment type, recurrence status, and specific maternal problems.

Given these problems with the current literature, the objectives of this correlational study are (a) to examine the predictive power of nine characteristics from three domains—demographic variables, maltreatment aspects, and maternal family problems—on the decision to place the child or to provide continuing services to the family and the decision to provide continuing service or to close the case at the end of intake; (b) to identify interactions between maltreatment type, recurrence status, maternal problems, and other variables included in the model; and (c) to assess the predictive efficiency of each of the two models.

Methodology

SUBJECTS

Study subjects include 1,034 families reported for child physical abuse or neglect to the Baltimore City Department of Social Services' Division of Child Protective Services during the 1-year period from 1 January to 31 December 1988. All families were substantiated for one of the two types of maltreatment by 1 May 1989 and met five other study criteria. We used a family rather than child unit of analysis because we believe that it is less likely to confound study findings for two reasons. First, when families have two or more children, inclusion of all children is likely to result in overestimation of the partial regression coefficients for predictors that are characteristic of these families and underestimation of those for one-child families. Second, use of only the first child (Runyan et al., 1981) or random selection of a child could lead to selection effects.

A two-step procedure was used to select families for study inclusion. First, from the 8,620 reports made during 1988, we identified all families (n = 2,902) who met study criterion 1: at least one report of physical abuse or neglect made during 1988 that was substantiated prior to 1 May 1989. Excluded from selection were reports on foster parents, children living in group homes, and day-care centers. After stratifying the 2,902 families who met criterion 1 by the month of their first substantiated report, we randomly selected approximately 45% of the families from each month (total n = 1,675) for step 2 screening.

Second, we examined the CPS case records of the 1,675 families selected during step 1 to determine those that met the remaining four eligibility criteria and to abstract information on placement predictors. Of the 1,675 families, we were able to access and screen for eligibility the records of 95% (n = 1,583). To ensure inter-rater reliability among the nine staff who worked on this step, a detailed manual with operational definitions for each variable was developed, all raters were thoroughly trained, and each case record was independently read by two raters. In the event of unresolvable differences between the two raters, a third reader settled the conflict. Of the 1,583 families, 1,035 were eligible for the study.

The remaining four criteria included (a) family residence within the geographical limits of the city at maltreatment occurrence; (b) caregiving provided by maltreated child's biological mother at the time of the 1988 index incident; (c) families experiencing a placement had at least one child remaining in care at the close of the CPS investigative phase (thus, no temporary or short-term foster care placements, those where children were returned prior to the close of intake, were included among the cases or comparisons [n = 141] because we feared they might confound the findings); and (d) the maltreatment characteristic of each family met the study operational definition of either physical abuse or neglect.

The latter criteria required that the allegation(s) of maltreatment reported to public CPS meet two additional criteria: each allegation had to (a) adhere to the definitions of maltreatment set forth in state laws (operationalized as "confirmation of the allegations by the investigative caseworker") and (b) meet the minimum maltreatment severity standards established by the authors for the study. These criteria, operationalized by measures established by individual researchers, vary from study to study (Zuravin, 1991). The definitions of type as well as the severity criteria for study inclusion are adaptations of measures developed by Magura and Moses (1986). Following are the definitions of the three types of maltreatment found among study families.

Physical abuse

A physically abused child is a minor who has been the victim of excessive and inappropriate use of physical force by a parent, parent substitute, or temporary caregiver. Severity of harm is measured at the ordinal level and divided into four categories: (a) *no injury*—child was the victim of unacceptable modes of physical discipline or aggression (e.g., hitting with a fist, kicking, choking, holding under water) that endangered well-being but did not result in physical injury; (b) *mild injuries*—welts, cuts, abrasions, bruises, and first-degree burns localized in one or two areas and involving no more than two separate injuries in each area; (c) *moderate injuries*—mild concussions, broken teeth, cuts or gashes requiring sutures, second-degree burns, fractures of small bones (e.g., fingers, toes); and (d) *serious injuries*—third-degree burns, brain or spinal cord injuries, eye injuries, fractures of bones other than the fingers or toes, severe concussions, and internal injuries. A child is assigned a severity code on the basis of the most severe injury sustained.

Child neglect

Child neglect refers to ten types of omissions in care by the child's primary caregiver. The first eight subtypes are inadequate physical health care, mental health care, supervision of child activities, household sanitation, household safety, personal hygiene, choice of a temporary caregiver(s), and nutrition. The remaining two subtypes are diagnosed non-organic failure to thrive and instability of living conditions. Each subtype has two severity levels. Level 1 indicates that the child is at risk for negative consequences but at the point of the CPS investigation was not showing obvious signs of significant harm (injury, illness, developmental delay, or mental health problems). Level 2 indicates that the child suffered negative consequences. Consequences vary by subtype.

Sexual abuse

Sexual abuse (SA) was included because some of the families who were substantiated for physical abuse or neglect were also substantiated for SA. The operational definition, taken from Russell (1983), classifies SA by perpetrator (extrafamilial and intrafamilial), child age, and severity. For extrafamilial SA, definitions differ by age. For children aged 13 years and younger, SA is one or more unwanted sexual experiences ranging from molestation to intercourse with any person unrelated by blood or marriage. For adolescents aged 14 to 17, SA is restricted to completed or attempted forcible rape by any person unrelated by blood or marriage. Intrafamilial SA is any exploitive sexual behavior ranging from molestation to intercourse that occurs before the age of 18 between relatives, no matter how distant the relationship. SA has four severity levels: (a) uncertain—used for cases where abuse is confirmed but workers are unable to determine exactly what occurred; (b) molestation—fondling genitals, breasts, or anal area as well as having children exhibit themselves; (c) nonpenile intercourse—penetration of the vagina or rectum with any object other than the penis; and (d) penile intercourse including oral, anal, or genital penetration.

MEASURES

Dependent

Two dichotomous dependent variables were created. To examine the first, service status, cases closed at the end of intake were coded 0, while those that were referred for continuing services were coded 1 (foster care is excluded from this category). To examine the second variable, foster care status, cases that were referred for continuing service were coded 0, while those where at least one child was placed in foster care and remained in care at the close of intake were coded 1.

Independent

Nine variables from three domains were selected for examination. The three demographic characteristics include maternal age at first birth, maternal race, and family status regarding Aid to Families with Dependent Children (AFDC). The first variable is ordinally measured and was included so that we could examine whether the rise in adolescent first births has affected placement decision making. Maternal racial status (0 = white, 1 = African American) was included to examine the possibility of racially biased decision making. AFDC status (0 = no, 1 = yes), a crude marker of family socioeconomic status (case records did not include better indices), was included to minimize the possibility of its confounding results for race and to assess the possibility of socioeconomically biased decision making.

The four potential maternal problems—AOD, emotional difficulties, developmental delay or limitations, and domestic violence—were included for two reasons: (a) to determine if parental functioning has an important impact on placement decision making and (b) to test whether the increase in AOD has translated into a stronger effect on placement decision making for this problem than the remaining three. Although we realize that the problems of other caregivers living in the home, particularly the father or the mother's partner, are likely to influence placement decision making, we were constrained to operationalize these variables only for the mother because the case record included little, if any, information about other caregivers. Emotional problems, domestic violence, and developmental delay are dummy variables. AOD is a three-level categorical variable where 0 = no, 1 = alcohol, 2 = drug(s) or alcohol and drug(s).

To obtain a positive rating for variables in the maternal problem domain, the case record narrative must have included evidence to indicate that the specific problem significantly interfered with the mother's ability to parent at any time. Evidence included any of the following: (a) mother admits having the problem, (b) family member(s) or relevant other(s) testify that mother has the problem, or (c) caseworker witnesses an occurrence of the problem or its effect on the mother. Additional criteria for AOD and mental health problems included hospitalization or outpatient treatment, whereas for domestic violence other criteria included residence in or attendance at sessions conducted by a shelter for battered women or other relevant programs.

The two maltreatment characteristics included a history of a prior maltreatment incident(s) and maltreatment type–number. They were included to assess both their main and interaction effects. The former variable is dichotomous; families with no substantiated incidents prior to the 1988 index were coded 0, and families with at least one prior substantiated report were coded 1. Codes for the latter variables were neglect = 0, physical abuse = 1, and multiple types including sexual abuse = 2. These codes indicated whether physical abuse or neglect were the sole types of substantiated maltreatment ever or whether the family had been substantiated for multiple types including any combination of physical abuse, neglect, and sexual abuse. It was necessary to use this inherently interactive variable rather than three separate variables—physical abuse only, neglect only, and multiple types of maltreatment—because severe multicollinearity between the three caused matrix problems.

DATA ANALYSIS STRATEGY

Two sets of analyses were run for all procedures: one for each dependent variable. First, crude odds ratios were calculated to estimate the likelihood of placement associated with each predictor (Table 1). Then, hierarchical maximum likelihood logistic regression analyses with deviation contrasts were conducted to identify the effect of the three domains as well as each predictor on the likelihood of placement and the likelihood of continuing service. Demographic variables were entered in a block first, followed by maltreatment characteristics, maternal problems, and each multiplicative, first-order interaction term separately. The final hierarchical model for service status (closure at the end of intake vs. referral to continuing service), the one used to estimate the predictive efficiency of the model, included 9 predictors, all of the original variables. The final model for foster care status (referral to continuing service vs. foster care placement) included 11 predictors, the 9 original variables plus 2 interaction terms that were significant at $p < .05$. To assure that partial logistic regression coefficients from the two models were independent so that they could be compared, the 370 cases that were referred to continuing service were randomly divided into two groups of 185 cases, and a different set of 185 was used for each of the two sets of analyses. Thus, the sample size for the service status analyses was 391, and the sample size for the foster care status analyses was 643.

Presented in Tables 2 and 4 are logits (the log of the odds ratio) and relative odds ratios (estimates of the likelihood of placement or continuing service given a one-unit change in each predictor, controlling for all other variables in the model). Odds ratios greater than one indicate that a unit change in the predictor increases the likelihood of placement, whereas ratios less than one indicate the opposite. To assess model predictive efficiency we developed specificity, sensitivity, and predictive values (Tables 3 and 5) by comparing actual and predicted placement status for the families included in the foster care analysis and the families included in the service status analysis.

Findings

SERVICE STATUS (CASE CLOSURE VS. CONTINUING SERVICE)

Crude odds ratios

Examination of the crude odds ratios for the nine potential predictors (see Table 1, column 3) revealed that six of the nine variables were statistically significant. Families who were receiving or had received AFDC, whose 1988 index report represented a recurrence of maltreatment, and who included a mother with mental health or alcohol problems were more likely to be referred to continuing service. On the other hand, families where the mother was older than 18 at first birth and where the maltreatment included physical abuse only (as opposed to multiple types of maltreatment) were less likely to be referred to continuing service.

Logistic regression findings

Logistic regression results differ somewhat from those for the bivariate analyses (see Table 2). Findings reveal that the first block of variables ac-

Table 1. Percentages and Crude Odds Ratios Estimating the Likelihood of Placement

Variables	Case Clos.	Cont Serv.	Odds Ratio	Cont. Serv.	Foster Care	Odds Ratio
Race						
Other	18.0	19.5	.91	26.5	21.0	1.36
Afr-Amer	82.0	80.5		73.5	79.0	
AFDC						
No	45.1	30.8	1.85**	38.9	31.2	1.40
Yes	54.9	69.2		61.1	68.8	
Mom's age 1st birth						
Greater 18	60.7	50.3	.81*	47.6	45.9	.97
Less 18	39.3	49.7		52.4	54.1	
Maltreatment type						
Multiple	24.3	33.5		27.0	46.5	
Physical Abuse	34.0	14.1	.30***	18.4	13.1	.73*
Neglect	41.7	52.4	.91	54.6	40.4	.76*
Recurrence						
No	79.1	69.7	1.65*	72.4	56.6	2.02***
Yes	20.9	30.3		27.6	43.4	
AOD problems						
No	90.3	80.5		78.9	46.7	
Alcohol	1.0	5.4	2.78*	4.3	10.3	1.54
Drugs or drugs & alcohol	8.7	14.1	.80	16.8	43.0	1.67**
Developmental problems						
No	99.5	97.8	4.49	93.0	92.8	1.03
Yes	.5	2.2		7.0	7.2	
Mental health problems						
No	98.1	91.4	4.78**	92.4	80.3	2.98***
Yes	1.9	8.6		7.6	19.7	
Domestic violence						
No	91.3	89.2	1.27	82.7	80.6	1.15
Yes	8.7	10.8		17.3	19.4	

*$p<.05$ **$p<.01$ ***$p<.001$

Table 2. Logistic Regression Results for Case Closure vs. Continuing Service (Logits and Odds Ratios)

Variables	Step 1		Step 2		Step 3	
	Logit	Odds Ratios	Logit	Odds Ratios	Logit	Odds Ratios
Race	-.16	.85	-.17	.85	-.15	.86
AFDC	.30	1.35**	.19	1.21	.15	1.16
Mom's age 1st birth	.19	1.20	.18	1.20	.24	1.27*
Maltreatment type						
Abuse vs multiple types			-.66	.51***	-.62	.54***
Neglect vs multiple types			.34	1.41*	.30	1.35*
Recurrence			.15	1.16	.04	1.05
AOD						
Alcohol					.93	2.54
Drug/drug & alcohol					-.27	.76
Developmental problems					.65	1.92
Mental health problems					.71	2.04
Domestic violence					.06	1.07
Constant	-.06		-.06		1.82**	
$x2$	12.52**	$df=3$	17.79***	$df=3$	14.63**	$df=5$

$*p<.05$ $**p<.01$ $***p<.001$

Note: n = 391

Table 3. Comparison of Actual Continuing Service Referral With Predictions From Logistic Regression Model

| | | Predicted | | |
		Continue	Closure	Total
Actual	Continue	109	76	185
	Closure	71	135	206
	Total	180	211	391

Sensitivity	58.6%
False Positive Rate	39.4%
Positive Predictive Value	60.6%
Specificity	64.0%
False Negative Rate	36.0%
Prevalence of Foster Care	47.3%

counted for a significant amount of the likelihood of being referred to continuing service. Of the three variables, AFDC status was significant. Families who were receiving or had received AFDC were approximately 35% more likely to be referred to continuing service than families who had not received this form of assistance.

The second block of variables, the two maltreatment characteristics (recurrence status and maltreatment type and number) led to a significant improvement in the ability of the model to predict a continuing service referral over a model including only the constant and the family demographic variables. Only the variable for maltreatment type and number of types was significant. Findings revealed that abusive families were about half as likely to be referred for continuing service as families with multiple types of maltreatment, whereas neglectful families were 41% more likely to be referred. It is important to note that once this block was entered into the model, AFDC, the one statistically significant predictor from the first block, became insignificant.

The third block of variables, the four maternal problems, led also to a significant improvement in the ability of the model to predict continuing service referral status over a model including the constant plus the first two blocks. Only one of the four variables was significant. Mothers with mental health problems were 104% more likely than those who did not have such problems to be referred to continuing service. Of the 22 interaction terms entered separately in the fourth step, none were significant (findings not shown).

Sensitivity and specificity

Analyses (see Table 3) reveal that the model performs very poorly relative to prediction of the actual continuing service decision for each family. Information presented in Table 3 identifies high rates of both false positives and false negatives. The former rate indicates that the model wrongly classified 39.4% of the families as being referred to continuing service when in fact they were not, and the latter rate indicates that the model wrongly classified 36% of the families as not being referred when in fact they were.

FOSTER CARE STATUS (CONTINUING SERVICE VS. FOSTER CARE)

Crude odds ratios

Examination of the crude odds ratios for the nine potential predictors (see Table 1, column 3) revealed that four are statistically significant. Families whose 1988 index report represented a recurrence of maltreatment and included a mother with drug or mental health problems were more likely to experience the placement of a child in foster care. On the other hand, families where the maltreatment included physical abuse only or neglect only were less likely to have at least one child placed in foster care than families where children experienced multiple types of maltreatment.

Logistic regression findings

Logistic regression results (Table 4) show that the first block of variables, the three demographic characteristics (race, AFDC status, and mother's age at first birth), failed to account for a significant amount of the likelihood of placement. The second block of variables, the two maltreatment characteristics (recurrence status and maltreatment type and number), led to a significant improvement in the ability of the model to predict placement status over a model including only the constant and the family demographic variables. Both variables were statistically significant. Specifically,

74

Table 4. Logistic Regression Results for Continuing Service vs. Foster Care (Logits and Odds Ratios)

Variables	Step 1		Step 2		Step 3	
	Logit	Odds Ratios	Logit	Odds Ratios	Logit	Odds Ratios
Race	.12	1.13	.15	1.16	.17	1.18
AFDC	.15	1.16	.12	1.13	-.03	.97
Mom's age 1st birth	.01	1.01	.01	1.01	.02	1.02
Maltreatment type						
Physical abuse vs multiple types			-.18	.83	.14	1.01
Neglect vs multiple types			-.27	.76*	-.49	.62**
Recurrence			.22	1.24*	.18	1.20
AOD						
Alcohol					.26	1.30
Drug/drug & alcohol					.69	1.99**
Developmental problems					.03	1.03
Mental health problems					.50	1.66**
Domestic violence					-.11	.89
Constant	.80*****		.85*****		1.68*****	
x2	4.84	df=3	26.16	df=3	67.70*****	df=5

findings revealed that (a) neglectful families were about 25% as likely to experience a placement as families with multiple types of maltreatment, whereas abusive families were equally as likely to experience a placement, and (b) families whose index incident represented a recurrence were about 25% more likely to experience a placement than those whose incident represented a first-time reported occurrence.

Entry of the third block of variables, the four maternal problems, led to a significant improvement in the ability of the model to predict placement status over a model including the constant plus the first two blocks. Two of the four variables were significant. Families where mothers had drug or drug and alcohol problems were almost 100% more likely to experience a placement than those without such problems, whereas those with only alcohol problems were equally as likely as those without substance problems to experience a placement; and families where mothers had mental health problems were 66% more likely than those without such problems to experience a placement. It is important to note that once this block was entered in the analysis, recurrence status (second block) no longer had a significant impact on the likelihood of placement.

Of the 22 interaction terms entered separately in the fourth step, two interactions, AFDC status by recurrence status and mental health problems by substance problems, led to a significant improvement in the predictive ability of the model. Examination of the interactions for mental health problems by substance problems revealed that families where mothers had mental health problems but no substance problems were more likely to experience a placement than those without mental health problems, whereas those families where mothers had both mental health problems and substance problems were not more likely to experience a placement than those with only substance problems. Findings with regard to AFDC status by recurrence status revealed that families whose index did not represent a recurrence were not more likely to experience a placement if they were receiving AFDC, whereas those whose index did represent a recurrence were more likely to experience a placement if they were receiving or had ever received AFDC.

Sensitivity and specificity
To assess predictive efficiency a final analysis with the two significant interaction terms entered in a fourth block was conducted. Findings (not shown) revealed that the two interaction terms together improved the pre-

Table 5. Comparison of Actual Foster Care Placements With Predictions From Logistic Regression Model

		Predicted		
		Continue	Closure	Total
Actual	Continue	413	45	458
	Closure	123	62	185
	Total	536	107	643

Sensitivity	90.2%
False Positive Rate	22.9%
Positive Predictive Value	77.1%
Specificity	57.9%
False Negative Rate	42.1%
Prevalence of Foster Care	71.2%

dictive efficiency of the model over one including the third block ($x^2 = 7.013$, $df = 3$; $p < .07$; 2 log likelihood = 666.074, $df = 628$, $p < .14$). Sensitivity and specificity analyses showed that the model does not perform very adequately relative to prediction of the actual placement decision for each family. Information presented in Table 5 identifies high rates of both false positives and false negatives. The former rate indicates that the model wrongly classified 22.9% of the families as experiencing a placement when in fact they did not. The latter rate indicates that the model wrongly classified 42.1% of the families as not experiencing a placement when in fact they did.

COMPARISON OF FINDINGS FROM THE TWO MODELS

To statistically compare the logits of identical predictors across analyses for the two dependent variables, a z statistic was computed by taking the difference of the two logit coefficients and dividing by the square root of the sum of the two standard errors squared. When the z statistic was 1.96 or greater, the difference was considered significant at the $p < .05$ level. Comparison of logits for the nine predictors across the two final models (i.e., the one with all three blocks entered into the equation) identified two predictors that differed significantly—maltreatment type/number of types and substance abuse problems. In addition to these two differences, sensitivity and specificity findings suggest that the foster care model has greater predictive efficiency than the case closure vs. continuing service model.

Discussion and Implications

CPS intake caseworkers routinely face difficult decisions about the type of service(s) to provide to maltreating families—i.e., close the case at the end of intake services because the risk of recurrence is low, refer the family to continuing services for intervention, or place a child(ren) in foster care. What factors influence decision making? Do they differ by type of decision to be made? Empirical study of judgment predictors is practically important because of their potential for guiding agency policy and program decision making. For example, knowledge of considerations that drive judgments can help to determine if caseworkers are adhering to clinical guidelines, risk assessment criteria, or empirical predictors of recurrence. In turn, such information can provide important insights for shaping the development of training programs and supervisory oversight. In an effort to fill gaps in knowledge about decision-making factors, the data presented in this chapter had one main focus—to determine if decision-making factors differ by the type of decision to be made.

STUDY LIMITATIONS

Prior to the summary and discussion of results, it is important to specify two limitations on interpretation that stem from the retrospective case record study design, the most widely used approach for conducting such studies. First, inclusion of all possibly relevant decision-making factors is not possible because case records vary considerably with regard to the information recorded by different workers. Consequently, model misspecification errors may occur and lead to over- or underestimation of the statistical parameters of variables included in the equation. Second, information on variables included in the model may be erroneous because of variation among caseworkers relative to the thoroughness of both the investigation and case record narratives of findings as well as competency in recognizing specific problems. For example, caseworkers' failure to record the existence of family and maternal problem(s) or to recognize difficulties like domestic violence, substance abuse, and maternal mental health problems would lead to some families being assigned a negative status on these predictors, when in fact they should have been assigned a positive status. Depending on the extensiveness of such inaccuracies, findings for the four maternal difficulties may be falsely negative or fail to reflect the true magnitude of the variable's effect on the decision.

SUMMARY OF FINDINGS, INTERPRETATIONS, AND IMPLICATIONS

Analyses identified three significant predictors of referral to continuing service—mother's age at first birth, maltreatment type/number of types, and maternal mental health problems—and five significant predictors of foster care placement—maltreatment type/number of types, maternal substance problems, maternal mental health difficulties, and two interactions, AFDC status by recurrence status and maternal mental health problems by maternal substance problems. Comparison of predictors across the two models identified two that differed significantly—maltreatment type/number of types and maternal substance problems. With regard to the former, findings showed that for the model of case closure vs. referral to continuing services, neglect increases the likelihood and physical abuse decreases the likelihood of a referral compared to multiple types of maltreatment, whereas findings for the model of referral to continuing services vs. foster care placement revealed almost the opposite—that is, neglectful families were less likely than those characterized by multiple types of maltreatment to experience a placement, whereas abusive families were equally as likely to experience a placement. Importantly, they also revealed that maternal substance abuse increased the likelihood of a family experiencing a foster care placement but not a referral to continuing service.

Information obtained from discussions with caseworkers and administrators provided some insight into the rationales underlying results. First, the increased probability of a continuing service referral for neglectful families was associated, at least according to the caseworkers, with two characteristics—the likelihood of the neglect being ongoing and pervasive—as well as the notion that continuing surveillance might be effective in promoting better care of the children. The decreased likelihood of placement was associated with the caseworkers' observations that neglect rarely resulted in severe physical injuries. Caseworkers gave the opposite explanation for physical abuse. Because of concerns about the high likelihood of recurrences that could result in severe physical injuries and even death (particularly when children were young), caseworkers were more likely to make the decision to place children from families where abuse had either occurred alone or in combination with other types of maltreatment. Second, the greater likelihood of both continuing referrals and foster care placement of children from families with mothers who had mental health problems reflected the caseworkers' notion that such children were at higher risk for being maltreated again than children from families not typified by such problems. Third, the greater probability of experiencing a foster care placement typical of families with a substance-abusing mother was caused by the caseworkers' belief that recurrence was extremely likely and, unlike maternal mental health problems, could best be alleviated by placement.

Equally as important as the positive findings are the negative ones. Unlike those from earlier efforts (e.g., Lindsey, 1992), they do not suggest that decision making is racially biased. African-American families are no more likely to be referred to continuing services or to experience a foster care placement than white families. Possible socioeconomic bias appeared to exist in only one situation—when the index incident represented a recurrence. In this one instance, families were more likely to experience a placement if they were receiving AFDC at the time of the index or had ever received such funding.

Because the primary purpose of CPS is to prevent recurrences of maltreatment, accuracy of decision making can be assessed and implications for future research can be derived from comparing findings to those from predictive studies of maltreatment recurrence. To date, only one comprehensive review of the recurrence empirical literature (DePanfilis & Zuravin, 1996) exists. Although this extensive examination of multiple regression–type studies does not present information on conflict among findings from different research efforts regarding individual variables (it offers instead data on the number of studies that identified a significant finding for a particular predictor), it is not without value for the above purposes. Review of results revealed that all four of the maternal problems constructs we examined were associated with recurrence by at least one study. Particularly impressive with respect to positive findings was the construct of maternal emotional health. Five different studies (Baird, 1988; Baird, Wagner, & Neuenfeldt, 1993; Johnson, 1994; Pianta, Egeland, &

Erickson, 1989; and Wagner, 1994) found some version of this construct (e.g., history of depression, self-esteem, emotional stability, impulse control) associated with recurrence, thus suggesting that clinical models (DePanfilis & Scannapieco, 1994) and casework judgment are not faulty in using this construct as a decision-making factor. Also noteworthy were findings relevant to type of maltreatment and recurrence status at the index report. Seven studies (Baird, 1988; Baird, Wagner, & Neuenfeldt, 1993; DePanfilis, 1993; Johnson, 1994; Schuerman, Rzepnicki, & Littell, 1994; Wagner, 1994; and Wood, 1995) found that families who had a history of recurrences at the index incident were at increased risk for future recurrences, and six studies (Baird, 1988; Berkeley Planning Associates, 1983; DePanfilis, 1995; Fryer & Miyoshi, 1994; Marks & McDonald, 1989; Pianta, Egeland, & Erickson, 1989) found that neglect rather than other types of maltreatment was most likely to recur, suggesting that making decisions based on these factors is not faulty.

Particularly interesting and informative with regard to the low predictive efficiency of our models, as well as providing recommendations for future research and training efforts, are findings from a survival analysis (DePanfilis, 1995) of 10 predictors of recurrence. After controlling for foster care placement status, this study identified as predictors of the time until recurrence several variables that have been examined only a few times or not at all. Child vulnerability (an index consisting of child mental health problems, developmental disability, and young age), family chronic strain (an index consisting of mother's age at first birth, number of children, span of childbearing years), lack of social support (an index consisting of no extended family to provide support, no neighbors or friends to provide support, and poor use of informal support system), and domestic violence all increased the likelihood of a shorter span of time until recurrence.

References

Baird, S. C. (1988). Development of risk assessment indices for the Alaska Department of Health and Social Services. In T. Tatara (Ed.), *Validation research in CPS risk assessment: Three recent studies* (Occasional Monograph Series No. 2, pp. 84–142). Washington DC: American Public Welfare Association.

Baird, C., Wagner, D., & Neuenfeldt, D. (1993). Actuarial risk assessment and case management in child protective services. In T. Tatara (Ed.), *Sixth National*

Roundtable on CPS *Risk Assessment summary of highlights* (pp. 152–168). Washington DC: American Public Welfare Association.

Berkeley Planning Associates. (1983). *Evaluation of the clinical demonstrations of the treatment of child abuse and neglect: Vol. 2. The exploration of client characteristics, services, and outcomes: Final report and summary of findings* (HEW 105–78–1108). Washington DC: U.S. Department of Health and Human Services, National Center on Child Abuse and Neglect, Office of Human Development Services.

DePanfilis, D. (1993). *A proximate test of the construct and predictive validity of the Child At Risk Field decision-making system.* Unpublished manuscript. University of Maryland at Baltimore, School of Social Work.

DePanfilis, D. (1995). *The epidemiology of child maltreatment recurrences.* Unpublished doctoral dissertation, University of Maryland, School of Social Work.

DePanfilis, D., & Scannapieco, M. (1994). Assessing the safety of children at risk of maltreatment: Decision-making models. *Child Welfare, 63*(3), 229–245.

DePanfilis, D., & Zuravin, S. (1996). Predictors of child maltreatment recurrences: Review of the literature. Unpublished manuscript, University of Maryland, School of Social Work.

English, D., & Pecora, P. (1994). Risk assessment as a practice model in child protective services. *Child Welfare, 63,* 451–473.

Fryer, G. E., & Miyoshi, T. J. (1994). A survival analysis of the revictimization of children: The case of Colorado. *Child Maltreatment, 18,* 1063–1071.

Hunter, W., Coulter, M., Runyan, D., & Everson, M. (1990). Determinants of placement for sexually abused children. *Child Abuse and Neglect, 14,* 407–417.

Jeter, H. (1963). *Children, problems, and services in child welfare programs.* Washington DC: Children's Bureau.

Johnson, W. (1994). Maltreatment recurrence as a criterion for validating risk assessment instruments. In T. Tatara (Ed.), *Seventh National Roundtable on* CPS *Risk Assessment summary of highlights* (175–182). Washington DC: American Public Welfare Association.

Kadushin, A., & Martin, J. (1988). *Child welfare services.* New York: Macmillan.

Leifer, M., Shapiro, J., & Kassem, L. (1993). The impact of maternal history and behavior upon foster placement and adjustment in sexually abused girls. *Child Abuse and Neglect, 17,* 755–766.

Lindsey, D. (1991). Factors affecting the foster care placement decision: An analysis of national survey data. *American Journal of Orthopsychiatry, 6*(2), 272–281.

Lindsey, D. (1992). Adequacy of income and the foster care placement decision. *Social Work Research and Abstracts, 28*(3), 29.

Magura, S., & Moses, B. (1986). *Outcomes measures for child welfare services.* New York: Child Welfare League of America.

Marks, J., & McDonald, T. (1989). *Risk assessment in child protective services: Predicting the recurrence of child maltreatment.* Portland: University of Southern Maine, National Child Welfare Resource Center for Management and Administration.

Pianta, R., Egeland, B., & Erickson, M. (1989). Results of the mother–child interaction research project. In D. Cicchetti & V. Carlson (Eds.), *Child maltreatment: Theory and research on the causes and consequences of child abuse and neglect* (pp. 203–253). New York: Cambridge University Press.

Pellegrin, A., & Wagner, W. (1990). Child sexual abuse: Factors affecting victims' removal from home. *Child Abuse and Neglect, 14,* 53–60.

Runyan, D., Gould, C., Trost, D., & Loda, F. (1981). Determinants of foster care placement for the maltreated child. *American Journal of Public Health, 71,* 706–11.

Russell, D. (1983). The incidence and prevalence of intrafamilial and extrafamilial sexual abuse of female children. *Child Abuse and Neglect, 7,* 133–146.

Schuerman, J. R., Rzepnicki, T. L., & Littell, J. H. (1994). *Putting families first: An experiment in family preservation.* New York: Walter de Gruyter.

Tatara, T. (1990). *Children of substance abusing and alcoholic parents in public child welfare.* Washington DC: American Public Welfare Association.

Wagner, D. (1994). The use of actuarial risk assessment in criminal justice: What can we learn from the experience? In T. Tatara (Ed.), *Seventh National Roundtable on CPS Risk Assessment: Summary of highlights* (pp. 211–223). Washington DC: American Public Welfare Association.

Wood, J. M. (1995, 14–16 June). *NCCD predictors of re-abuse and re-neglect in a predominantly Hispanic population.* Paper presented at the ninth National Roundtable on CPS Risk Assessment, San Francisco.

Zuravin, S. (1991). Research definitions of child physical abuse and neglect: Current problems. In R. Starr Jr. & D. Wolfe (Eds.), *The effects of child abuse and neglect: Issues and research.* New York: Guilford Press.

Zuravin, S., & DePanfilis, D. (in press). Factors affecting foster care placement of children receiving child protective services: Literature review and presentation of data. *Social Work Research.*

Zuravin, D., Orme J., & Hegar, R. L. (1995). Substantiation of child physical abuse reports: Review of the literature and text of a predictive model. *Children and Youth Review 17*(4): 547–566.

4

Foster Care and the Special Needs of Minority Children

Anthony J. Urquiza, Jane Wu, and Joaquin Borrego Jr.

The literature has consistently demonstrated that abused and neglected children experience a wide range of psychological and behavioral problems resulting from abuse or neglect (Barahal, Waterman, & Martin, 1981; Browne & Finkelhor, 1986, Crittenden, 1984; Deitrich, Starr, & Weisfield, 1983; Kinard, 1982). Thus, maltreated children who enter child welfare systems constitute a high-risk group for serious impairment in various mental health and developmental domains (Benedict, Zuravin, Somerfield, & Brandt, 1996; Garland, Landsverk, Hough, & Ellis-MacLeod, 1996; Simms & Halfon, 1994). For these children, the additional stressors of parental separation (even from abusive or neglectful parents), multiple out-of-home placements, lack of appropriate caretaking by foster parents or other caregivers, and a failure to identify or address medical and psychosocial issues may compound their preexisting problems (Dale, Kendall, & Schultz, chapter 8 of this book; Fanshel, 1981; Knitzer, 1978). A clear understanding of the psychosocial problems of children in foster care is essential in order to develop appropriate interventions.

Although there continues to be a paucity of data on the mental health status of foster care children (Kazdin, 1993; Landsverk & Garland, chapter 9 of this book; Urquiza, Wirtz, Peterson, & Singer, 1994), there has been considerable attention given to the topic in recent years. There is virtually no empirical data or conceptual/anecdotal literature addressing the unique problems of abused and neglected ethnic minority children in foster care (Courtney et al., 1996). Though ethnic minority children comprise 20% of the national population, they represent 61% of all children in out-of-home care (Tatara, 1993). Given this, there has been a concern for foster care children from different ethnic or cultural backgrounds (Roys, 1984). It can be argued that ethnic minority children in foster care may be at a greater disadvantage than nonminority children as a result of inadequate or inappropriate social service responses to their cultural or ethnic needs.

There has been a significant increase in the ethnic minority population in the United States, and with this increase comes challenges to all levels of the child welfare system. One challenge involves addressing changes in the way services are delivered to these children and families (Friesen, 1993); another involves offering services that are culturally competent (Knitzer, 1993). The need to provide culturally sensitive and culturally competent services in the mental health system has been well described (Bernal & Castro, 1994; Betancourt & Lopez, 1993; Keys, 1991; Rogler, 1989; Rogler, Cortez, & Malgady, 1987). There is a need for mental health workers to meet different ethical, social, and political responsibilities (Yutrzenka, 1995). In discussing *culture*, we use Urquiza and Wyatt's (1994) definition of the term as a set of beliefs, attitudes, values, practices, and standards of behavior shared by groups distinguished by race, ethnicity, gender, and sexual orientation. For our purposes, we focus on ethnic minority children. We define *cultural competency* as the ability to understand, to the best of our knowledge, the worldview of different people and make appropriate changes (Abney, 1996).

This chapter provides a brief overview of some of the common mental health problems noted in foster care and describes some institutional biases affecting ethnic minority children in out-of-home care. It also addresses a broad range of practical and policy-oriented issues that need to be raised in order to administer culturally competent policy and services.

Problems in Foster Care

Preliminary research dealing with the mental health needs of abused children entering the foster care system has described problems across several domains (Hoschstadt, Jaudes, Zimo, & Schachater, 1987; Klee & Halfon 1987; Runyan, Gould, Trost, & Loda, 1982). Foster care children usually have physical, emotional, and behavioral problems (Benedict et al., 1996; Simms & Halfon, 1994). In turn, these problems tend to affect their everyday functioning. In a study of 149 abused and neglected children entering foster care, Hochstadt et al. (1987) reported that 38% of the children under the age of five were suspected to have some type of developmental delay. In addition, many of the older children presented with symptoms of antisocial behavior (30%), cognitive, academic, or learning disability (47%), psychotic behavior (12%), or sexual behavior disturbance (7%). In a foster care preschool sample of 113 children, Simms (1989) found that 61% had developmental delays and 40% had behavioral disturbances. When considering both developmental and emotional problems, Halfon, Mendonca, and Berkowitz (1995) found that 84% of their sample exhibited such problems. Runyan and Gould (1985a, 1985b) reported that abused and neglected children in the foster care system are at greater risk for becoming involved in delinquent behavior and having some type of academic problem.

McIntyre and Kessler (1986) administered the Achenbach Child Behavior Checklist (CBCL) to children 4–18 years of age who were in foster care and documented the full spectrum of clinical syndromes identified by the CBCL. Forty-nine percent of the children manifested at least one syndrome. There was a 2–32% risk increase for behavioral disturbance associated with foster care status versus home-reared children. In comparing foster care children with both a clinical and community sample, Stein and colleagues (Stein, Evans, Mazumbar, & Rae-Grant, 1996) found that foster care children were similar to the clinical sample in the number and types of symptoms exhibited. Both groups had higher psychiatric symptom levels than the community sample. These findings tend to suggest foster care children have as many problems as children who are referred to treatment. From these studies (a more complete description of the problems of children in foster care is presented by Dale, Kendall, and Schultz, chapter 8 of this book; and Landsverk and Garland, chapter 9), it is apparent that maltreated children entering foster care have a wide range of developmental, behavioral, or emotional problems that require intervention in order to (a) avert more significant forms of psychopathology in the future, (b) ease the management of these children within their foster care placement, and (c) facilitate later reunification with their family of origin.

Often absent in the discussion of children's emotional and psychological well-being in out-of-home care is the impact of loss, change, or shift in their cultural environment. One of the primary objectives for all levels of the child welfare system is to respect and maintain children's cultural rights and to address other types of specific population characteristics (i.e., ethnicity, gender) that may influence their physical and mental health status.

In examining institutional responses to children in out-of-home care, it appears that these children face unique problems. Ethnic minority children (e.g., African-American, Hispanic, Asian-American, and Native American children) tend to be overrepresented in the child protection system (Abney, 1996), to remain in out-of-home placement substantially longer than nonminority children (Barth et al., 1986; Gurak, Smith, & Goldson, 1982; McMurtry & Lie, 1992), and to receive differential treatment (Harris, 1990). This is supported by Horwitz, Simms, and Farrington (1994), who indicate that being nonwhite and having one or more developmental problems were predictors of longer out-of-home care. Additionally, in an interesting (albeit descriptive) study, Pellowe (1990) suggests that when social service caseworkers and African-American clients are of similar ethnicity, the clients are perceived as more cooperative and more successful in completing assignments or requirements than mixed-ethnicity worker-client dyads. Although little research has been conducted on the health status of ethnic minority children in out-of-home care, Porte and Torney-Purta (1987) found that Indo-Chinese children placed in white homes had higher depression scores than those living with ethnic minority families. Although limited, these findings suggest that ethnicity appears to have an impact on the duration of the out-of-home placement, institutional responses, and mental health status of minority foster care children.

Delivery of Culturally Competent Services in the Foster Care System

One of the primary goals of this chapter is not simply to document that children (minority and majority) in foster care have a range of problems but to delineate strategies that address and alleviate problems unique to ethnic minority children as they enter and move through the foster care system. Prior to addressing these points, reasons for addressing cultural issues for minority foster children, their families, and child welfare agencies are noted. The primary assertion is that improvement of mental health problems or reduction of child maltreatment risk cannot be addressed outside of a natural context (e.g., cultural upbringing). Individuals develop in psychologically healthy ways because they are provided the opportunity to develop and grow in a safe, secure, and nurturing environment. In many families outside of the child welfare system, we tend not to focus on issues of cultural appropriateness or competence. In general, families generate their own culture, belief systems, ideals, and values. However, whenever children are removed from their own family and cultural context—that is, removed from their family of origin, from consistent contact with extended family members, from their community or neighborhood, or from situations in which care providers and social contacts have similar behaviors, values, and traditions—they no longer possesses the support and familiarity afforded by these social institutions. It is understood that families and cultural contexts can sustain a duality of both child maltreatment and support, which should not be perceived as inferring that any specific culture condones or promotes maltreatment. Therefore, ethnic minority children in child welfare systems require continued contact with their own culture in order to develop within social, intrapersonal, and behavioral domains. Further, effective coping strategies are facilitated by maintenance in interpersonal and cultural styles that are familiar and consistent in their social environment (e.g., family, extended kin, church, community). Also, the alleviation of interpersonal problems (e.g., poor academic performance, behavioral problems) and intrapersonal problems (e.g., traumatic symptoms, emotional distress) is more likely to result from continued reliance on culturally familiar coping strategies.

Conversely, moving to an environment where there is little acknowledgment and appreciation of children's cultural context will likely result in significant emotional discord, which may create more stress, behavioral problems, and poorer functioning. Intrapersonal child resources may be diverted from addressing important problems in their lives (e.g. learning new and different family rules, traditions, beliefs) to learning to accommodate to different household and family characteristics outside their culture. Finally, with the objective of reunifying children with their families (whenever this is a reasonable and safe possibility), it is suggested that it is most appropriate to maintain children in a foster placement with similar cultural values and behaviors while the biological parent is working toward reunification. This not only eases the transition of children from their biological parents to their foster families but also increases the likelihood of transition back to their biological families. In most cases where families are reunifying, it is necessary to address the problems resulting from out-of-home placement (e.g., reconnecting parent–child relationships, reinstituting parent domain and authority, coping with adaptive changes that have occurred). It is suggested that if parents and children make changes and adapt within the confines of their cultural context, then addressing re-unification will be much easier. In order to ensure and protect the welfare of ethnic minority children and their families, we assert that they have unique cultural rights that need to be upheld throughout each family's involvement with social service programs.

BASIC CULTURAL RIGHTS

An essential part of effective intervention services with ethnic minority families and children includes recognizing their ethnic or cultural differences from the mainstream and maintaining or reinforcing the positive cultural aspects in the children's foster care situation. Children and families have basic cultural rights:

1. Families have the right to make social service agencies aware of their ethnicity and culture and what their children need in order to maintain their cultural identity while in foster care (e.g., attending church on weekends).
2. Families have the right to expect that social service agencies will preserve their children's ethnic identity as the family understands it to be (e.g., a family might identify themselves as Hispanic, Chicano, Mexican American).
3. Families have the right to retain their primary language when receiving child welfare services (e.g., family reunification, family preservation).
4. Families have the right to culturally specific services if they prefer such services (e.g., counseling through a church).
5. Children in long-term care and children who will not be reunified with their parents have the right to be fully informed about their biological family history and culture.
6. Children in care have the right to ongoing interaction with adults and peers who share their ethnicity or culture (e.g., having a Japanese child spend play time with other children who speak Japanese).
7. All children in care have the right to have family and fictive kin (individuals who serve in the role of a family member or extended family member, but who have no formal blood ties; e.g., a *compadre* in the Hispanic culture) considered first as placement options (e.g., extended family members).

89

These cultural rights are an important aspect of ethnic identity, which, in turn, is critical to the development of self-esteem and mental health (Ocampo, Knight, & Bernal, 1997; Phinney, 1991). However, it is suggested that continued involvement in a child's own culture (which may be facilitated by culturally competent case management) is also likely to promote family reunification by enhancing the child's psychological health. It is suggested that while the maintenance of a child's culture and heritage must be held at all levels of child welfare institutions, the agents of policies involving children's culture are primarily the foster care family.

WHAT DO MINORITY CHILDREN NEED WHEN IN FOSTER CARE AND HOW CAN FOSTER PARENTS HELP?

A child's transition from his or her family to foster care is traumatic, even when the move is to a home perceived to be more stable and nurturing. Stress, loss, inability to develop emotional attachments, and a myriad of other psychosocial problems plague abused and neglected children who move in and out of the system and from foster home to foster home. These problems are magnified when ethnic minority children are placed into mainstream foster homes where the cultural environment is distinctly different from their own (e.g., a Spanish-speaking child in a predominantly English-speaking foster home). Additionally, some children may have learned not to trust "the system" (e.g., law enforcement, social workers, therapists, in-home support workers) and perceive foster parents as an extension of an authoritarian state.

Facilitating a comfortable transition is critical to the emotional well-being of all foster children. At the very minimum, ethnic minority children need to speak their own language, to continue eating food familiar to them (with culturally appropriate eating utensils), and to have sleeping arrangements that are comforting rather than anxiety inducing. For example, if siblings are placed together and are used to sharing the same bed, this practice should be continued (unless there is a problem with the physical or sexual safety of the children). The issue of sleeping arrangements should be evaluated and discussed with the children, especially with older children who may be serving a caregiver role.

Providing continuity in health care is also important. Foster parents need to understand different health, dietary, and hygiene requirements of each of their foster children. Providing cookies and milk to a child is a kindly act, but offering milk to a child who has a hereditary intolerance to lactose is an avoidable error. Foster parents need to know how to care for different types of skin and hair, what different cultural values and actions are attached to young menstruating adolescent girls, what alternative medical remedies the child is accustomed to receiving (i.e., herbal infusions vs. Western pills or injections) and from whom.

Minority children also need to maintain a link with their ethnic community. Many ethnic groups see all of their children as part of a larger family community—some related by blood, others not. Fictive kin can be instrumental in shaping the life of a child and are often more helpful as supports because they are not as closely involved in the family politics.

Whether or not children return home, ongoing interaction with their ethnic communities is essential for individual and group ethnic or cultural identification and growth. Continued ties to culturally familiar relationships involving peers, religion, and community or after-school activities can maintain children's sense of cultural identity—even during out-of-home placements. Foster parents can also help bridge the gap between foster care and the children's heritage by helping them to problem-solve utilizing the cultural values and beliefs of their ethnic communities, supporting them in their cultural activities, and encouraging ethnic pride.

CULTURALLY DEVELOPMENTAL ACTIVITIES THAT FOSTER PARENTS CAN INITIATE

Minority children lose not only their families when placed in foster care; they often also lose contact with their extended families, friends, and surrounding communities. It is in these instances that reconnecting children to their extended families and communities is important. Some appropriate connecting or reconnecting activities are listed below.

Infancy

Babies need comforting smells and faces for a smoother transition into foster care. Foster parents should try to duplicate some scents that would be familiar to the baby. Foster parents should try to replicate the same holding and sleeping patterns that are familiar to the infant. If the child was swaddled or carried in a pack, these practices should continue. Leaving an infant in a crib alone may be traumatic if the baby is used to sleeping with the parents in the same bed or room. Foster parents should be cautious about baby formulas and cognizant of the infant's ability to digest dairy products.

Preschool

Toddlers and preschoolers need to be exposed to their primary languages, culturally congruent play activities, familiar foods, and familiar styles of clothing. Foster parents should continue to support and practice the child-rearing values of their children's ethnic communities and should facilitate access to people with whom the children can identify within their ethnic communities. Access to the families of origin (if possible) and extended families should be stressed. Foster parents can also read ethnic or cultural stories and myths and can introduce children to music, art, and religion that is culturally congruent. It is not ethical or within the scope of the foster parents' role to change children's religious views.

Latency

During latency, all of the above practices apply. Additionally, foster parents can facilitate religious schooling, primary language schooling, and primary language support systems, and can enroll children in after-school activities that either include peers from their ethnic communities or focus on cultural aspects. Foster parents should seek adult mentors from the children's communities to provide cultural leadership and support. Most important at this developmental stage, foster parents can assist children with problem-solving skills regarding discrimination, racism, and harassment, whether observed globally or experienced directly or indirectly.

Adolescence

In adolescence, the above practices apply, but in addition to supporting youth in their efforts to identify and integrate with their own racial or ethnic group, the foster parent needs to help them function effectively in a bicultural environment. It is during these developing adolescent times of independence and separation from adults and mentors that minority adolescents may need guidance in deciding what to integrate from their childhood, heritage, and ethnic communities.

WHAT ABOUT BIRACIAL OR MULTIRACIAL CHILDREN?

The most important aspect of foster care for multiracial children is to consider the biological parents' identification of their children. If a family is multiethnic (e.g., Latino and African American) and describes itself as one ethnicity (Latino), this request should be honored. Typically, families with biracial children have a predominant cultural preference. This can be explored by social workers as part of case management and decision making regarding placement in practice. For example, if a child is partly Chinese American and African American and the mother identifies the child as Chinese American, there will be difficulties in helping the child cope with the perceptions of society, especially if the child has darker skin and different racial features than the general Chinese-American mainstream. It is far better for foster parents to acknowledge the rich heritages of biracial or multiracial children and to support the concept of diversity in its fullness.

WHO MAKES A GOOD CANDIDATE FOR CROSS-CULTURAL PARENTING?
Any foster parent placed in the situation of caring for a child from a different cultural or ethnic group faces a complex and difficult task. This would include European-American foster families responsible for fostering minority children as well as minority foster parents who are caring for children of a different cultural or ethnic group (e.g., an African-American foster parent serving as caregiver for a Cuban child). However, it may be that minority foster parents are better able to understand the diversity that accompanies ethnic and cultural lifestyles. That is, minority foster parents, comprising a population that has traditionally been oppressed or economically disadvantaged due to skin color, behavior, or religious beliefs, may be more likely to appreciate and respond to different cultural characteristics of the children to whom they provide foster care. However, it is important that *all* foster parents be willing to work hard to accommodate the differences in minority foster children, rather than try to make a child fit into their own family system. They must engage in honest self-examination to ascertain how they feel about their own cultural beliefs. Are these beliefs similar? How are they different? Can the foster parents accommodate the differences? What are the foster parents willing to do in order to step out of their comfort zones to meet the children's cultural needs? This may mean attending an African-American church, celebrating Chinese New Year, attending a powwow, learning some Spanish language skills, or interacting with the children's families on a regular basis. It may mean seeking nontraditional services such as provided by a *curandero*, a shaman, or an herbalist when going to the local pediatrician is standard practice.

Culturally supportive foster parents acknowledge that in the larger community, minority children will be faced with racism, discrimination, or harassment and will need to learn coping skills to deal with these problems. Racial harassment, slights, or insults result in minority children feeling "negatively different" or "less than" children in the mainstream population. Foster parents who have never experienced discrimination may need specialized training in talking with youth about discrimination and helping them with problem-solving skills around such issues. Further, families who work with culturally diverse foster children must be prepared to deal with society's response to racism and judgments made on the basis of their foster children's skin color, appearance, or cultural stereotype.

TRAINING FOR CULTURAL COMPETENCE IN OUT-OF-HOME CARE
The child welfare system must acknowledge that foster parents do not come equipped with all of the answers for our diverse youth. Training is a necessity and should be geared to meet the needs of the community. Basic training should help foster parents to:

understand one's own culture and biases;
cope with racism and discrimination and maintain self-esteem;
identify the health, hygiene, and dietary needs of specific ethnic groups;
incorporate cultural practices of specific ethnic groups;
access local resources to find cultural supports;
work with biological families and receive positive results;
support biracial youth;
transition minority children back home after being in a completely different environment; and
work with refugee or immigrant children and families.

Providing culturally appropriate services requires a commitment of time and financial support. Foster parents may need to travel frequently or long distances to get children back into their own cultural environments. Arranging for specialists to do training in cultural sensitivity and cultural competence or to provide information regarding a particular cultural group may be expensive. Special language and arts classes may not always be expensive, but they require a commitment of time and resources that is difficult. However, minority children have the right to maintenance and support of their cultures throughout their experience with the public child welfare system.

Summary

Since demographics for ethnic minorities in the United States are rapidly changing, more and more ethnic minority children will be entering the social welfare system. Given this, the social welfare system has to become culturally responsive to these populations. The social welfare system must be responsive to cultural differences such as communication style, religious views, discipline strategies, and normative parent–child relationships. As social welfare changes occur, services for these children and their families should be developed (Bryant & Snodgrass, 1992). One possible avenue can be increasing the amount of research regarding kinship care with ethnic minority children. As with other types of child welfare research, kinship care has received minimal attention (Berrick & Barth, 1994).

Though being *all-knowing* about a particular culture or knowing about *all* cultures is unrealistic, it is still possible to work effectively with people from different cultures. It is apparent that abused and neglected children in out-of-home placement have a wide range of behavioral and emotional problems (Rosenfeld et al., 1997). Culturally sensitive services provided to ethnic minority children may lessen the traumatic impact of being separated from their families *and* from being in a majority-culture public child welfare system. If both ethnic minority children and their parents feel more comfortable and better able to focus on their presenting problems, successful outcomes in out-of-home placement are more likely.

References

Abney, V. D. (1996). Cultural competency in the field of child maltreatment. In J. Briere, L. Berliner, J. A. Bulkley, C. Jenny, & T. Reid (Eds.), *The APSAC handbook on child maltreatment* (pp. 409–419). Thousand Oaks CA: Sage.

Barahal, R. M., Waterman, J., & Martin, H. P. (1981). The social cognitive development of abused children. *Journal of Consulting and Clinical Psychology, 49*, 508–516.

Barth, R. P., Snowden, L., Ten Broeck, E., Clancy, T., Jordan, C., & Barusch, A. (1986). Contributors to reunification or permanent out-of-home care for physically abused children. *Journal of Social Services Research, 9*(2/3), 31–45.

Benedict, M. I., Zuravin, S., Somerfield, M., & Brandt, D. (1996). The reported health and functioning of children maltreated while in family foster care. *Child Abuse and Neglect, 20*, 561–571.

Bernal, M. E., & Castro, F. G. (1994). Are clinical psychologists prepared for service and research with ethnic minorities? *American Psychologist, 49*, 797–805.

Berrick, J. D., & Barth, R. P. (1994). Research on kinship foster care: What do we know? Where do we go from here? *Children and Youth Services Review, 16*, 1–5.

Betancourt, H., & Lopez, S. R. (1993). The study of culture, ethnicity, and race in American psychology. *American Psychologist, 48*, 629–637.

Browne, A., & Finkelhor, D. (1986). The initial and long-term effects of child sexual abuse. In D. Finkelhor (Ed.), *A sourcebook on child sexual abuse.* Beverly Hills: Sage.

Bryant, B., & Snodgrass, R. D. (1992). Foster family care applications with special populations. *Community Alternatives: International Journal of Family Care, 4*, 1–25.

Courtney, M. E., Barth, R. P., Berrick, J. D., Brooks, D., Needell, B., & Park, L. (1996). Race and child welfare services: Past directions and future directions. *Child Welfare, 75*(2), 99–137.

Crittenden, P. (1984). Sibling interaction: Evidence of a generational effect in maltreating infants. *Child Abuse and Neglect, 8*, 433–438.

Deitrich, K., Starr, R., & Weisfield, G. (1983). Infant maltreatment: Caretaker-infant interaction and developmental consequences at different levels of parental failure. *Pediatrics, 73*, 532–540.

Fanshel, D. (1981). Decision making under uncertainty: Foster care for abused or neglected children? *American Journal of Public Health, 71*, 685–686.

Friesen, B. J. (1993). Overview: Advances in child mental health. In H. C. Johnson (Ed.), *Child mental health in the 1990s* (pp. 12–19). Rockville MD: U.S. Department of Health and Human Services.

Garland, A. F., Landsverk, J. L., Hough, R. L., & Ellis-Macleod, E. (1996). Type of maltreatment as a predictor of mental health service use for children in foster care. *Child Abuse and Neglect, 20*, 675–688.

Gurak, D. T., Smith, D. A., & Goldson, M. F. (1982). *The minority foster child: A comparative study of Hispanic, black, and white children.* New York: Fordham University, Hispanic Research Center.

Halfon, N. G., Mendonca, A., & Berkowitz, G. (1995). Health status of children in foster care: The experience of the center for the vulnerable child. *Archives of Pediatric and Adolescent Medicine, 149*, 386–392.

Harris, N. (1990). Dealing with diverse cultures in child welfare. *Protecting Children, 7*, 6–7.

Hochstadt, N. J., Jaudes, P. K., Zimo, D. A., & Schachater, J. (1987). The medical and psychosocial needs of children entering foster care. *Child Abuse and Neglect, 11*, 53–62.

Horwitz, S. M., Simms, M. D., & Farrington, R. (1994). Impact of developmental problems on young children's exit from foster care. *Developmental and Behavioral Pediatrics, 15*(2), 105–110.

Kazdin, A. E. (1993). Adolescent mental health: Prevention and treatment programs. *American Psychologist, 48*, 127–141.

Keys, H. (1991). The CLWA cultural responsiveness initiative: A status report. *APSAC Advisor, 4*, 12–13.

Kinard, E. M. (1982). Experiencing child abuse: Effects on emotional adjustment. *American Journal of Orthopsychiatry, 52*(1), 82–91.

Klee, L., & Halfon, N. (1987). Mental health care for foster children in California. *Child Abuse and Neglect, 11*, 63–74.

Knitzer, J. (1978). Responsibility for delivery of services. In J. Mearig (Ed.), *Working with children*. San Francisco: Jossey-Bass.

Knitzer, J. (1993). Children's mental health policy: Challenging the future. *Journal of Emotional and Behavioral Disorders, 1*, 8–16.

McIntyre, A., & Keesler, T. (1986). Psychological disorders among foster children. *Journal of Clinical Child Psychology, 15*, 297–303.

McMurtry, S. L., & Lie, G. W. (1992). Differential rates of exit of minority children in foster care. *Social Work Research and Abstracts, 28*, 28–42.

Ocampo, K. A., Knight, G. P., & Bernal, M. E. (1997). The development of cognitive abilities and social identities in children: The case of ethnic identity. *International Journal of Behavioral Development, 21*, 479–500.

Pellowe, D. (1990). *Race and culture in family first*. Chicago: University of Chicago, Chapin Hall Center for Children.

Phinney, J. S. (1991). Ethnic identity and self-esteem: A review and integration. *Hispanic Journal of Behavioral Sciences, 13*(2), 193–208.

Porte, Z., & Torney-Purta, J. (1987). Depression and academic achievement among Indochinese refugee unaccompanied minors in ethnic and non-ethnic settings. *American Journal of Orthospychiatry, 57*, 536–547.

Rogler, L. H. (1989). The meaning of culturally sensitive research in mental health. *American Journal of Psychiatry, 146*(3), 296–303.

Rogler, L. H., Cortez, D. E., & Malgady, R. G. (1987). What do culturally sensitive services mean? A case of Hispanics. *American Psychologist, 42*, 565–570.

Rosenfeld, A. A., Pilowsky, D. J., Fine, P., Thorpe, M., Fein, E., Simms, M. D., Halfon, N., Irwin, M., Alfaro, J., Saletzky, R., & Nickman, S. (1997). Foster care: An update. *Journal of the American Academy of Child and Adolescent Psychiatry, 36*, 448–457.

Roys, P. (1984). Ethnic minorities and the welfare system. *International Journal of Social Psychiatry, 30*, 102–118.

Runyan, D. K., & Gould, C. L. (1985a). Foster care for child maltreatment: Impact on delinquent behavior. *Pediatrics, 75*(3), 562–568.

Runyan, D. K., & Gould, C. L. (1985b). Foster care for child maltreatment: Impact on school performance. *Pediatrics, 76*, 841–847.

Runyan, D. K., Gould, C. L., Trost, D. C., & Loda, F. A. (1982). Determinants of foster care placements for maltreated children. *Child Abuse and Neglect, 6*, 343–350.

Simms, M. D. (1989). The foster care clinic: A community program to identify treatment needs of children in foster care. *Journal of Developmental and Behavioral Pediatrics, 10*, 121–128.

Simms, M. D., & Halfon, N. (1994). The health care needs of children in foster care: A research agenda. *Child Welfare, 73*, 505–524.

Stein, E., Evans, B., Mazumbar, R., & Rae-Grant, N. (1996). The mental health of children in foster care: A comparison with community and clinical samples. *Canadian Journal of Psychiatry, 41*, 385–391.

Tatara, T. (1993). *Characteristics of children in substitute and adoptive care, fiscal year 1989.* Washington DC: American Public Welfare Association.

Urquiza, A. J., Wirtz, S., Peterson, M. S., & Singer, V. (1994). Screening and evaluating abused and neglected children entering foster care. *Child Welfare, 73*(2), 155–171.

Urquiza, A. J., & Wyatt, G. (1994). Culturally relevant violence research with children of color. APSAC *Advisor, 7*, 16–20.

Yutrzenka, B. A. (1995). Making a case for training in ethnic and cultural diversity in increasing treatment efficacy. *Journal of Consulting and Clinical Psychology, 63*, 197–206.

5

Incorporating the Perspectives of Youth Placed in Family Foster Care: Selected Research Findings and Methodological Challenges

Mary C. Curran and Peter J. Pecora

In 1996, approximately 970,000 children were found by child protective agencies to be victims of child abuse or neglect, and an even greater number of families received counseling and other services from child and family service agencies in America (National Center on Child Abuse and Neglect, 1998, pp. 2–5). Furthermore, although the substitute care child population had fallen from 502,000 in 1977 to 276,000 in 1985, the volume of child entries, exits, and returns to care has increased significantly—the system was estimated to have served an annual total of 710,000 children and adolescents in 1995 (Tatara, 1992, p. 1; Tatara, 1997, pp. 1–2).

An extensive analysis of the characteristics of children in substitute care for 1988 revealed that 37.2% (estimated at 123,700) had been in substitute care for 2 years or more, and 11.6% (39,400) had been in care for more than 5 years (Tatara, 1992, pp. 111–113).[1] For all children remaining in substitute care, 12.4% (an estimated 42,160 children, based on reports from 29 states) had long-term foster care as the primary placement goal (Tatara, 1992, pp. 107–108).

Thus, although family-based service placement prevention programs (e.g., Kinney, Haapala, & Booth, 1991; Wells & Biegel, 1991), family reunification programs (Maluccio, Abramczyk, & Tomlinson, 1996; Fraser, Walton, Lewis, Pecora, & Walton, 1996), and aggressive adoption pro-

This chapter was inspired by the need to document the value and perceptions of youth being served in the foster care system. Chris Downs, Trudy Festinger, Rap Howell, Kathy Kingery, Ruth Massinga, Ken Perry, Jim Traglia, Tom Wedeven, and Linda Wilson provided valuable consultation and support in that regard.

grams are reducing the numbers of children spending long periods of time in substitute care, a significant number of America's children will "grow up" in foster care. The increasing backlog of children in foster care (Wulczyn & Goerge, 1992), investigative reports, and class-action lawsuits indicate the need for program refinements. Although foster families are more frequently involved in various research studies, children in foster care constitute the ultimate consumers of child welfare services. Surprisingly, few evaluation studies directly involve youth themselves.

Relatively few researchers have interviewed youth directly about their experiences in this delivery system, yet these youth are the primary stakeholders in this service delivery system and constitute an important source of information that could be used to refine services to them and their families—both birth and foster families. This chapter discusses the importance of consumer feedback in foster care, reviews the major research that has involved foster children, and presents some recommendations for further research. Note that the term *children*, as used in this chapter, includes both younger children and adolescents.

Why Involve Children in Evaluation Studies?

OVERVIEW

Why gather information from children about consumer satisfaction and their perspectives of service delivery? Traditionally, program evaluation studies in child welfare have not focused on client satisfaction or client reports of improvement. Part of the reason for this gap in the literature may be the problems associated with consumer recall and various types of response bias (Austin et al., 1982; Sudman & Bradburn, 1974). Satisfaction ratings have often been considered "soft measures" by social scientists. However, low reliability and validity do not appear to be intrinsic qualities of satisfaction measures: rather, they may result from the manner in which these measures are designed or implemented (Warfel, Maloney, & Blase, 1981, p. 154). The authors note that five important factors will increase the reliability of satisfaction measures: credibility, knowledgeable population, specificity, adequate response rates, and proper presentation of findings. In short, the authors believe that consumer feedback can create a cooperative and professional liaison from which both consumers and providers benefit.

From a "quality improvement" perspective (e.g., Deming, 1986), providers must place a high importance on what consumers have to say in order to improve services with an attitude of openness. Ultimately, consumer feedback may dictate which programs are accepted and which will succeed. For example, children's satisfaction with and commitment to their placements are crucial to successful placement outcomes (Colton, 1989).

Bush and Gordon (1982) are convinced that "there is an untapped potential for improving social services and contributing to family stability by seeking out and paying attention to children's views" (p. 309). Their study found enough commonalties in what the children defined as supportive care that children's placement selection criteria could be used along with the official criteria. Children have the ability to verbalize what makes an environment nurturing and healthy, and have been found to be more satisfied with placements that they were able to help choose. They also can be excellent sources of information about who in the community might be able to take care of them. As indicated by attachment research, children who want to maintain relationships with both birth and surrogate parents must be aided in doing so, whenever appropriate.

Involving youth allows them to express how they see their situation. Most children are able to state whether they are comfortable with a particular placement. In fact, engaging children as a source of information may both increase the number of options available to providers and empower clients to be experts in managing their own lives.

Finally, Rapp and Poertner (1987, 1992) have argued that the central challenge facing human service managers today is "moving clients to center stage." This goal involves a client-centered philosophy and renewed attention to two aspects of service delivery, process and outcome:

There are two major elements in what we are referring to as client-centeredness. The first focuses attention on the "process" of service provision—the degree to which the practice and the behavior of personnel, and the organizational structures and operating processes reflect a preoccupation with clients and their well-being. It includes having the client treated with the highest degree of dignity, respect, and individuality. It involves the design and implementation of intake procedures, service accessibility, courtesy of receptionists, provisions for client input into individual case and programmatic decisions, flexibility to tailor services to individual client needs and desires, etc. The list can be extended tenfold.

The second element of client centeredness is the organizational focus on service effectiveness, client outcomes, [and] results. While the terms vary by author, the central notion is that the centerpiece of agency performance is the benefits accrued by clients as a result of our efforts. (Rapp & Poertner, 1987, p. 23)

In summary, obtaining the child or parent's perspective in assessing service effectiveness has been emphasized by a number of program evaluation experts in child welfare and other fields (see, for example, Ellsworth, 1975; Giordano, 1977; Hargreaves & Attkisson, 1978; Magura & Moses, 1984; Maluccio, 1979; Millar and Millar, 1981). These and other researchers have highlighted a number of benefits associated with consumer evaluation data: (a) client empowerment is modeled; (b) attainment of organizational goals is increased through improved organization–client relations; (c) consumer observations and recommendations may identify areas for improvement and solutions that other evaluation methods did not discover, in effect broadening the range of measures that are used to quantify "agency effectiveness"; and (d) children and parents bring an outside perspective to the evaluation process compared to using only worker-generated data.

Challenges to Gathering and Using Consumer Satisfaction Data

NEED FOR SERVICES REFINEMENT

Historically, data related to client satisfaction or self-reports of improvement have not been included in more evaluations of social services such as family foster care, in particular, for several reasons. First, relatively few formal program evaluation studies have been conducted in this field.[2] The few foster care agencies that are systematically gathering consumer satisfaction data generally use it only to gauge consumer satisfaction rather than as a formal means of program evaluation. In few cases are children formally involved in consumer satisfaction research, even though their perceptions are often gathered informally.

In addition, there are a variety of difficulties associated with assessing consumer viewpoints of services received. In contrast to the studies noted earlier, most of this research has used global measures of client satisfaction instead of problem-specific questions or behaviorally anchored scales. Interpreting satisfaction scores is also difficult because of an absence of normative data (Hargreaves & Attkisson, 1978) and a general distrust of satisfaction measures (Miller & Pruger, 1978). More specifically, there are a variety of methodological limitations associated with consumer satisfaction research. For example, in many situations, people seem satisfied with everything about which they are asked. Furthermore, consumers tend not to show high levels of dissatisfaction in areas where it is "common knowledge" that people are dissatisfied (e.g., 61% of respondents reported satisfaction with public assistance offices even though experts knew that the opposite was true). Ware (personal communication, 15 June 1996) recently noted how the New England Medical Center was using new scale anchors in response to this problem (e.g., the highest satisfaction area was described as where there was no possible way to improve the service). Finally, in some programs, consumers may not respond honestly for fear that future services may be withheld or sanctions of some kind (e.g., child replacement, restricted child visitation) may be imposed.

There also exists a discrepancy between the evaluation of one's own experience and the evaluation of a program in general (Gutek, 1978). The preexisting negative attitudes that people hold about an organization or program may contrast greatly with the actual results of service, resulting in inflated satisfaction ratings—a "contrast effect" (Katz, Gutek, Kahn, & Barton, 1975, as cited in Gutek, 1978). Furthermore, distinctions are rarely drawn between whether clients like, relate to, or trust certain groups of professionals, and whether those professionals are effective in treating or helping their clients (Giordano, 1977, p. 36). Finally, evaluation studies rarely take into account the influence of the organization (e.g., coercive power), client backgrounds, and other "intervening variables" upon client responses (Giordano, 1977).

One recommendation for improving satisfaction studies involves using a combination of more specific satisfaction measures instead of one subjective or global question. However, studies of job satisfaction using this approach have found that specifying various facets of satisfaction account for only about 50% of the variance in global satisfaction (Gutek, 1978). Yet the use of more specific measures may provide more information on what determines consumer satisfaction and on how to refine services.

Developing more objective outcome measures modeled after the interview schedules developed by Magura and Moses (1986) and others that focus on specific areas of child, parent, or family functioning may also improve satisfaction outcome studies. In addition, approaches that attempt to incorporate consumers' opinions about quality of service or their "cognitive meaning" of satisfaction appear worthwhile. These methods take into account how consumers conceptualize satisfaction, and use a variety of questions to examine the dynamics involved in interviewing consumers (e.g., parents may or may not identify suggestions for improvement, people rate satisfaction in comparison to what they or others they know have experienced, "happiness" or "contentment" with a service is viewed as being different than "satisfaction") (Taylor, 1977; Gutek, 1978). The next section addresses the extent to which the consumer-oriented research involving children in foster care has addressed these concerns.

Selected Studies of Children Currently in Foster Care

OVERVIEW

Unfortunately, foster care research frequently ignores those who know the system best: the children and families. Hampson and Tavormina (1980) suggest, "Why not ask the foster parents themselves?" (p. 109), and urge professionals to stop blaming the foster parents for the downfalls of the foster care system. Instead, professionals should elicit ideas as to the type of support parents and children need in an effort to improve the quality of care. However, researchers have rarely drawn out the opinions of children. In fact, numerous studies have noted the lack of channels for feedback from children in out-of-home care (e.g., Jacobson & Cockerum, 1976; Festinger, 1983; Gil & Bogart, 1982). As foster care agencies become more concerned with service effectiveness, studies of consumer feedback will become increasingly important.

GIL AND BOGART STUDY

Gil and Bogart (1982) conducted a study on behalf of the San Francisco Child Abuse Council in an effort to allow foster care children to speak for themselves about the quality of care they received, what sort of expectations they had about their future, and what kinds of suggestions they would make to improve the foster care system. Volunteers interviewed a total of 100 children (50 living in group homes and 50 living in foster family homes) selected at random from a list of children served by the San Francisco Department of Social Services. The children ranged in age from 8 to 18 years and came from a variety of ethnic backgrounds. Two questionnaires were used, one for the 8- to 12-year-olds and one for the 13- to 18-year-olds (p. 8). The questionnaires were divided into four sections and included the following: the Coopersmith Self-Esteem Test, the Parks Career Role Inventory, a specially designed behavior checklist, and four open-ended questions intended to evoke children's perception of foster care: "The best place I ever lived was _____"; "This was because _____"; "Is there something you would recommend that could make things better for children and teenagers in foster care?"; and "Why are you now in foster care?"

The Gil and Bogart study found that children in family foster care generally have a higher level of self-esteem than children living in group homes: 88% of the children in family foster care responded that they felt safe and secure as compared with only 47% of the children in group homes. In addition, 81% of the children in family foster homes reported enjoying their current placement, as opposed to 47% of the group home children (p. 8). These findings concur with a study done by Colton (1989) that noted children in family foster care were more satisfied with their placements than children in residential treatment. The Colton study also found foster children tended to have a higher level of identification with and involvement in their environments. (Unfortunately, studies controlling for type of previous child maltreatment, current functioning, and other key factors need to be conducted.)

Gil and Bogart report that in terms of improving foster care, the children in family foster homes suggested foster parents play games with them, offer plenty of love and affection, and allow them to make their own choices. Youth placed in group homes wanted more staff, more homes, and more money for the program. This study highlighted two major areas of concern. First, the educational needs of these children were not being met. Many of the children interviewed could not read the questionnaire or write responses. Second, there was a marked lack of understanding among the foster children concerning their foster care status and reason for placement. Thus, one of the study's major implications was that children must be made aware of the overall case plan and the most realistic placement options.

CASEY CHILD INTERVIEW STUDY

The Casey Family Program undertook an evaluation of the status, feelings, and beliefs of about 100 Casey youth in 1993 and 1995 (Allen, Barenblat, Le Prohn, & Pecora, 1996). The information obtained in the first round of interviews provided a profile of youth attitudes about the program prior to a series of program redesign efforts. This study used an extensive set of closed and open-ended interview questions. Through analysis of the 104 second-round interviews and comparison with the earlier interviews, the study found that most children perceived Casey as helpful and caring. Those youths who would change some aspects of Casey made suggestions that included improving group work, encouraging different levels of social worker contact, and allowing more input from Casey youths.

Seventy-nine percent of the children interviewed reported participating in some type of Casey-sponsored group; they found group work increasingly useful in meeting their needs. Many children also expressed a strong interest in being more involved in planning for their futures and in receiving more help to ease the transition to living on their own after emancipation through skills groups and Casey alumni groups. A major concern of many children was a perception that they lacked control over decision making about their lives. The interviews also suggest that the Casey program has more work to do before it fully meets its goal of helping children develop stronger ethnic identities. One-third of the children said that their foster families had not given them an opportunity to learn about their ethnic backgrounds.

Finally, these children place great value on receiving the same treatment as all other children in the foster home. They seemed happy with their foster parents and content with the guidelines set for them. Eighty percent of the respondents said that their foster parents treated them kindly and accepted them as part of the family "a lot."

ADDITIONAL CONSUMER STUDIES

When children in foster care are given the chance to express their opinions, their perceptions are often both insightful and crucial to effective social work practice. As long as agencies continue to discount what children have to say, the less likely children will see staff members as caring adults. Kufeldt (1984) looked at a sample of 40 children aged 9–15 years, from 28 families, all of whom were taken into care between the ages of 6 and 12 years. The author presents a descriptive look at children in foster care but highlights the children's feelings about foster care. A second part of the study interviewed members of the "foster care role-set," consisting of foster mothers, social workers, birth mothers, and children.

The study indicated that children were more likely to look toward environmental factors as reasons why they ended up in foster care. In general, children wanted to be able to visit with birth parents, although they wanted to help decide when the visits would take place. For example, one child was quoted as saying, "The child will think that the parents don't care if they don't know when they're seeing each other" (Kufeldt, 1984, p. 260). In fact, the research pointed out that denial of parental visits pushes kids to run away. Inclusive fostering is an approach highlighted by the article, particularly in regard to the information both children and birth parents can provide to the agency and foster family. Children saw their biological parents as playing a crucial role in making the transition into foster care easier. Birth parents know and can give foster parents ideas about how their children act and can talk about the child's problems (p. 261).

Kufeldt was distressed by the fact that children's relationships with their social workers are not stable ones. "Opportunities to develop a familiar and trusting relationship with a worker are further reduced by the fact that only 2% of all contacts recorded on agency files during the first year in care were between social worker and child alone" (p. 261). As a result, children often held negative attitudes toward their social workers. Kufeldt stresses that although the reliability of children's responses as a research tool has been questioned, it is a disservice to all participants when providers choose not to use children's feedback.

Aldgate, Stein, and Carey (1989) state that the reality depicted by consumer surveys often differs dramatically from that intended by policy. The young people interviewed came from both group settings and foster homes. The researchers noted that, "in both the United Kingdom and the United States, children from ethnic minority families seem to be even more disadvantaged when exposed to the institutional racism inherent in the 'white,' ethnocentric care system" (p. 62). Their study highlights four areas of particular concern and the congruence between consumer feedback in the United Kingdom and the United States. First, the young people reported having little say in whether they participated in life-altering decisions. Most felt that they had no control over what happened to them. This was particularly acute for those who entered care at a young age.

These youth often went through a tremendous amount of change that had ripple effects throughout many aspects of their lives. They often blamed themselves or felt responsible if their placement disrupted.

In addition, Aldgate et al. point out that this continual movement wreaked havoc on foster children's educational progress. Respondents in Stein and Carey's (1986) "Leaving Care" study reported very low levels of educational attainment, with few children taking any British qualifying exams, and not one child staying in school after age 16 (as cited in Aldgate et al., 1989, p. 67). In addition, foster children's social networks often broke down as a result of placement disruption and the collapse of their peer relationships once they switched neighborhoods or schools. Berridge & Cleaver (1987) found "that of children experiencing placement breakdowns, four-fifths joined new schools when departing from the foster home" (p. 84). Children who changed schools were twice as likely to experience a breakdown in their foster home placement than those children who remained in the same school when switching foster homes. However, Berridge and Cleaver also discovered that placing siblings together often enhanced placement outcomes.

Selected Studies of Foster Care Alumni

THE FESTINGER STUDY OF CHILDREN IN NEW YORK CITY

In part three of the landmark study "No One Ever Asked Us," Festinger (1983) interviewed 277 former foster children about their satisfaction with foster care. Her study noted that, in general, youth were relatively happy with their experience in foster care, although children in foster homes expressed more satisfaction than those who were in group settings. One of the major factors linked to satisfaction was whether the child perceived his or her placement as a necessity. Those who felt that placement in foster care was their only option—the vast majority—were more satisfied than those who did not. In addition, those children who could better understand the reasons behind their placement, such as the death or emotional impairment of their parents, seemed to be more comfortable in their foster placement.

Children who had developed a close relationship with their foster parents tended to be more satisfied. Interestingly, children who were more satisfied with their foster care situation were the ones who felt that the amount of contact with their biological parents was sufficient. The underlying point was that these former foster children wished that their own preferences regarding contact with birth parents had been allotted more significance. In the words of one: "It was always the grownups who were making the decisions . . . I was treated like a child . . . never consulted even in my teens" (p. 91).

Among the many concerns raised by this study is that youth wanted to be asked their opinions about decisions affecting them. Many children also felt that the screening process for foster parents needed to be improved. The interviewees were steadfast in their belief that "siblings should not be separated."[3] In addition, these former foster children wanted accurate information about their backgrounds. Seven out of ten children indicated "they wished they had known more about their family background during their placement" (p. 266). Their interest in their family background came about from their struggle to gain a sense of self, as well as the more practical concern of needing to know such things as family medical history. About two-thirds of those interviewed felt that they had gained in terms of economic advantage by their placement in foster care. In general, foster children experienced themselves as being different than their peers. They often felt labeled and singled out at school. Almost "58% of the respondents said it was very or pretty true that at times they did not want to acknowledge being a foster child" (p. 273). These former foster children strongly believed they had been shifted around too much while in foster care, and as a result, they suffered, especially in terms of their education.

Education was an area of major youth concern, both in respect to their foster parents placing importance on it and to the low standard of education accepted by their foster care agency. This lack of educational opportunities factored into why these children felt very ill-prepared to live independently. In fact, "close to 71%, males and females alike, chose job preparation and career planning as one of the most important aspects in terms of independent living, but only 23.4% thought their agency had prepared them well" (p. 284). The need to refine this area of service was also noted by some Casey alumni in a more recent follow-up study in Idaho (Wedeven, Pecora, Hurwitz, Howell, & Newell, 1994).

Foster parents also confirmed these views of independent living preparation. A study conducted by Kluger, Fein, Maluccio, and Taylor (1986) found that only 35% of foster parents felt foster children were prepared or very well prepared for emancipation as compared to 52% of the social workers (p. 229). This discrepancy highlights the very different perceptions that exist among the participants of the foster care system. Often those making decisions regarding services fail to understand what children and foster parents see as their level of need (Kluger et al., 1986).

Many of these children wished that some sort of support services had been provided to them after discharge from foster care, especially educational and employment support services. In closing, Festinger notes that, in particular, three aspects were neglected in the provision of foster care services: (a) the ability of those in foster care to participate in decisions affecting their lives; (b) educational services; and (c) preparation of these children for independent living.

THE BARTH STUDY OF YOUTH IN CALIFORNIA

Barth (1990) located 55 former foster care recipients in order to look more closely at the needs of youth in foster care. The youth studied had departed foster care in the San Francisco Bay Area, had been out of care for longer than a year, and were at least 16 years of age. The researchers sent out flyers to various public agencies, foster parents, social workers, and group care providers in order to advertise the study. Even though the findings may not be representative because of the sampling method, the study data are intriguing. Part of the interview consisted of questions concerning life skills preparation, health, educational preparation, amount of contact with birth parents and former foster parents, substance use, criminal activity, income level, and the type of housing accessed. In addition, the study explored how satisfied the youth were with their foster care experience and what sort of suggestions they would make to improve foster services.

Youth interviewed averaged 21 years of age; their ethnic background was white (72%), black (13%), or Latino (9%); and slightly more than half (53%) were female (p. 423). They had experienced an average of three different foster home placements. In terms of the results, nearly one-third (29%) of the youth identified their dearth of education and skills as the greatest obstacle to securing desirable employment. Most youth (89%) indicated that they had remained in contact with their former foster parents, and slightly under half (40%) occasionally communicated with their social worker. The youth felt their foster parents and social workers should have helped more in their process of emancipation. They saw it as crucial for foster children to have more preparation in building independent living skills. Over half of the youth did not have a high school degree upon exit of foster care. On average, foster care alumni appear to be susceptible to a high number of health problems and experience a higher level of depression.

In general, those interviewed saw their foster care experience as being "somewhat good" to indifferent. They indicated that one of the most important things that happened to them in foster care was when they felt accepted by their foster family. Indeed, most of the youth looked at foster care as critical to their well-being, and most felt their lives would have been much worse without it. The study noted that the youth were involved in a substantial degree of criminal activity—both during and after foster care. In looking at their transition to independent living, the youth experienced a considerable amount of hardship. In fact, 29% replied there was more than one time in which they did not have a home or moved approximately every week or more. Nearly two-thirds mentioned that they often worried about whether they would have enough money for food.

In terms of improving social services, the former foster children believed it imperative that social workers put more emphasis on teaching youth life skills as well as providing more tools to secure adequate and affordable housing upon emancipation. In addition, the youth recommended to other foster children that they save more money while still in care, utilize counseling services, and prepare themselves in the area of budgeting and planning.

THE FANSHEL, FINCH, AND GRUNDY STUDY

A "life course" research study was conducted by Columbia University researchers for the Casey Family Program in the late 1980s that involved an extensive case record review and interviews with 106 alumni of the program (Fanshel, Finch, & Grundy, 1988, 1990). A variety of study limitations were present, but the data have important implications for program refinement in family foster care.[4]

Some of the indicators of life functioning that were examined by this aspect of the life course study are listed below:

Children who were not involved with drugs and who were at an age-appropriate grade level at case closure reported greater involvement with friends as an adult.

Most respondents (66%) were wage earners, with 10% receiving public assistance. Yet, almost one-third regarded their finances as inadequate and found themselves worried about finances (Fanshel et al., 1990, p. 99).

Of those alumni who were working, about 83% were somewhat or very satisfied with their current jobs (p. 100). This high figure may be a result of some of the special services that have been implemented by the program to support development of self-sufficiency skills (Wedeven & Mauzerall, 1990).

Two-thirds still maintained contact with foster families. Alumni–foster family contact, however, varied with the amount of time that had passed since the person had left the program.

Most (87%) reported that while they were with Casey, their social worker visited them regularly and cared about what was happening to them. When asked, "Was the social worker someone you could depend on for help with problems?" 70% of those interviewed said yes, and 26% responded in a negative fashion (Fanshel et al., 1990, pp. 95–96).

Achieving emancipation at case closure was negatively correlated with criminal activity (Fanshel et al., 1988, pp. 6.32).

Data indicating less positive outcomes for some children are discussed in this section, but it is important to reiterate that the sample size for the follow-up study was small (106 children) and not randomly selected. Nevertheless, these findings may indicate a need for further program refinements if they have not yet been addressed.

Some alumni experienced severe corporal punishment and physical abuse while in family foster care. A small but significant proportion of the alumni (25%) reported being "whipped or physically punished in a severe way" by foster parents (Fanshel et al., 1990, pp. 91, 341). In recent years, Casey and other foster care agencies have developed policy statements banning the use of corporal punishment and have strengthened foster parent screening, training, and supervision. Furthermore, social workers now meet with children monthly to interview them in private regarding their progress in foster care and to discuss any concerns they might have.

About one in eight (13%) of those alumni interviewed reported "extreme difficulty with drug use" (p. 104). About one-third of the alumni reported using marijuana one to two times per week in the last year, and 18% used it every day. One-third of those interviewed had used cocaine on one or more occasions (p. 104). Alcohol abuse had been a major problem for 13% of the respondents at some point in their lives, and somewhat of a problem for 25% of the alumni (p. 105). These data indicate that further program refinements are necessary regarding approaches to preventing drug and alcohol abuse, but these incidence levels also need to be examined in relation to national surveys of drug and alcohol use and follow-up data from comparable foster care programs regarding drug and alcohol use.

There appears to be a strong association between physical abuse and drug usage and other law violations in adulthood (pp. 106–107). Besides their implications for treating children in the program, these data underscore the importance of prompt intervention by child protective services to stop physical abuse, which may be at the root of these problem behaviors.

BOISE ALUMNI STUDY

Wedeven et al. (1994, 1997) recently conducted a survey of 69 Casey alumni from the Boise Division of the Casey Family Program who were discharged between the years of 1974 and 1992. The alumni ranged in age from 17 to 35 years, and a surprisingly high percentage (94.1%) completed high school, either through obtaining a diploma (79.6%) or a GED (11.8%). The majority of alumni perceived their experiences with the agency as favorable, indicated a desire for a continuing relationship with Casey, and saw agency support as important. In addition, many alumni expressed a desire to connect with other alumni and to be involved in alumni activities. A majority expressed a willingness to contribute to the division and to help "Casey kids" currently in foster homes.

In addition to expressing positive feelings for their foster families, a large number of alumni considered agency activities such as the Wilderness Work Program, the Lemon Grove semi-independent living experience, and work and recreational activities as highly influential. Groups, survival trips, camps, and the "Anytown" leadership experiences were also perceived as worthwhile. Turning points for over one-third of the alumni came when they assumed the adult responsibilities of marriage and having children. These experiences seemed to provide the occasion to apply the relationship and parenting skills modeled in their foster homes. Others referred to entering college or vocational technical school as a critical time in their lives. A third group singled out placement in a Casey foster home as a key factor in their lives.

Matching youth with families, joint case planning, and careful listening to youth in care were mentioned as areas for program refinement. Results suggest the importance of early work on transitions, self-sufficiency, and career track choices. Vocational counseling was suggested by 70% of the alumni as an option that would have been helpful to them when transitioning from their foster homes. While 4 of the 69 alumni were incarcerated, the vast majority of the respondents were working, self-supporting citizens.

EXAMINING THE PERCEPTIONS OF STREET YOUTH

Holdaway and Ray (1992) set out to explore street kids' attitudes regarding foster care. They interviewed 47 street youth aged 14 to 17 who utilized services in drop-in centers in three western cities: Seattle, San Francisco, and Spokane. The authors developed a 50-item instrument to elicit youth attitudes about foster care, from which four categories were created: control, peer influence, fear of failure, and family loyalty. Of the children interviewed, 29 had previously been in foster care. Although the responses varied, the youth who viewed their foster care experience as positive commonly spoke of having a sense of belonging.

In terms of the attitude questions, most children said the best thing about living on the streets was the freedom it allowed. It is this sense of having control of their lives that appeared to be the most important factor for street youth. In addition, the children placed a high value on both peer loyalty and a sense of community, which detoured them from living in a foster home. However, a majority did not believe that the "fear of being rejected" is what kept them out of foster care. It was more of a combination of seeing (or experiencing) physical and sexual abuse in some of the foster homes, experiencing too strict foster parents, and resenting the favoritism that some foster parents showed to their own children.

BARTH AND BERRY LITERATURE REVIEW

Finally, other research studies in foster care have demonstrated how information gathered from children is essential for program planning. Barth and Berry (1987) reviewed a number of research studies regarding preferred permanency planning outcomes (reunification, adoption, guardianship, and long-term foster care). Studies of child satisfaction were included as part of their review, with the following observations noted:

1. All but one of the children who returned home preferred their present home to their foster home.

2. Most children preferred their current setting compared to their previous family or out-of-home setting, with satisfaction highly associated with the child's sense of permanence.
3. Children who had multiple placements and who sought a sense of belonging preferred adoption.
4. Children living in institutions felt less comfortable, not as happy, less loved, less looked after, less trusted, and less cared about than did children in other forms of surrogate care or children reunified with their families.
5. Children who had some choice in their foster care placements were significantly more satisfied in their placements than were children with no choice (Barth & Berry, 1987).

Discussion

MAJOR THEMES

Some major themes have emerged in this review of the literature. The majority of children spoke about two areas where planning and preparation were lacking. One area centered on the sharing of information. Foster children need to be given accurate information about their backgrounds and the reasons for their placement. This information includes knowledge of their birth families' history, both cultural and medical.

The second area, the lack of planning and preparation for leaving care, elicited some of the strongest responses from foster children. A number of respondents believed they could have received much more aid in the form of counseling about career options and strategies to cope with independent living (Aldgate et al., 1989; Allen et al., 1996; Barth, 1990; Festinger, 1983; Nollan et al., 1997). The Kluger et al. (1986) study listed job training as the area of greatest need in preparation for emancipation.

In addition, these studies stressed foster children's concern over their lack of education. Numerous children felt their educational needs had been neglected, both by the foster care agency and their foster parents. Some even felt that there was not enough emphasis on selecting foster parents who valued education, although this situation may have changed significantly since some of these studies were undertaken (Festinger, 1983). Yet, as noted in Barth (1990), Fanshel et al. (1990), and elsewhere, children in foster care are much more likely to be behind in school than their peers.

This discrepancy is in part due to a lack of available services or inadequate use of them as reflected by Kluger et al. (1986), who found that "almost half of the children and youth (48%) needed help with school, but only 37% were receiving such services" (p. 160). The number of placement disruptions was also associated with the lack of educational attainment (Proch & Taber, 1987).

Another prevalent theme was that these youth wanted to have a sense of belonging; they desired to be part of a safe family living situation. This desire is tied to the tremendous amount of instability that these youth have experienced. Igelhart (1992) commented that the worker-youth relationship plays an important role in providing consistent support for the youth trying to endure foster care instability. In two studies (Jacobson & Cockerum, 1976; Holdaway & Ray, 1992) respondents spoke of the sexual and physical abuse they had experienced within foster homes. Some children gave abuse as the reason why they were currently living on the street (Holdaway & Ray, 1992). Finally, foster children emphasized that they should be active participants in the planning and decision making that affect their lives. They need to be listened to and to have their opinions taken seriously. The respondents in many of these studies expressed a genuine feeling of exasperation regarding a lack of control over their foster care experience and the choices made for them as well as their lack of preparation for independent living.

STUDY LIMITATIONS

In examining and applying the results of the research, a number of limitations must be kept in mind. First, in several studies, the sample size was small, typically between 7 and 55 (e.g., Jacobson & Cockerum, 1976; Gil & Bogart, 1982; Rice and McFadden, 1988; Barth, 1990; Holdaway & Ray, 1992). Some of the studies also had a sample that was not chosen randomly or systematically, so the group of respondents represented only a particular type of youth, such as those who frequented social service agencies or who were self-selected (e.g., Jacobson & Cockerum, 1976; Rice and McFadden, 1988; Holdaway & Ray, 1992). Oftentimes the questions asked were general in nature, and as a result, data interpretation was somewhat subjective (e.g., Jacobson & Cockerum, 1976; Rice and McFadden, 1988).

In addition, many of the research studies did not assess child safety while in care or did not employ standardized measures of behavior, educational functioning, physical health, mental health functioning, cultural identi-fication, relationships with family and friends, community involvement, life satisfaction, self-esteem, or other important dependent variables. Con-sequently, both validity and reliability may have been reduced, and there are few comparisons with the general population of youth of that age, gen-der, or ethnicity. With the exception of Allen et al. (1996), who noted the need for more attention to cultural identity, Festinger (1983), who exam-ined some gender differences, and Igelhart (1992), who found that both Af-rican Americans and females were much more likely to be placed in foster care, none of these studies explored the issues of race and gender and how those variables affect the responses of foster children. Finally, the studies did not use control or comparison groups as a way of assessing the impact of time spent in foster care.

Recommendations for Further Research and Practice

In reviewing the research studies, we have drawn a number of implications for research and practice, including asking more specific questions, using varied data collection approaches, and talking more with younger chil-dren. In addition, we need to go beyond asking questions about general well-being. We thus conclude with the following set of recommendations:

1. Ask more specific questions

Evaluation studies need to delve deeper and avoid using mostly global questions of child well-being or satisfaction. Researchers should instead focus on major outcome areas such as educational development, physical health, and mental health in terms of youth functioning, specific behav-iors, family adjustment, and peer relationships. Preadolescents and adoles-cents have specific opinions about service needs and report being very con-cerned about their development in areas such as sex education, career planning, and self-sufficiency (Hanlon, 1992).

The research literature indicates that children placed in foster care want to give feedback but often lack outlets to do so. The studies also highlight areas where children have concerns and point out what sorts of questions will help identify those needs. In addition to using more focused items, questions need to look at how children feel about their placements, such as "What do you like and not like about foster homes? If you could do one thing with a magic wand, what would you do to change foster homes?" (Rice and McFadden, 1988, p. 233).

It is also imperative to find out what sort of preparation was given to these youth before they entered their foster placements—for example, "What were you told upon entering foster care?" How children feel about their agencies and social workers is also a crucial area in which to elicit feedback. Maluccio (1979) posed this general introductory question: "What did you like or dislike about your social worker's approach and your agency as a whole?" (p. 397). A question like this can be a good segue into more specific queries. Festinger's (1983) study explored how children felt about being moved around in their own lives and how they felt numerous placements affected other children in foster care. A fundamental question posed by Gil and Bogart (1982) was, "Is there something you would recommend that could make things better for children and teenagers in foster care?" (p. 8).

Furthermore, research needs to examine the preparation for independent living that foster children receive. More specifically, it is necessary to look at the level of educational support they have received from both their foster parents and their foster agencies and what skills they are learning. Foster children want to be asked how they feel about keeping in contact with their biological families. Respondents in the Festinger study stated, "You are never asked if you want contact with your families . . . they seem to forget all about your parents" (p. 268). This is a serious problem and is another indicator that family reunification efforts need to be strengthened in many states as documented by the growing backlog of youth remaining in foster care (Goerge, Wulczyn, & Harden, 1996).

2. Pay attention to cultural factors

In many studies, ethnicity and gender are not considered during study planning or data analysis. These issues must be addressed in any survey measuring children's opinions about foster care. For example, the amount of re-placements she saw in the foster care system and the disproportionate number of African Americans and females in family foster care disturbed Igelhart (1992). Kluger et al. (1986) also found that minority children were much more likely than white children to be placed in foster care at a younger age. In addition, their study noted that "Black children and youth had fewer contacts with their biological families than White youngsters" (p. 258).

Study questions might focus upon what the children see as necessary before they can be reunified with birth parents or other family members. Other questions include the following: What is the level of safety children feel in their environment? Do they fear being sexually or physically abused in their foster homes? Have they been treated fairly? Do they feel like the culture with which they identify is incorporated into their lives? Have they been given enough information about their backgrounds to explore their ethnicity, and have their foster parents and social worker supported that exploration? Do they feel comfortable discussing their ethnicity with their foster parents? Do they feel the foster system is biased against them? If so, what changes need to be made? (See Allen et al., 1996; Festinger, 1983; Kufeldt, Armstrong, & Dorosh, 1995; and the other research cited in this chapter for useful questions.) Additional recommendations are listed in the following sections.

3. Organize groups of foster children

In Madison County, Illinois, a group of foster children united to form their own association. The purposes of the association were to "(1) improve the quality and quantity of foster homes; (2) enhance communication among foster children and advocate for their legal and natural rights; (3) improve the image of foster children in the community, and (4) promote the development of programs, resources, and recreational activities for foster children" (Perozzi, 1977, author abstract). The association was successful in changing some agency policies, holding training workshops for foster parents, sponsoring recreational programs, and involving the media to improve the image of foster children. In New York City, New Youth Connections publishes a bimonthly magazine written mainly by teenagers in the child welfare system.

4. Use varied data collection approaches

Researchers need to move beyond exclusive reliance on face-to-face or phone interviews in this field. Focus groups composed of various children of similar ages (Hanlon, 1992; Stewart & Shamdasani, 1990) can be used to elicit opinions and ideas. These groups produce a "synergy" that often results in children becoming empowered in their roles as consumers so that they feel that they have something to offer in the way of service refinement. Many of the same benefits can sometimes be achieved through the use of youth "panels" such as the ones organized by Jacobsen and Cockerum (1976), the results of which are discussed earlier in this chapter.

We have to think more creatively about how to help children express themselves. Card-sort methods being pioneered by the Behavioral Sciences Institute (the agency that developed the Homebuilders program) are helping staff members better assess the values, attitudes, and service goals of clients of all kinds. Many of these cards are being used with youth. Although special consumer satisfaction-oriented cards need to be developed, this approach has much potential for engaging youth in a relaxed but focused manner.

"Draw a picture" and "complete the sentence" approaches may prove useful in this area as well (e.g., "The best foster family I ever knew was _____"; "The most important opportunity that the agency provided for me last year was _____").

Food can play a relaxing and nurturing role in these types of events. Discussions held over lunches or potluck dinners may incorporate some skill-building and socialization activities into a program refinement–oriented activity.

5. Talk with younger children

Typically many agencies neglect to talk with younger children in an organized way because of the needs of the adolescents in care and concern about troubling the younger children. Yet if conducted in a developmentally appropriate and sensitive manner, a variety of individual interview and group-oriented data-gathering methods could be used with children as young as 3 or 5 years old. What we will gain from children in the interviewing process will depend on their level of "communicative competence," the style and personal characteristics of the interviewer, the objective behind seeking the information, and the particular interviewing techniques employed (see, for example, Garbarino, Stott, & Associates, 1989).

Conclusion

In the human services, it is often easy to lose track of our fundamental responsibility to the children and parents as consumers, especially in the context of funding shifts and crises that at times require a focus on the service delivery process rather than program quality and effectiveness. However, as the above studies have shown, not only do children in foster care want to be asked about how these services affect their lives, but they can also offer both vital information and creative solutions regarding the provision of foster care. In utilizing the perspective of these "system insiders," we improve our ability to provide effective services.

Programs that actively seek consumer feedback and use it as an aid in guiding policy will help ensure a more client-centered approach to practice. In the case of children in foster care, this goal cannot be emphasized enough. A foster child's life is one that too often can be characterized by both instability and a lack of control. If we can encourage children's feedback on their level of satisfaction with foster care, we will let them know that they matter, and we will increase the likelihood of implementing successful programs—programs that make sense to the people who use them. Allowing these children to participate in the decision-making process gives them a sense of their own worth and control, which will facilitate more positive client outcomes and ease the transition toward independent living.

Notes

1. The 1988 VCIS national statistics for the lengths of time spent in foster care are based on reports from 23 states representing 65.9% of the foster care population.

2. More studies reporting the views of children in care appear to have been conducted in Great Britian (see Colton, 1989).

3. Berridge & Cleaver (1987) report that in a sample of placements in Great Britain where siblings were separated from each other, the failure rate was 50%. Yet there are some family situations where separation of siblings for a period of time may be the best approach.

4. Because alumni from only two divisions of the Casey Family Program were included in the study, some of the follow-up data may not reflect the experience of children in other divisions. Services changed over time, as the study period covered children who were admitted from 1966 and exited from the program by 31 December 1984. The study therefore represented an evaluation of Casey as a new and evolving social program (pp. 82, 204). More recent admissions and some of the more positive cases were still being served by the program at the time of the research project. These children were therefore not eligible to be interviewed and were not included in the study (p. 86).

References

Aldgate, J., Stein, M., & Carey, K. (1989). The contribution of young people and their families towards improving foster family care. In J. Aldgate, A. Maluccio, & C. Reeves (Eds.), *Adolescents in foster families* (pp. 61–76). Chicago: Lyceum Books.

Allen, R., Barenblat, M., Le Prohn, N., & Pecora, P. (1996). *Quality service redesign project: Child interview report.* Seattle: Casey Family Program.

Austin, M. J., Cox, G., Gottlieb, N., Hawkins, J. D., Kruzich, J. M., & Rauch, R. (1982). *Evaluating your agency's programs.* Newbury Park CA: Sage.

Barth, R. P. (1990). On their own: The experience of youth after foster care. *Child and Adolescent Social Work, 7*(5), 419–440.

Barth, R. P., & Berry, M. (1987). Outcomes of child welfare services under permanency planning. *Social Service Review, 61*(1), 71–90.

Berridge, D., & Cleaver, H. (1987). *Foster home breakdown.* Oxford: Basil Blackwell.

Bush, M., & Gordon, A. C. (1982). The case for involving children in child welfare decisions. *Social Work, 27*(4), 309–314.

Colton, M. (1989). Foster and residential children's perceptions of their social environments. *British Journal of Social Work, 19,* 217–233.

Deming, W. E. (1986). *Out of the crisis.* Cambridge: Massachusetts Institute of Technology, Center for Advanced Engineering Study.

Ellsworth, R. B. (1975). Consumer feedback in measuring the effectiveness of mental health programs. In M. Guttentag & E. L. Struening (Eds.), *Handbook of evaluation research* (Vol. 2). Newbury Park CA: Sage.

Fanshel, D., Finch, S. J., & Grundy, J. F. (1988). *Foster children in life course perspective: The Casey Family Program experience.* New York: Columbia University, School of Social Work.

Fanshel, D., Finch, S. J., and Grundy, J. F. (1990). *Foster children in life course perspective.* New York: Columbia University Press.

Festinger, T. (1983). *No one ever asked us: A postscript to foster care.* New York: Columbia University Press.

Fraser, M. W., Pecora, P. J., Bennett, R. B., & Haapala, D. A. (1989). Placement outcomes: Did treatment affect placement prevention rates? In M. W. Fraser, P. J. Pecora, and D. A. Haapala (Eds.), *Families in crisis: Findings from the family-based intensive treatment project* (Technical Report). Salt Lake City: University of Utah, Graduate School of Social Work, Social Research Institute, and Federal Way WA: Behavioral Sciences Institute.

Fraser, M. W., Walton, E., Lewis, R. E., Pecora, P. J., & Walton, W. K. (1996). An experiment in family reunification: Correlates of outcome at one-year follow-up. *Children and Youth Services Review, 18*(4–5), 335–361.

Garbarino, J., Stott, F. M., & Faculty of the Erickson Institute. (1989). *What children can tell us.* San Francisco: Jossey-Bass.

Gil, E., & Bogart, K. (1982, January/February). Foster children speak out: A study of children's perception of foster care. *Children Today, 11*(1), 7–9.

Giordano, P. C. (1977). The client's perspective in agency evaluation. *Social Work, 22*(1), 34–39.

Goerge, R. M., Wulczyn, F. H., & Harden, A. (1996). New comparative insights into states and their foster children. *Public Welfare, 54*(3), 12–25, 52.

Gutek, B. A. (1978). Client satisfaction. *Journal of Social Issues, 34*(4), 44–56.

Hampson, R. B., & Tavormina, J. B. (1980). Feedback from the experts: A study of foster mothers. *Social Work, 25*(2), 108–113.

Hanlon, C. (1992, May). *Assessment of need for independent living preparation services in the Austin Division of the Casey Family Program.* Mimeograph report, Casey Family Program and University of Texas, School of Social Work.

Hargreaves, W. A., & Attkisson, C. C. (1978). Evaluating program outcomes. In C. C. Attkisson, W. A. Hargreaves, M. J. Horowitz, & J. E. Sorensen (Eds.), *Evaluation of human service programs.* New York: Academic Press.

Hill, M., & Triseliotis, J. (1990). Supported Adoption in Britain. *Community Alternatives: International Journal of Family Care, 2*(1), 91–111.

Holdaway, D. M., & Ray, J. (1992). Attitudes of street kids toward foster care. *Child and Adolescent Social Work Journal, 9*(4), 307–317.

Iglehart, A. P. (1992). Adolescents in foster care: Factors affecting the worker youth relationship. *Children and Youth Services Review, 14,* 305–322.

Jacobson, E., & Cockerum, J. (1976, November/December). As foster children see it: Former foster children talk about foster family care. *Children Today, 5*(6), 32–36, 42.

Katz, D., Gutek, B. A., Kahn, R. L., & Barton, E. (1975). *Bureaucratic encounters: A pilot study in the evaluation of government agencies.* Ann Arbor MI: Institute for Social Research.

Kinney, J. M., Haapala, D. A., & Booth, C. (1991). *Keeping families together: The Homebuilders model.* Hawthorne NY: Aldine de Gruyter.

Kluger, M., Fein, E., Maluccio, A., & Taylor, J. (1986). *An examination of long-term foster care: Final report.* Hartford CT: Research Department, Hartford Child and Family Services.

Kufeldt, K. (1984). Listening to children—Who cares? *British Journal of Social Work, 14,* 257–264.

Kufeldt, K., Armstrong, J., & Dorosh, M. (1995). How children in care view their own and their foster families: A research study. *Child Welfare, 74*(3), 695–715.

Magura, S., & Moses, B. S. (1984). Clients as evaluators in child protective services. *Child Welfare, 63*(2), 99–112.

Magura, S., & Moses, B. S. (1986). *Outcome measures for child welfare services: Theory and applications.* Washington DC: Child Welfare League of America.

Maluccio, A. N. (1979). Perspectives of social workers and clients on treatment outcome. *Social Casework, 60*(7), 394–401.

Maluccio, A. N., Abramczyk, L. W., & Tomlinson, B. (1996). Family reunification for children in out-of-home care: Research findings, issues and perspectives. *Children and Youth Services Review, 18*(4–5), 287–305.

Millar, R., & Millar, A. (Eds.). (1981). *Developing client outcome monitoring systems: A guide for state and local social service agencies.* Washington DC: Urban Institute Press.

Miller, L., & Pruger, R. (1978). Evaluation in care programs: With illustrations from Homemaker-Chore in California. *Administration in Social Work, 2*(4), 469–478.

National Center on Child Abuse and Neglect, Children's Bureau, (1998). *Child maltreatment 1996: Reports from the states to the National Child Abuse and Neglect Data System.* Washington DC: U.S. Department of Health and Human Services.

Nollan, K. A., Pecora, P. J., Downs, A. C., Wolf, M., Horn, M., Martine, L., & Lamont, E. (1997). Assessing life skills of adolescents in out-of-home care. *International Journal of Child and Family Welfare, 97*(2), 113–126.

Perozzi, W. T. (1977). The Illinois Foster Children's Association. *Children Today, 6*(6), 16–17, 34–46. East St. Louis IL: Illinois Department of Children and Family Services. (From *Social Work Abstracts,* 1977, Abstract No. 1570)

Proch, K., & Tabor, M. A. (1987). Alienated adolescents in foster care. *Social Work Research and Abstracts, 23*(2), 9–13.

Rapp, C. A., & Poertner, J. (1987). Moving clients center stage through the use of client outcomes. In R. J. Patti, J. Poertner, and C. A. Rapp (Eds.), *Managing for services effectiveness in social welfare organizations* [Special issue], *Administration in Social Work, 11*(3–4), 23–38.

Rapp, C. A., & Poertner, J. (1992). *Social administration: A client-centered approach.* New York: Longman.

Rice, D. L., & McFadden, E. J. (1988). A forum for foster children. *Child Welfare, 67*(3), 231–243.

Stewart, D. W., & Shamdasani, P. N. (1990). *Focus groups: Theory and practice.* Newbury Park CA: Sage.

Sudman, S., & Bradburn, N. M. (1974). *Response effects in surveys: A review and synthesis*. Chicago: Aldine.

Tatara, T. (1992, May). *Characteristics of children in substitute and adoptive care—A statistical summary of the VCIS national child welfare data base*. (VCIS Research Notes No. 3, 1–4). Washington DC: American Public Welfare Association.

Tatara, T. (1997, March). *U.S. child substitute care flow data and the race/ethnicity of children in care for FY 1995, along with recent trends in the U.S. child substitute care populations*. (VCIS Research Notes No. 13). Washington DC: American Public Welfare Association.

Taylor, J. C. (1977). Job satisfaction and quality of working life: A reassessment. *Journal of Occupational Psychology, 50*, 243–252.

Warfel, D. J., Maloney, D. M., & Blase, K. (1981). Consumer feedback in human service programs. *Social Work, 26*(2), 151–156.

Wedeven, T., & Mauzerall, H. (1990). Independent living programs: Avenues to competence. In A. N. Maluccio, R. Krieger, & B. A. Pine (Eds.), *Preparing adolescents for life after foster care: The central role of foster parents* (pp. 91–105). Washington DC: Child Welfare League of America.

Wedeven, T., Pecora, P. J., Hurwitz, M., Howell, R., & Newell, D. (1994). *The Boise Division alumni survey: Summary report*. Boise ID and Seattle WA: Casey Family Program.

Wedeven, T., Pecora, P. J., Hurwitz, M., Howell, R., & Newell, D. (1997). Examining the perceptions of alumni of long-term family foster care: A follow-up study. *Community Alternatives: International Journal of Family Care, 9*(1), 88–106.

Wells, K., & Biegel, D. E. (Eds.). (1991). *Family preservation services: Research and evaluation*. Newbury Park CA: Sage.

Wulczyn, F. H., & Goerge, R. M. (1992). Foster care in New York and Illinois: The challenge of rapid change. *Foster Care, 66*(2), 278–294.

Policies and Practices

6

Foster Care and the Costs of Welfare Reform

Mark E. Courtney

Foster care remains a poorly studied and poorly understood social service program despite the sensationalized media coverage of some particularly tragic cases. A current case in point concerns the unexamined relationship between foster care and the Aid to Families with Dependent Children (AFDC) program. The makers and analysts of poverty policy have largely ignored foster care, even though about half of the children in care come from families that are eligible for or receiving AFDC. This lack of attention to foster care is a serious and potentially costly oversight. In light of the steadily increasing foster care caseload, current welfare reform initiatives may well reap unanticipated—and expensive—consequences by placing even greater stress on the foster care system.

Background

Federal assistance to help states make maintenance payments for children placed out of their homes by a child welfare agency was first provided in 1961 under the old Aid to Dependent Children (ADC) program (Title IV-A of the Social Security Act), now known as AFDC. The federal role grew out of the recognition that some states were denying ADC payments to children whose homes were deemed "unfit." The 1961 regulations required that states either continue ADC payments and improve conditions in the home or provide out-of-home care for the child. Federal financial participation was available only for the placement of children who had been receiving ADC in the month preceding foster care placement. Later amendments made the program permanent and mandatory for states and allowed for

Figure 1. Federal spending on Title IV-E foster care and AFDC compared, fiscal years 1985–1995.

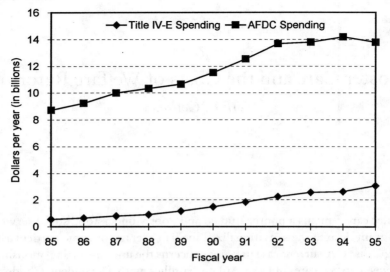

payments to children in private, not-for-profit institutions. Eventually, eligibility included children from families who were eligible for ADC when the children were removed from the home, regardless of whether the family was actually receiving ADC at the time.

The size of the AFDC foster care program relative to its "mother" program, AFDC, highlights the need to understand the relationship between foster care and overall poverty policy.[1] The number of child recipients of AFDC increased by 29% over a recent 7-year period, from approximately 7 million in 1985 to about 9 million in 1992. Over the same period of time, the foster care population grew by 60% —twice the rate of AFDC growth— from 276,000 in 1985 to about 442,000 in 1992 (Tatara, 1993).

The relative growth in the federal costs of both programs provides an even more striking contrast (see Figures 1 and 2). Federal expenditures on AFDC benefits and administration grew from $7.76 billion in 1981 to $13.79 billion in 1995. In contrast, federal expenditures for foster care maintenance payments and administration leapt from $309 million to $3.05 billion over the same period. Under current law, it is estimated that by 1999 federal foster care expenditures will increase to $3.79 billion, representing a growth of 1,100% from 1981 levels!

The higher per capita cost of foster care partly reflects the much higher

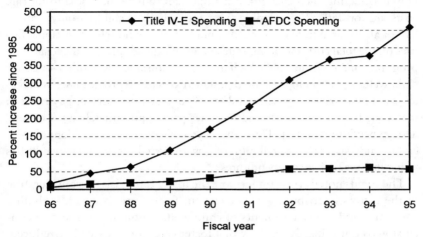

Figure 2. Percentage growth in federal spending on Title IV-E foster care and AFDC compared, fiscal years 1986–1995.

administrative costs of supervising the care of children than of distributing AFDC checks. It also costs more to entice foster care providers to raise children than we currently pay AFDC recipients. The median monthly AFDC payment for one child ($212) is about $100 per month less than the median foster care rate. Costs of group care (e.g., group homes and residential treatment centers) generally range from $2,000 to $6,000 per month for one child. Furthermore, foster care rates are proportional to the number of children placed (i.e., two children generate twice the foster care rate of one child), while AFDC per capita payment rates decrease with increased family size. Thus, the more children in a family, the greater the difference in cost between AFDC and foster care. The net effect of these differences is that the federal government spent about $10,945 per child on foster care maintenance and administration costs in 1993. In contrast, it spent about $975 in 1993 for each child receiving AFDC. In short, recent estimates suggest that it costs the federal government over 11 times as much per child to provide foster care as to provide basic income maintenance.

In essence, AFDC foster care is a government program that takes over primary child-rearing responsibilities from poor parents based on the assumption that it can and must do better. The numbers presented above imply that the federal government is already spending about one-fifth as much attempting to raise the children of poor families as it spends on the primary income support program for poor families.

In considering such changes, it is important to note that these foster care costs are for Title IV-E–eligible (i.e., AFDC-eligible) children only—about half of all children in foster care. Although there are no reliable national figures on the total cost (including state and local expenditures) of the foster care program, an American Public Welfare Association analysis of thirty-one state child welfare plans in 1990 found that states expected to provide 68.1% of foster care maintenance payments and 57.2% of foster care service payments in that year. In contrast, states and localities paid approximately 45% of total AFDC expenditures in 1993. Thus, an analysis of federal spending alone considerably understates the overall ratio of governmental foster care expenditures to income maintenance expenditures.

The trends noted above underscore the foster care crisis. A consideration of the factors contributing to the current foster care caseload, including legislative and judicial elements of child welfare policy, leads to two conclusions: (a) it is highly·unlikely that foster care caseloads will be reduced; and (b) this crisis presents problems for reform of public assistance programs. The ensuing discussion focuses primarily on the fiscal implications of the federal government's failure to address the foster care crisis.

The Child Welfare Services Morass: How Did We Get Here Anyway?

The federal government, by design and lack of enforcement of existing child welfare regulations (Ellertson, 1994), grants the states great latitude in administering child welfare programs. The consequent variation in foster care programs from one state to another makes difficult any effort to discuss "national" foster care policy. Nevertheless, federal legislation in conjunction with federal and state court decisions directly affected the foster care system. In particular, laws mandating that child abuse be reported and that public agencies respond to such reports, the "permanency planning" movement, and court decisions leading to the growth of kinship foster care have altered the foster care landscape. At present, the child welfare system is also being overwhelmed by more clients who are increasingly troubled.

THE RESPONSE TO CHILD ABUSE AND NEGLECT

The "rediscovery" of child abuse and neglect during the 1960s and early 1970s led to federal legislation that has done much to increase the "demand" for foster care. Spurred on by the focus on "the battered child" during that period, state legislatures began to enact laws requiring that child abuse be reported by professionals who interact with children, such as teachers and doctors (Antler, 1978; Stein, 1984). By 1974, the Child Abuse Prevention and Treatment Act (CAPTA, Public Law 93-247) was passed by Congress, providing federal financial support to states that chose to develop programs for the prevention, identification, and treatment of child abuse and neglect. As part of the law and its revisions, states, which receive assistance, must enact laws that require various professionals (e.g., teachers, physicians, social workers, psychotherapists) to report suspected incidents of child maltreatment to law enforcement officials.

Mandated child abuse and neglect reporting has profoundly influenced the foster care system, since these reports must be responded to by child welfare authorities and are the primary means by which children come to the attention of the child welfare system. In addition, since the passage of CAPTA and supporting legislation by the states, the reported prevalence of child abuse and neglect has dramatically increased, placing still further demands on child welfare services including foster care (Besharov, 1990; Kamerman & Kahn, 1990). In 1994, the number of children reported as abused or neglected exceeded 3 million, an increase of 63% since 1985 (National Committee to Prevent Child Abuse, 1995). In contrast, about 670,000 reports were filed in 1976 (American Humane Association, 1989).

PERMANENCY PLANNING

By the late 1970s, interest in finding adoptive homes for hard-to-adopt or "special needs" children in foster care (e.g., ethnic minorities, older children, children with disabilities), along with the perception that many children were inappropriately being placed in foster care or were spending inordinate amounts of time in the system, led to demands for reform of the existing child welfare services system. The primary legislative consequence of this reform movement was the Adoption Assistance and Child Welfare Act of 1980 (Public Law 96-272).

Public Law 96-272 transferred the foster care program from Title IV-A to a new Title IV-E. The law altered the funding mechanism for foster care by retaining its entitlement status but linking it to Title IV-B (Child Welfare Services) spending in order to encourage states to use their IV-B monies for prevention of out-of-home placement and rehabilitation of families. Previously, many states had used much of their Title IV-B funding to help defer state costs of foster care placement. It also created a program of adoption assistance payments to parents who adopt children with special needs.

In order to obtain maximum federal financial participation in state child welfare programs, PL 96-272 requires the states to implement a number of programs and procedural reforms: a statewide information system and inventory of children in foster care; a preplacement preventive services program providing "reasonable efforts" to prevent child placement; procedural safeguards regarding child removal and placement; a detailed case plan for every child in care; standards for care emphasizing placement in a "least restrictive" environment, in close proximity to parents and with kin when possible; judicial or administrative case reviews done every 6 months and a dispositional hearing within 18 months of a child's placement; and services to reunite children with their families or find another "permanent" placement. In essence, the focus on "permanency planning" in Public Law 96-272 calls for prompt and decisive action to maintain children in their own homes or to place them, as quickly as possible, in permanent homes with other families (preferably guardianship or adoption).

Although the procedural and programmatic requirements associated with permanency planning make sense, in practice they lead to time wasted on paperwork and court on the part of child welfare workers. These reforms were put in place just as reports of child abuse—the primary source of "demand" for child welfare services—were beginning to skyrocket. Unfortunately, although foster care spending has grown with the foster care caseload, the funding for casework services under Title IV-B Child Welfare Services has not (see Figure 3). For example, although IV-E spending grew over 900% between 1981 and 1995, IV-B spending increased only about 80% over the same period, from $163.4 million in 1981 to an estimated $291.9 million in 1995. Even after adjusting for inflation, federal foster care spending grew by over 400% between 1981 and 1993 whereas IV-B spending only grew by about 14%. Furthermore, although an unknown portion of funds provided by the Title XX social services block grant is spent by the states on child protective services, these funds have declined in real terms since the early 1980s. Thus, after the implementation of CAPTA and PL 96-272, the child welfare services system was left providing fewer services to a much larger clientele (Kamerman & Kahn, 1990; Maluccio & Fein, 1992).

Figure 3. Federal spending on Title IV–B child welfare services and Title IV–E foster care compared, fiscal years 1985–1995.

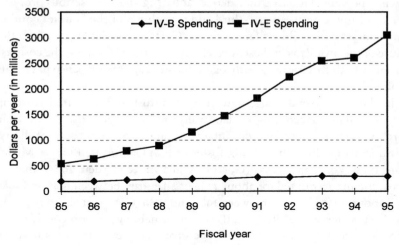

THE CHANGING CHARACTERISTICS OF THE FOSTER CARE CASELOAD

If foster care is intended to be the "life raft" for children who can no longer remain safely at home, then the boat is being swamped, not only by the sheer number of its passengers but also by their numerous and expensive special needs. Various studies have found that up to 60% of foster children suffer from moderate to severe mental health problems and that about 40% have physical health problems (Halfon, English, Allen, & DeWoody, 1994). Recently the U.S. General Accounting Office conducted a study of a random sample of children under the age of three who had entered out-of-home care in 1986 or 1991 in Los Angeles County, New York City, and Philadelphia County and found that over 80% of these young children had one or more serious health problems (U.S. General Accounting Office, 1994).

The mental and physical health problems of foster children create a significant, although for the most part unquantified, impact on the need for services. For example, a recent study of the utilization of Medi-Cal—California's version of Medicaid—found that foster children are almost 10 times more likely to use mental health services and are likely to be hospitalized almost twice as long as other children on Medi-Cal (Halfon, Berkowitz, & Klee, 1990). Thus, while foster children make up only about 4% of California children on Medi-Cal, they account for 40% of all Medi-Cal mental health expenditures. Furthermore, recent surveys of child welfare agency personnel indicate that alcohol and drug abuse is a serious problem for somewhere between one-third and two-thirds of the families coming into contact with child welfare agencies (Curtis & McCullough, 1993). Because of the problems in these severely dysfunctional families, the costs associated with foster care greatly exceed foster care maintenance payments alone.

In the past several years, new entrants into foster care are becoming much younger. According to data from the Multistate Foster Care Data Archive, between 1990 and 1993 infants accounted for about 24% of all first admissions of children entering foster care in California, Illinois, Michigan, New York, and Texas (Goerge, Wulczyn, & Harden, 1995). In contrast, infants accounted for about 23% of all entries between 1987 and 1989 and about 16% of entries between 1983 and 1986 (Goerge et al., 1995). In all of these states except Texas, infants are remaining in care considerably longer than children in any other age group, and even in Texas they are staying longer than all but adolescents. The likelihood of these infants being adopted after they spend any significant time in foster care is quite low (Barth, Courtney, Berrick, & Albert, 1994). Thus, the recent rise in foster care caseloads includes a foster care "baby boom" that will almost inevitably result in a historically unprecedented number of children being raised in some form of foster care.

African-American children are particularly likely to wind up in foster care. In 1990, the likelihood that African-American children would be in foster care ranged from 3 times (Texas) to over 10 times (New York) that of white children (Goerge, Wulczyn, & Harden, 1994). The overall foster care prevalence rate in 1990 for African-American children was about 4.4% in California and 4.2% in New York, the states with the largest foster care populations. Over 5% of African-American infants in these two states lived in foster care at any given time in 1990.

Of course, an overall point-in-time prevalence rate likely underestimates the proportion of children who will spend some time in foster care. For example, like other children, many African Americans born in the past several years who did not enter care in their first year will do so before they reach adulthood, given that about three-quarters of first entries to foster care happen after the age of 1 year. Furthermore, since best estimates indicate that nearly two-thirds of children entering care exit within 3 years (Goerge et al., 1994) and that fewer than one-third of these reenter care

(Courtney, 1995; Wulczyn, 1991), prevalence rates for older children are not exclusively, or even largely, a function of infants or other young children staying in the system indefinitely. Thus, although an accurate estimate is not possible at this time, current data suggest that a large proportion of African Americans in at least some of our largest states, if not across the country, will have spent some time in foster care.

KINSHIP CARE

Landmark federal legislation and the myriad problems facing America's children are not the only contributors to the current face of foster care. The relatively recent development of paid foster care by relatives of court dependents—kinship care—has changed the types of settings in which foster children are likely to grow up. For example, whereas in the early 1980s placements with kin accounted for fewer than 10% of foster care placements in such large states as California, Illinois, and New York, they accounted for about half of all placements by the end of the decade (Courtney, 1994; Goerge et al., 1994; Goerge, 1990; Wulczyn & Goerge, 1992).

Early evidence indicates that the shift toward kinship care affects permanency outcomes for children entering foster care, including slower family reunification rates and lower adoption rates (Barth, Courtney et al., 1994; Courtney, 1994; Goerge, 1990; Thornton, 1991). In other words, children entering kinship care are more likely than children placed in foster family homes or group care to remain in the foster care system for a long period of time, if not indefinitely. Even if child welfare authorities wished to alter this trend, it would be very difficult, given that the number of non-kinship foster family homes in this country declined from about 147,000 in 1984 to 100,000 in 1990 (National Commission on Family Foster Care, 1991).

What are the reasons for the phenomenal growth of kinship care? Various states and localities, as well as social workers and judges, have played a role in ways that cannot be easily observed, let alone described, given the decentralized nature of child welfare services. However, certain factors besides the lack of other placement options appear to have caused this increase.

In response to PL 96-272, current permanency planning philosophy in child welfare places emphasis on keeping children "with family" even when they are removed from the home of their birth parents. For the vast majority of children entering the foster care system, the permanency plan involves returning the child home to the birth family. Common sense suggests that a stay with a relative is likely to be less traumatic for a child removed from parental care than placement with unfamiliar foster parents or group care providers. In addition, it is also possible that the option of paying kin to care for a child, as opposed to having to find an appropriate foster home, makes the difficult decision to remove a child from home easier for social workers and judges.

Anecdotal (and some empirical) evidence suggests that child welfare workers believe that placement with kin reduces the need to provide reasonable efforts to return children to their biological families (Barth, Berrick, & Needell, 1994; Iglehart, 1994). Presumably, kinship care frees up time for social workers to spend on casework activities related to other clients on their normally large and demanding caseloads. This relative lack of attention to kinship care may contribute to the slower rate of family reunification for children placed with relatives.

Though the emphasis in PL 96-272 on finding the most family-like and least restrictive placement for foster children helps to make kin an attractive placement resource, judicial rulings at the federal and state level have probably contributed most to the impetus to place children with kin by providing equitable financial support to relative caregivers (Gleeson & Craig, 1994). In particular, the ruling by the U.S. Supreme Court in *Miller v. Youakim* (1979) opened the way for kinship care by requiring that relatives not be excluded from the definition of foster parents eligible for federal foster care benefits. If a child considered for out-of-home placement comes from a birth parent's home that is AFDC eligible, relative caregivers are eligible for the same reimbursement provided to non-kin foster parents, as long as the kin can meet state standards for foster care. Relatives who care for children placed by court order who do not come from an AFDC-eligible family are eligible only for AFDC payments, rather than AFDC foster care payments. In practice, numerous states have established more lenient standards for the approval of relative foster care homes than for non-kin foster homes, and at least 16 states reimburse kin at the same rate as other foster care providers, regardless of whether the child in care is AFDC eligible (Gleeson & Craig, 1994).

The argument over the provision of foster care payments to relatives is understandable given the differences between AFDC and foster care reimbursement practices. In addition to being greater than AFDC rates, foster care rates are proportional to the number of children placed (i.e., two children of the same age will generate twice the foster care rate of one), whereas AFDC per capita payment rates decrease with increased family size. Thus, the larger the number of children in a family, the greater the difference between the amount of money the family may receive from AFDC and the amount it may receive in foster care reimbursement.

The decision to make foster care reimbursement the same for kin and non-kin foster families can be easily justified on the grounds of equity. Why should the state pay "strangers" more than kin to care for a child in need? Indeed, it is hard to envision a child welfare system consistent with our cultural or "family" values that did not support the ability of the extended kin network to care for children in a time of family crisis.

At the same time, current funding arrangements may provide a perverse financial incentive for AFDC families to have children placed in kinship care, since the higher foster care rates usually represent a net financial gain for the extended family. This financial incentive can be quite large when there are two or more children involved.

THE CLOTHES HAVE NO EMPEROR AND ARE NOT LIKELY TO FIND ONE SOON

Unfortunately, current child welfare policy reflects the conflicting values of child protection and family preservation, in addition to a lack of political will. For example, CAPTA enlists adults to protect children from maltreatment. Unfortunately, one of its effects has been to flood child protective services offices with child abuse reports. Thus, mandatory reporting has contributed to ever growing numbers of children in foster care. CAPTA largely reflects the American tradition of "child saving" but not family preservation.

In contrast, PL 96-272 and the court decisions supporting its implementation emphasize protecting children by keeping them "in the family." In the absence of adequate resources child welfare authorities are forced to engage in a process of triage. Agencies increasingly decline help to a growing proportion of families being reported for child abuse and neglect (Kamerman & Kahn, 1990) and shuttle an increasing number of children to kin with little provision of supportive or permanency planning services.

Further complicating the problems cited above is an apparent lack of political will to reform the child welfare system. At present, federal and state governments do not allocate sufficient resources to child welfare personnel. The $1 billion over 5 years in the Omnibus Budget Reconciliation Act of 1993 (PL 103-66) for an array of family preservation and family support services cannot be expected to reduce the growth of troubled families and the demand for foster care. One need only consider that under current funding projections the federal government will spend over $16 billion over the same period on foster care to appreciate that the family preservation and support initiative does not represent a significant fiscal commitment to supporting families and preventing out-of-home care.

It is hard to see how the child welfare system will cope with the growing foster care crisis in the absence of both a serious attempt to reconcile existing inconsistencies in child welfare policy and the emergence of a political commitment to allocate the resources necessary to implement such policy changes. Of course, the lack of rigorous program evaluation research in the area of child welfare services—partly a function of minimal federal funding—leaves policymakers and administrators with little concrete guidance as to what to do even if funds were forthcoming (Curtis, 1994).

It may not even be possible to reform the child welfare system within the context of our residual approach to supporting families and children (Pelton, 1989; Lindsey, 1993). Our society has a long tradition of coming to the aid of families only when parents have "failed" in some significant way to care adequately for their children. Even then we do so only grudgingly, and our efforts are feeble at best. As long as this is our approach, it is likely that we will find ourselves paying "strangers," or even more ironically, kin, much more to care for children than we will pay to support parents to care for their own.

Welfare Reform and Foster Care

In August 1996, President Bill Clinton signed into law H.R. 3734, the Personal Responsibility and Work Opportunity Reconciliation Act. Although the law is too complex to describe in detail here, certain elements that are most likely to affect the child welfare system and its clients include the following (Department of Health and Human Services, 1996):

the block granting of AFDC, Emergency Assistance, and the JOBS program into a single capped entitlement to states at an estimated funding level of $16.4 billion from 1996 through 2003, with state funding levels based on recent federal expenditures to each state for the block-granted programs;

no individual entitlement to assistance under the new programs;

a 5-year limit on the use of block grant funds for cash aid to families—shorter time limits at state option—with states able to exempt up to 20% of the caseload from the time limit;

a requirement that states must move families receiving assistance into work, with a 50% work participation rate for single-parent families by 2002 and 90% for two-parent families by 1999;

work requirements are less stringent for single-parent families than two-parent families and for single-parent families with young children;

states operating welfare programs under waivers of AFDC regulations are allowed to continue to operate their cash assistance programs under some or all of the waivers, although they will still receive funding at the block grant amount;

a contingency fund of $2 billion is established for states with excess need for assistance, with triggers for contingency funding based on state unemployment rates or food stamp utilization;

states must maintain a level of funding for the new workfare programs equal to 80% of FY 1994 funding on AFDC and related programs, 75% for states meeting work participation requirements;

unmarried minor parents are required to live with an adult or in an adult-supervised setting and participate in educational and training activities in order to receive assistance;

fiscal incentives are created for states to maximize work participation of program participants and to reduce out-of-wedlock births;

individuals convicted of drug-related felonies after enactment of the legislation are barred for life from receiving temporary assistance or food stamp benefits, although states will have the right to opt out of this provision;

maladaptive behavior is eliminated from the medical criteria used to evaluate mental disabilities in children, resulting in an estimated reduction of the Supplemental Security Income (SSI) caseload of about 315,000 low-income children by 2002 (Super, Parrott, Steinmetz, & Mann, 1996);

ssi and food stamp eligibility are eliminated for most legal immigrants until citizenship;

states are allowed to ban most legal immigrants from receiving benefits under the Medicaid (except for emergency services), Title XX Social Services, child care, and workfare programs until citizenship;

new child care funding is combined with the existing Child Care and Development Block Grant to provide $13.9 billion in mandatory funding for child care in FYS 1997–2002 and authorizes an additional $7 billion in discretionary funding for child care between 1996 and 2002; and,

when fully implemented, the bill reduces funding for the food stamp program by almost 20%. (Super et al., 1996)

In addition to broad changes in public assistance programs, the welfare reform law also made some relatively minor changes in federal child welfare programs. The law reinforces the growth of kinship foster care by requiring states to give preference to kinship placements, allows states to use IV-E funds to make foster care payments on behalf of children in for-profit children's institutions, extends enhanced federal funding for automated child welfare information systems through 1997, and appropriates $6 million per year from 1996 to 2002 for a random sample study of abused and neglected children.

Unfortunately, it is unlikely that welfare reforms currently under way will resolve the crisis in the child welfare system. How will welfare reform affect the foster care system and child welfare services in general? Clear answers are impossible to provide given the limited data on federal and state child welfare programs and their relationship to public assistance. However, there is some evidence from a study of child protective services referrals in Los Angeles County that cuts in AFDC benefit levels are associated with an increase in child maltreatment reports. In particular, a time-series analysis found that a 2.7% cut in benefit levels in 1991 was associated with an increase of about 12% in the monthly number of protective services referrals, whereas a 5.8% cut in AFDC benefits implemented in two phases during late 1992 was associated with an approximately 20% increase in referrals (Sherman, 1995).

Furthermore, the impact of welfare reform on children and the child welfare system will almost certainly vary considerably from state to state as a result of interstate variation in program implementation, size of the legal immigrant population, and economic conditions. Nevertheless, costs associated with the child welfare system are likely to increase regardless of the nature of program changes, for reasons discussed below.

MAKING LIFE HARDER FOR POOR CHILDREN AND THEIR FAMILIES

Cutbacks in support for poor families are likely to come about for a number of reasons in the post-reform era. First, many families will lose support due to the time-limit provisions of the new law. The Congressional Budget Office has estimated that between 2.5 million and 3.5 million children could be affected by the 5-year time limit on assistance when the law is fully implemented, even after taking into account the 20% hardship exemption (Super et al., 1996). Moreover, these numbers may be conservative since states may set much shorter time limits than 5 years. Second, an unknown number of families will lose cash and other benefits due to noncompliance with work requirements. Third, some legal immigrants will lose benefits that they use to help support their children, many of whom are U.S. citizens. Fourth, some people who are banned from program participation for life because of drug-related crimes will be parents. This provision of the welfare reform law may have a serious impact on the child welfare system, given the large proportion of families currently involved with the system who suffer from substance abuse problems. Lastly, since the individual entitlement to support has been eliminated, some states may simply cut off benefits when economic or political circumstances result in inadequate funds to continue assistance to all families in need.

Growth in child poverty owing to any or all of the reasons cited above is likely to lead to an increase in child maltreatment and a corresponding increase in demand for child welfare services, including substitute care. The vast majority of children in substitute care come from single-parent homes, and about half come from AFDC-eligible families. Poverty is the best predictor of child neglect, as well as a strong predictor of other forms of child maltreatment (Jones & McCurdy, 1992; Pelton & Milner, 1994; Sedlak, 1993). Most children are placed in foster care because of neglect or parental incapacity (e.g., chronic substance abuse) rather than physical or sexual abuse. Many of the families who are most likely to be unable or unwilling to find work or make use of education and training are, by and large, already at relatively high risk of neglecting or abusing their children.

Elimination or reduction of benefits to these families will heighten that risk.

The expansion of work requirements without adequate child care could also contribute to a movement of children into foster care. Many current AFDC recipients do not work because they devote all of their time to child care. Although the welfare reform law significantly increases federal child care funding, the additional funding may not be enough to cover the child care costs associated with moving welfare recipients into work programs. The Congressional Budget Office estimates that if states meet work participation goals by placing participants in work programs, by 2002 federal child care funding will fall $1.8 billion short of what will be needed to provide child care for low-income working families (Super et al., 1996). There is no guarantee of child care for program participants under the new law, and families with children over 6 years old can be penalized for failure to engage in work activities. Thus, many poor families may be faced with the choice of either losing benefits due to noncompliance with work requirements or leaving their children alone and unsupervised for long periods of time. In either case, the children in these families are at increased risk of neglect.

Narrowing the definition of child disability under the SSI program may also increase demand for substitute care. The debate over whether the children in question are "truly" disabled may be largely irrelevant if the children are a burden or are perceived to be so by their caregivers. Children who exhibit "maladaptive behavior" and are no longer eligible for SSI may be prime candidates for abuse, neglect, or abandonment when their caregivers can no longer rely on SSI for financial support.

KINSHIP CARE AND WELFARE REFORM

In the absence of significant legislative or judicial action regarding the status of kinship care, children from families hurt by reform efforts may simply end up with extended family, at a much greater cost than AFDC. Some state-level welfare reform proposals, as in Wisconsin, explicitly call for the development of kinship care programs to provide homes for children displaced by program changes (Legislative Fiscal Bureau of the State of Wisconsin, 1995). "Reform" of kinship care, like reform of AFDC, is easier said than done. Attempts to limit the growth of kinship care or deny assistance to kin who are willing to care for these children would fly in the face of society's commitment to keep children with family—a commitment that is manifest in the kinship care language of the welfare reform legislation—and restrict placement options to more expensive alternatives.

Current kinship care funding arrangements create the probability of confusion and fiscal shell games at the state level in the wake of welfare reform. Some states make significant use of both federal foster care funds and AFDC funds via payments to non–legally responsible relatives (NLRR) to support kinship foster care. Other states rely almost exclusively on NLRR payments to fund kinship care. In effect, these states have been financing a large part of their foster care system using AFDC funds. Still others appear to discourage the use of kin altogether, though every state makes some use of this placement resource. Under the welfare block grant some states may gain funding while others lose. For example, states with relatively high utilization of kinship care supported by NLRR payments may end up with a relatively larger proportion of the welfare block grant than states that have not historically made much use of NLRR for this purpose. Since federal foster care funding is left uncapped, states with large NLRR foster care caseloads may simply figure out a way to shift kinship care funding to the federal foster care funding stream, realizing a significant windfall. Of course, states that did not have significant numbers of children in kinship care prior to the passage of the welfare reform bill will not be able to take advantage of this funding scheme.

Other questions arise concerning the impact of changes in federal law on the conditions under which kin will provide state-supported care. For example, can kin participate in so-called workfare programs and provide kinship foster care at the same time? How will changes in the support kinship care providers receive affect the supply of kinship care?

Regardless of the role of kinship care in the wake of welfare reform, a significant increase in demand in the face of scarce placement resources will almost certainly lead child welfare agencies to develop new group care settings. These placements cost an average of about $3,000 per month. Thus, a major increase in the number of children coming to the attention of the child welfare system will increase not only the number of children needing substitute care but also the average per-child cost of substitute care.

THE NEW FEDERALISM AND THE HUMAN COSTS OF WELFARE REFORM
It bears repeating that this discussion has focused almost exclusively on the

fiscal implications of the foster care crisis and its relationship to welfare reform. Needless to say, this focus neglects the monumental and still unanswered questions about the effect of welfare reform on children. The increased demand for child welfare services resulting from welfare reform would have human as well as fiscal consequences. Given current federal and state child welfare policy, children who are put in harm's way by program cutbacks would not spontaneously appear at the doors of "orphanages" or other substitute care settings. Many if not most poor parents would attempt to raise their children by any means necessary. Only when their behavior resulted in a child maltreatment report would the child welfare system intervene. Many children may suffer considerable harm before such a report is made, and even the filing of a report does not guarantee timely intervention, given the precarious state of child welfare services. In fact, the additional maltreatment reports generated by increased stress on poor families would further stretch the already overwhelmed child welfare system. Furthermore, although research on the long-term functioning of children placed in foster care does not show them to fare worse than poor children in general, they do not appear to fare better, and they more often lack the long-term support afforded by family (McDonald, Allen, Westerfelt, & Piliavin, 1993). This is to say nothing of the fact that institutional care of very young children—the bulk of the AFDC caseload—has been considered anathema to healthy child development for many years, even among the staunchest advocates for children's institutions.

Of course, the impact of welfare reform is likely to be felt primarily at the state and local levels. Although welfare reform is likely to lead to an increase in child maltreatment reports, its implementation at the state and local level will play a large role in the magnitude of the increase. Unfortunately, the federal welfare reform legislation and existing state-level welfare reform initiatives make little attempt to reconcile the principles of the "new" safety net with those of the child welfare system. The new federal law and all of the high-profile state-level welfare reform plans are primarily concerned with encouraging parents to work instead of relying on public assistance. These reforms provide financial and in-kind incentives (e.g., child care and health care) for work and propose that parents who refuse to work, or who engage in activity that threatens their ability to work (e.g., substance abuse), will be "sanctioned" through denial of benefits. In contrast, the purpose of the child welfare system is to protect children from maltreatment while preserving the integrity of families whenever possible, based on the assumption that a child's family is generally the best place for a child to be raised. Whatever its limitations, the previous public assistance system complemented the child welfare services system: it provided minimal financial support and health care to poor families regardless of whether parents chose to or were able to work. In the process of trying to preserve families, the child welfare system often provides support to families in the form of targeted financial assistance (e.g., help with paying utilities or rent), in-kind benefits (e.g., child care), and various social services. However, provision of assistance to poor families by the child welfare system may be seen in some cases to undercut the work-related sanctions of welfare reform programs.

Will the conflicting demands of the new workfare programs and the child welfare system be reconciled, and if so, how? Will the child protective services system refuse to help families who have been denied benefits under the new workfare programs? Alternatively, will parental refusal or inability to participate in the new programs in and of itself be treated as evidence of child maltreatment? Answers to these questions are central to what welfare reform will mean to the most desperate of America's children.

The record of state and local governments in protecting children does not provide much reason for optimism regarding the rapid devolution of authority over social programs to the states. After all, it was the failure of the states to do anything about the condition of children in unsafe homes that led the federal government to provide financial support for out-of-home care in the first place. Moreover, in many ways, federal law remains the primary method of ensuring that states provide some basic level of child welfare services. Litigation intended to improve child welfare practice at the state and local levels has resulted in at least 21 states being required to operate part or all of their child welfare services programs under some form of court order (Pear, 1996).

Conclusion

The growth in the number of children in foster care, their numerous difficulties, and the rapidly rising cost of their care should have already drawn significant attention to the crisis in the child welfare system. This has not happened. It is usually the case that the cost of a government program bears little relationship to the public or political attention it garners: witness the long-term uproar over the relatively inexpensive AFDC program that, together with the SSI and food stamp programs, represented 0.7% of the gross domestic product and approximately 3.2% of the federal budget in 1990 (U.S. House of Representatives, 1994).

Perhaps the perilous relationship between foster care and its more "glamorous" forebear AFDC will finally awaken the makers and analysts of public policy to the importance of a better understanding of the foster care crisis. All other considerations aside, the ongoing development of workfare alternatives to AFDC *must* include a serious consideration of the impact of such policy and program changes on the foster care system and its clients. Furthermore, evaluation efforts should be required to take into account the impact of welfare reform on child well-being and foster care caseloads and weigh these costs against possible benefits. Policy analysts have too long neglected the importance of foster care as a de facto poverty program. If we continue to do so during this period of grand experimentation with the social safety net, we are only asking for a rude awakening at a later date.

Note

1. Unless otherwise noted, data on the AFDC and child welfare services programs, including foster care, come from the U.S. House of Representatives (1994).

References

American Humane Association. (1989). *Highlights of official aggregate child neglect and abuse reporting, 1987*. Denver: Author.

Antler, S. (1978). Child abuse: An emerging social priority. *Social Work, 23*(1), 58–61.

Barth, R. P., Berrick, J. D., & Needell, B. (1994). A comparison of kinship foster homes and foster family homes: Implications for kinship foster care as family preservation. *Children and Youth Services Review, 16*(1–2), 33–63.

Barth, R. P., Courtney, M. E., Berrick, J. D., & Albert, V. (1994). *From child abuse to permanency planning: Child welfare services pathways and placements*. New York: Aldine de Gruyter.

Besharov, D. J. (1990). Gaining control over child abuse reports. *Public Welfare, 48*(2), 22–29.

Courtney, M. E. (1994). Factors associated with the reunification of foster children with their families. *Social Service Review, 68*(1), 81–108.

Courtney, M. E. (1995). Reentry to foster care of children returned to their families. *Social Service Review, 69*(2), 226–241.

Curtis, P. A. (Ed.). (1994). A research agenda for child welfare. *Child Welfare, 73*(5).

Curtis, P. A., & McCullough, C. (1993). The impact of alcohol and other drugs on the child welfare system. *Child Welfare, 72*(6), 533–542.

Ellertson, C. (1994). The Department of Health and Human Services foster care review system needs a major overhaul. *Children and Youth Services Review, 16*(5–6), 433–444.

Gleeson, J. P., & Craig, L. C. (1994). Kinship care in child welfare: An analysis of states' policies. *Children and Youth Services Review, 16*(1–2), 7–31.

Goerge, R. M. (1990). The reunification process in substitute care. *Social Service Review, 64*(3), 422–457.

Goerge, R. M., Wulczyn, F. H., & Harden, A. W. (1994). *Foster care dynamics, 1983–1992: California, Illinois, Michigan, New York and Texas: A report from the Multistate Foster Care Data Archive.* Chicago: University of Chicago, Chapin Hall Center for Children.

Goerge, R. M., Wulczyn, F. H., & Harden, A. W. (1995). *Foster care dynamics, 1983–1993: California, Illinois, Michigan, New York and Texas: An update from the Multistate Foster Care Data Archive.* Chicago: University of Chicago, Chapin Hall Center for Children.

Halfon, N., Berkowitz, G., & Klee, L. (1990). *Health and mental health service utilization by children in foster care in California* (Report to the California Policy Seminar). Berkeley: University of California, Berkeley.

Halfon, N., English, A., Allen, M., & DeWoody, M. (1994). National health care reform, Medicaid, and children in foster care. *Child Welfare, 73*(2), 99–115.

Iglehart, A. (1994). Kinship foster care: Placement, service, and outcome issues. *Children and Youth Services Review, 16*(1–2), 107–122.

Jones, E. D., & McCurdy, K. (1992). The links between types of maltreatment and demographic characteristics of children. *Child Abuse and Neglect, 16*(2), 201–214.

Kamerman, S. B., & Kahn, A. J. (1990). If CPS is driving child welfare—where do we go from here? *Public Welfare, 48*(1), 9–13.

Legislative Fiscal Bureau of the State of Wisconsin. (1995, 24 November). *Report to the Assembly Committee on Welfare Reform on Assembly Substitute Amendment LRB 0286/1 to Assembly Bill 591: Summary of Wisconsin Works Proposal.* Madison WI: Author.

Lindsey, D. (1993). *The welfare of children.* New York: Oxford University Press.

Maluccio, A. N., & Fein, E. (1992). Permanency planning: Another remedy in jeopardy? *Social Service Review, 66*(3), 335–348.

McDonald, T., Allen, R., Westerfelt, A., & Piliavin, I. (1993). *Assessing the long-term effects of foster care: A research synthesis.* Madison: University of Wisconsin, Institute for Research on Poverty.

Miller v. Youakim. (1979). Supreme Court 440 U.S. 125.

National Commission on Family Foster Care. (1991). *A blueprint for fostering infants, children, and youth in the 1990s.* Washington DC: Child Welfare League of America.

National Committee to Prevent Child Abuse. (1995). *Fact sheet: 1994 child abuse and neglect statistics.* Chicago: Author.

Pear, R. (1996, 17 March). Many states fail to meet mandates on child welfare. *New York Times*, 1, 14.

Pelton, L. (1989). *For reasons of poverty: A critical analysis of the public child welfare system in the United States.* New York: Praeger.

Pelton, L. H., & Milner, J. (1994). Is poverty a key contributor to child maltreatment? In E. Gambrill & T. J. Stein (Eds.), *Controversial issues in child welfare* (pp. 16–28). Needham Heights MA: Allyn & Bacon.

Sedlak, A. J. (1993). *Risk factors for child abuse and neglect in the U.S.* Expanded version of paper presented at the fourth European Conference on Child Abuse and Neglect, Padua, Italy, March 1993.

Sherman, R. E. (1995). *Unpublished report of Robert E. Sherman to Norm Zimlich of the Institute for Human Services Management, April 5, 1995.* Seattle WA: Institute for Human Services Management.

Stein, T. J. (1984). The Child Abuse Prevention and Treatment Act. *Social Service Review, 58*(2), 302–314.

Super, D. A., Parrott, S., Steinmetz, S., & Mann, C. (1996, 13 August). *The new welfare law.* Washington DC: Center on Budget and Policy Priorities.

Tatara, T. (1993). *U.S. child substitute care flow data for FY 92 and current trends in the state child substitute care populations.* (VCIS Research Notes No. 9, pp. 1–14). Washington DC: American Public Welfare Association.

Thornton, J. L. (1991). Permanency planning for children in kinship foster homes. *Child Welfare, 70*(5), 593–601.

U.S. Department of Health and Human Services, Office of the Assistant Secretary for Planning and Evaluation. (1996, 7 August). *Summary of provisions: Personal Responsibility and Work Opportunity Reconciliation Act of 1996 (H.R. 3734).* Washington DC: Author.

U.S. General Accounting Office. (1994). *Foster care: Parental drug abuse has alarming impact on young children*. Washington DC: Author.

U.S. House of Representatives, Committee on Ways and Means. (1998). *1998 green book: Background material and data on programs within the jurisdiction of the Committee on Ways and Means*. Washington DC: U.S. Government Printing Office.

Wulczyn, F. H. (1991). Caseload dynamics and foster care reentry. *Social Service Review, 65*(1), 133–156.

Wulczyn, F. H., & Goerge, R. M. (1992). Foster care in New York and Illinois: The challenge of rapid change. *Social Service Review, 66*(2), 278–294.

7

Recent Trends in Kinship Care: Public Policy, Payments, and Outcomes for Children

Jill Duerr Berrick and Barbara Needell

The expansion of kinship foster care is, perhaps, the most dramatic shift to occur in child welfare practice over the past 15 years. In some large states, kinship care has fundamentally changed child welfare services. For example, in Illinois, the kinship foster care caseload increased from 3,700 children in 1986 to over 16,000 children 6 years later (Testa, 1997). New York saw kinship care grow at a more accelerated pace, increasing from about 100 children to about 24,000 children during this same period (Takas, 1993). Similar growth has been witnessed in California (Needell, Webster, Barth, Armijo, & Fox, 1997) and other large states (Goerge, Wulczyn, & Harden, 1995).

Some of this growth was ushered in by the landmark 1979 decision by the Supreme Court (*Miller v. Youakim*, 1979), which ruled that states were required to pay foster care board rates to relatives who met foster care licensing requirements, thereby encouraging the greater inclusion of kin as foster parents. In fact, much of the overall growth in the foster care caseload throughout the late 1980s was absorbed by kin (Wulczyn & Goerge, 1992). Without this safety valve in the child welfare system, the current crisis in foster care might be even more acute.

Since the *Miller v. Youakim* decision, various states have adopted different approaches to kinship foster care in philosophy, practice, and funding.

Funding for this study was supported by the California Department of Social Services, the Stuart Foundations, and the David and Lucile Packard Foundation. We appreciate Dr. Richard P. Barth's thoughtful review of this chapter.

Recent reviews of state policies (Gleeson & Craig, 1994; Hornby, Zeller, & Karraker, 1996) indicate that some states do not view kin as principal foster care providers but, rather, as a diversion into informal family care outside of the child welfare system (18 states). Other states embrace the use of kin and either require a diligent search for relative caregivers before placing children with non-kin (8 states) or identify relatives in statute as the first priority placement (21 states).

Just as states have followed distinctive paths in implementing kinship care policies, funding for kinship placements also has been diverse. Some states will allow kin to receive federal Title IV-E foster care payments only if kin meet the same licensing standards as non-kin foster parents. Other states have special approval standards for kin that permit them to receive board payments for specific children in care. Until recently, Illinois paid the foster care rate to all approved relative caregivers; for those children who were not federally IV-E eligible, state funds were utilized to pay the full foster care rate (Testa, 1997). Six states (California, Colorado, New Jersey, North Carolina, Oregon, and Pennsylvania) offer a dual payment structure to kin caregivers. In California, foster parent licensure is not required for kinship caregivers; however, kin are eligible to receive the full IV-E (or AFDC-FC) foster care payment when the placement of children in their care meets the following conditions:

> The placement was the result of a judicial determination to the effect that continuation therein would be contrary to the welfare of such child; the child's placement and care are the responsibility of the State agency; and the child received aid (AFDC) . . . in or for the month in which such agreement was entered into or court proceedings leading to the removal of such child from the home were initiated, or would have received such aid . . . if application had been made; or had been living with a relative . . . within six months prior to the month in which such agreement was entered into. (*42 U.S.C. 672[a]*; Act of 22 December 1987, PL 100-203)

Those kinship caregivers who do not meet the above criteria may receive AFDC (i.e., "welfare") payments for the children in their care. In California, almost 60% of the kinship caregivers receive the AFDC-FC payment rate, while the remaining receive the lower AFDC payment. The differences between the two rates are not insignificant. AFDC payments are means-tested and are based upon the number of children in the household. As the num-

Figure 1. AFDC vs. AFDC-FC payments for formal kinship foster care in California, March 1997.

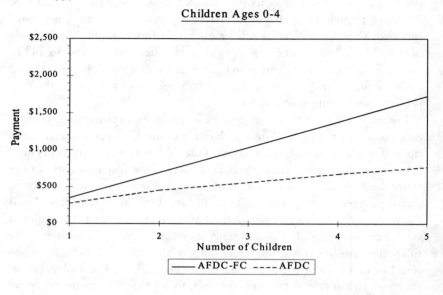

Children Ages 0-4

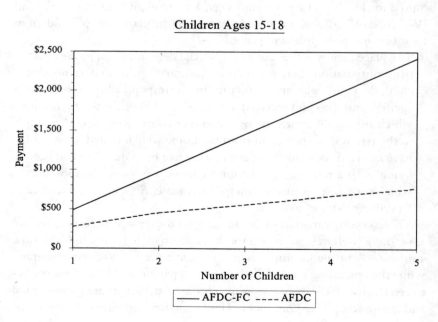

Children Ages 15-18

Table 1. AFDC vs. AFDC-FC Payments for Formal Kinship Foster Care in California, March 1997

No. of children	AFDC payment	AFDC-FC children 0–4	AFDC-FC children 15–18
1	$ 279	$ 345	$ 484
2	$ 456	$ 690	$ 968
3	$ 563	$ 1,035	$ 1,452
4	$ 673	$ 1,380	$ 1,936
5	$ 767	$ 1,725	$ 2,420

ber of children in the home increases, the payment rises incrementally. The payment for one child is $279 per month. For two children, the caregiver receives $456, and for three children, the payment increases to $563. (These rates are reviewed annually by the state legislature and, until 1998, had been reduced each year for the previous 5 years.)

Kinship foster parents receiving the AFDC-FC rate are paid on a per-child basis—two children double the amount of money a caregiver is paid. The funding these caregivers receive also increases with the age of the child. Caregivers are given $345 per month for a very young child (ages 0–4), with payments graduated to a rate of $484 per month for the oldest children in care (ages 15–18). In addition to the higher regular payment rate, these caregivers also may be eligible for specialized care increments (i.e., additional payments for special-needs children), infant supplement payments, and clothing allowances. The children may also take part in the Independent Living Program when they reach adolescence. Figure 1 and Table 1 show the payment differential between the two rates, depending upon whether the kinship foster parent is receiving AFDC or AFDC-FC, the age of the children in care, and the number of children being served.

States such as California, which have implemented two-tiered payment structures, now face a policy dilemma as child welfare practice interfaces directly with welfare reform. Although welfare payments for kinship caregivers have received little discussion in current debates about welfare policy (Mullen, 1996), the implications of reform for kin caregivers could be significant (Minkler, Berrick, & Needell, 1998). Under the Personal Responsibility and Work Opportunity Reconciliation Act of 1996 (PL 104-193), welfare policy has been fundamentally transformed. In a block grant environment, where children's caregivers are no longer entitled to AFDC, important questions will be raised about whether kinship foster care is philosophically and practically more similar to foster family care, or whether it more closely resembles informal family care. If kinship foster care squarely fits within the conceptual framework of foster family care, states may need to consider adopting policies that increase payments to some kin to match the AFDC-FC rate. These kinship caregivers would also need to be fully embraced as foster parents by the child welfare system and exempted from new provisions under the Temporary Assistance to Needy Families (TANF) regulations, such as time limits, family caps, work requirements, and benefit reductions. If these kinship caregivers are maintained at the AFDC rate, however, states will need to extend the new welfare policies to relatives or devise exemptions specifically for this population. These policy choices could have considerable and unintended consequences for income maintenance programs, the foster care caseload, and family dynamics. Understanding more about the dynamics of kinship foster care and the effect of payment levels on these outcomes will help policymakers develop informed approaches to serving children and families.

In order to examine these issues, we first review what is known about the benefits afforded through kinship foster care. We place this discussion within the context of *benefits,* as the literature on kinship foster care generally suggests a variety of positive features regarding this form of care for children (Child Welfare League of America, 1994; Meyer & Link, 1990; Minkler & Roe, 1992). Child welfare service providers solidly support the greater use of kin as children's foster caregivers (Berrick, Needell, & Barth, 1998); and the incorporation of kin into the foster care system has been so prevalent in many large, urban communities (Goerge, Wulczyn, & Harden, 1995) that to rely less on the use of kin now would be unfeasible. Given that the government's responsibility in developing policy for children and families must be aimed at enhancing their well-being, states will need to devise kinship care policies that acknowledge and promote the benefits of kinship care.

In spite of the known benefits of kinship foster care, we also acknowledge that much remains unknown about this form of caregiving. The quality of care children receive in kin and non-kin settings has been much discussed but has not been adequately studied (Berrick, 1996). Information about children's outcomes, including their health, education, and well-being after placement in kin and non-kin settings, is emerging (Benedict, Zuravin, & Stallings, 1996), but children's perceptions of placement are largely unknown. It is incumbent upon child welfare services systems to ensure the protection of dependent children and to promote children's well-being in care. Greater efforts to study these issues and to promote positive outcomes for children are therefore encouraged.

After reviewing the literature on kinship care, we next examine data from California's foster care system to illustrate the association between benefit levels and outcomes for children. We conclude with an analysis of the possible consequences that may result from various policy choices regarding kinship foster care and suggest an approach to kinship policy and funding that reflects the principal values of child welfare practice: to protect children from harm, to support families, and to promote permanence (Berrick, Needell, Barth, & Jonson-Reid, 1998).

The Private and Public Benefits of Kinship Care

Several aspects of the relationship between the kinship caregiver, the birth parent, and the child appear to have a significant effect on the kinship care dynamic. For example, children living in kinship foster homes appear to have greater access to their birth parents than children in non-kin homes. A study conducted by LeProhn (1993) showed that children placed with kin were more likely to see their birth mothers, fathers, and siblings than children placed with foster parents. A California-based study (Berrick, Barth, & Needell, 1994) also found that consistent contact with birth parents was more regularly maintained with kin than with foster parents (81% vs. 58%). About half (56%) of children placed with kin saw their birth parents more frequently than once a month, in comparison to about a third (32%) of foster children. Very few children in foster care saw their parents regularly (3%), but nearly one-fifth (19%) of children in kinship care saw a parent at least once a week. Visitation arranged by kin tended to be informal; nearly four-fifths (79%) of the caregivers arranged visits directly with the birth parents. In contrast, over half (54%) of the foster parents had visits arranged by the courts or social service agency. Given that continuing parent-child contact is one of the most important variables affecting placement outcomes (Fanshel & Shinn, 1978; Meezan & Shireman, 1985; Rowe, Cain, Hundleby, & Kean, 1984), and that the maintenance of family ties is crucial to the central tenets of child welfare services, these data suggest that kinship foster care is more facilitative of the values of family preservation than conventional foster care.

In addition to parent-child visitation, it appears that the physical proximity between children in kinship foster homes and their birth parents may be especially close. A study conducted by Goerge, Harden, and Lee (1993) showed that almost one-fifth (17%) of children placed with relatives in Chicago did not move when they were first "placed." An additional 10% of children moved to within one-half mile of their previous home. Testa (1997) later examined this same issue and found similar results. (These findings could be somewhat unique to Illinois, which allows kinship foster care payments in "nonremoval" cases where the child resides with both mother and kin and the mother agrees to leave the home.)

Goerge and associates shed light on the relationship between the child and caregiver prior to placement. If children are living in the same communities as their relatives, it is likely that these children had a relationship of some nature prior to the children's placement in the relatives' homes. Berrick, Barth, and Needell's study (1994) showed that nearly one-third (31%) of kinship caregivers not only knew the children prior to placement but also knew the children's circumstances so well that the caregivers originated the call to the protective services agency. The fact that children placed in kinship homes generally have a relationship with the caregiver prior to placement has led many observers to note that kinship placements may be less traumatic to the child at the time of placement (Child Welfare League of America, 1994).

In addition to the qualitative aspects of caregiver-child relationships, kinship foster care appears to promote greater placement stability while children reside in out-of-home care. In California, less than one-fifth (18%) of young children aged 0–5 remaining in kinship care 4 years later had been in three or more homes, whereas over 35% of young children in foster care had more than three placements (Berrick, Needell, Barth, & Jonson-Reid, 1998). These differences were also evident among older children. The stability of kinship placements for adolescents was corroborated by Iglehart (1994), who compared the placement histories of 352 adolescents in kinship care to 638 in foster care and found that adolescents in kinship care were more likely to have had fewer placements than their non-kin counterparts. Even when they move to a new placement, most children initially placed with kin remain in the family through placement with a different relative (Courtney & Needell, 1997).

Some of the outcomes associated with kinship care also may be considered beneficial to children. Early studies on the topic indicated that children placed with kin were less likely to reunify with their parents than children residing in foster family care (Benedict & White, 1991; Wulczyn & Goerge, 1992). (Indications from child welfare workers in one state suggest that the urgency of reunification may be less profound for children placed in kinship foster care than conventional foster care since the children's caregivers are well known to the birth parents [Berrick, Needell, & Barth, 1995]). More recent evidence, however, suggests that children placed with kin are considerably less likely to be reunified during the first year of placement, but the rates of reunification are similar for children in kin and non-kin settings after 1 year (Courtney, 1994), ensuring the rough equivalence of the two placement settings in this regard, when examined across a long enough span of time (i.e., 4 years).

The benefits of kinship care placements are especially notable when reentry rates are examined. Reunification of children and their birth families can usually be considered a successful outcome only if there is no subsequent abuse or neglect following return. The few studies that have been conducted on recidivism have found that 15–30% of children who are reunified come back into care at some point, and that children who experience placements of fewer than 90 days have the highest rates of reentry (Courtney, 1995; Rzepnicki, 1987; Wulczyn, 1991). Findings using a cohort of all children exiting foster care in the last half of 1989 in California provide evidence that children placed with kin and subsequently reunified are less likely to reenter foster care than children placed in foster homes (Courtney, 1995). More important, when analyzing the net permanence rate (i.e., the children placed in a family minus those who later reenter care), Needell and associates (1997) found that kin and non-kin homes were essentially equivalent on this outcome. Thus, early reunification and adoption rates appear to be greater for children in non-kin care, but rates of reentry to care are lower for children placed with kin.

Few studies have been conducted that review the differential effects of payment levels on outcomes for children in kinship foster care. Courtney (1994) examined reunification rates for children in kin and non-kin care and found that AFDC-eligible children in kinship care (i.e., those whose caregivers were likely receiving AFDC-FC payments) generally had a lower rate of reunification than non-AFDC eligible children. Needell (1996) also studied this issue by analyzing outcomes for infants placed in kin and non-kin care and found that AFDC eligibility was associated with a lower likelihood of reunification and a longer length of stay when all exits from kinship care were considered. Recent work by Piliavin and Courtney (1996) suggests that eligibility status, while diminishing the likelihood of reunification for children in kinship care, may not have a significant effect on reentry.

The Effects of Benefit Levels on Outcomes for Children

In this study we utilized data from California's Foster Care Information System (FCIS), reconfigured at the University of California, Berkeley, as part of the California Children's Services Archive. The archive includes all children in foster care in California since January 1988 and is updated yearly. It currently lists over 280,000 dependent children; as of December 1996, California's foster care caseload reached 98,589 children.

The data in the archive have been reconfigured into a longitudinal, relational database that allows for analyses of children's pathways in and out of foster care. The database indicates the reason for children's removal from home (e.g., physical abuse, sexual abuse, and various forms of neglect including severe neglect, general neglect, and caretaker absence or incapacity), the age of the children at placement, and the reason for their exit (e.g., reunification, exit to adoption, exit to guardianship, or other).[1] The database also indicates the setting in which the children were placed. We defined children's placement setting as *kinship care* or *non-kin care*, depending upon where they spent the majority of their time during their first spell (i.e., their primary placement while in care). Non-kin care includes only those children in regular foster family care and excludes children placed in group homes, specialized foster care, or other placements. For purposes of these analyses, the children's first spells in care were examined (for each *spell* in out-of-home care, children may experience one or more *placements*).

In addition to these general descriptors of children and their circumstances, an aid-status code is included in the database. Children are designated as either *IV-E eligible* or *non-IV-E eligible*, based upon the last known eligibility assigned to children in care.[2] For simplicity, we refer to these federally eligible and non–federally eligible caregivers as those families who receive AFDC-FC vs. AFDC respectively.[3]

For our analyses we examined three indicators commonly related to the principal goals of the child welfare system. These outcome indicators included: (a) outcomes from care, including reunification, adoption, guardianship, or remaining in care; (b) length of stay in care; and (c) reentry following reunification.

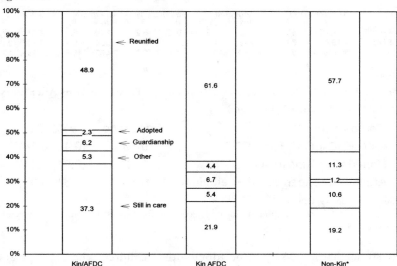

Figure 2. Outcomes from kin and non-kin foster care.

★All receive AFDC-FC

Outcomes From Care

Data for this analysis include all children who entered care for the first time in the years 1989–1991 and who were placed in kin (n = 32,946) and non-kin (n = 32,586) foster homes. Four years after their initial placement, we examined the number and proportions of children who were reunified with their parents, were adopted, exited to legal guardianship, or were still in their first spell in care.

Reunification

Considering children in kinship care only, we find that the proportion of children reunified with their birth parents within 4 years is much lower for those who are receiving AFDC-FC than those who are not. Almost half (49%) of children who are receiving AFDC-FC were reunified with their parents within 4 years compared with two-thirds (62%) of children who were receiving AFDC (see Figure 2 and Table 2). Among children in non-kin care, somewhat more than one-half of children had been reunified with their parents by this time (58%).

Adoption

Very few children placed in kinship foster care were adopted after 4 years compared to children in non-kinship care. AFDC-FC children in kinship care

Table 2. Outcomes From Kin and Non-kin Foster Care

	Reunited		Adopted		Guardianship		Other		Still in care	
	n	%	n	%	n	%	n	%	n	%
Kin/AFDC-FC	7,703	48.9	362	2.3	972	6.2	829	5.3	5,873	37.3
Kin/AFDC	10,605	61.6	749	4.4	1,149	6.7	934	5.4	3,770	21.9
Non-kin	18,816	57.7	3,680	11.3	380	1.2	3,465	10.6	6,245	19.2

Table 3. Likelihood of Reunification vs. Remaining in Care Four Years After Entry
(N = 7,178 Reunified, 2,831 in Care)

Comparison	Odds ratio	95% C.I.
Kin/AFDC-FC vs Kin/AFDC	0.49	(0.42, 0.54)
Non-kin* vs Kin/AFDC	1.02	(0.91, 1.14)
African-American vs other ethnicity	0.34	(0.31, 0.37)

*All non-kin receive AFDC-FC.

Note: 1991 entry cohort, one child randomly selected per family. Likelihood ratio: 2.71 with 2df (p = 0.2585).

were somewhat less likely to be adopted than children whose caregivers were receiving AFDC (2% vs. 4%), although these differences may be partly explained by the coding irregularity we have found in the aid-status code for preadoptive children. A much larger proportion of children in non-kin homes had exited foster care for adoption 4 years later (11%).

Guardianship

Regardless of eligibility status, children placed with kin were more likely to exit to guardianship (approximately 6%) than children placed with non-kin (1%), although this difference may be somewhat smaller than these data suggest.

Still in care

Children residing in kinship homes receiving AFDC-FC were more likely to be still in care after 4 years than AFDC children. Almost 40% (37%) of AFDC-FC children were still in care 4 years later compared to 22% of AFDC children. Approximately one-fifth (19%) of children in non-kin homes were still in care 4 years after placement.

Likelihood of Reunification

A logit model was developed to estimate the overall effect of AFDC eligibility on the odds of reunification vs. remaining in care, controlling for ethnicity. The findings reaffirm that AFDC-FC children are about half as

Figure 3. Probability of leaving care over time.

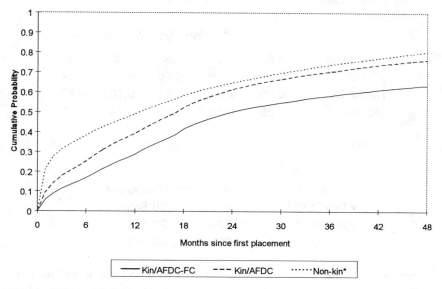

*All non-kin receive AFDC–FC

likely to be reunified as either AFDC children or children in foster care (Table 3). African-American children have greatly reduced odds of reunification, regardless of placement type or eligibility status.

Length of Stay in Care

Survival analysis was used to examine the length of stay for children first entering kin or non-kin foster care between 1989 and 1995 (n = 146,809). The cumulative probability of leaving care (Figure 3 and Table 4) was considerably lower for children who were federally eligible (AFDC–FC) and placed with kin than for either non-eligible children (AFDC) placed with kin or children placed in foster homes, with median stays in care of 23, 17, and 12 months, respectively. These differences were amplified when analyzed across ethnic groups. The median length of stay for African-American AFDC children residing with kin was 26 months, whereas the median length of stay for African-American AFDC–FC children in kinship homes was 47 months.

Reentry

Survival analysis was also used to consider the likelihood of reentry to care following reunification for children who exited kin or non-kin foster care

Table 4. Probability of Leaving Care Over Time

	Months since first placement				
Status	*6*	*12*	*24*	*36*	*48*
Kin/AFDC-FC	0.17	0.29	0.50	0.58	0.64
Kin/AFDC	0.25	0.39	0.61	0.70	0.77
Non-kin	0.38	0.49	0.65	0.74	0.80

Status	*N*	*No. leaving care*
Kin/AFDC-FC	38,012	20,546
Kin/AFDC	40,589	26,120
Non-kin	68,208	48,761

between 1989 and 1995 (n = 93,859). Children whose caregivers were receiving AFDC-FC and who were returned to their birth parents from a kinship home were more likely to return to foster care than children whose kin caregivers were receiving AFDC. The cumulative probability of reentry after 3 years was .23 for kin children in AFDC-FC homes and .10 for AFDC children. AFDC-FC children who were placed in kinship care and who were returned home had a reentry rate very similar to children placed in non-kin foster care (see Figure 4 and Table 5).

Kinship Dynamics, Payments, and Implications for Permanency
The data appear to suggest that the payment rates kinship caregivers receive may have an effect on a variety of outcomes in child welfare. Specifically, the payment rate appears to influence the rate of reunification and the overall length of time children remain in the foster care system. Focus groups with child welfare workers indicate that these longer stays in care may result from families attempting to maximize their total family income over a longer period of time. Since the families' overall income may be reduced profoundly upon reunification, there may be less incentive to seek reunification (Berrick, Needell, & Barth, 1998). Further, because the dynamics of kinship foster care are so fundamentally different from non-kin care and because boundaries between family and caregiver are generally

Figure 4. Probability of reentering care over time.

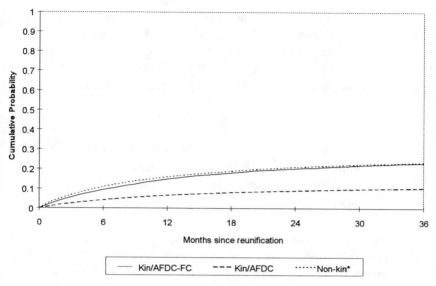

Months since reunification

| —— Kin/AFDC-FC | – – – Kin/AFDC | ·····Non-kin* |

*All non-kin receive AFDC-FC

more permeable (Berrick, Needell, & Barth, 1995), these patterns of relationship may be intertwined with financial effects.

These data also point to a possible payment effect on reentry rates. The lower welfare payment available to some families during a first spell in care may have a dampening effect on reentry rates. However, in light of research by other authors using multivariate techniques (Piliavin & Courtney, 1996), we suggest that this finding be interpreted with caution. Other analyses (not shown) indicate that payment rates have little effect on placement stability in kinship care; children who are AFDC eligible are slightly more likely to experience three or more placements during their first spell in care. Previous research has demonstrated that placement with kin is more stable than placement with non-kin, regardless of eligibility status (Needell et al., 1997).

Other factors may explain these presumed payment-level results that we cannot currently study. For example, differences in the amount or degree of services provided to kin by child welfare workers or lack of information about the child welfare system may contribute to differential outcomes, although these factors would likely explain overall differences between kin

Table 5. Probability of Reentering Care Over Time

Status	Months since reunification			
	6	12	24	36
Kin/AFDC-FC	0.09	0.15	0.20	0.23
Kin/AFDC	0.04	0.07	0.09	0.10
Non-kin	0.11	0.16	0.21	0.23

Status	N	No. re-entering care
Kin/AFDC-FC	22,588	4,425
Kin/AFDC	29,985	2,717
Non-kin	41,286	8,645

and non-kin and would not necessarily be related to eligibility status. Other considerations beyond payments, such as eligibility for specialized care increments, infant supplements, access to Independent Living Skills Programs, and other services for federal IV-E–eligible families may play a hidden yet important role in determining child welfare outcomes for children in kinship care.

Nevertheless, in view of the evidence, it seems likely that unless significant changes are developed in kinship care policy, California will continue to see considerable growth in its foster care caseload. Caseloads may increase when the number of admissions to the foster care system rise, but they are strongly affected by the number of discharges from the system as well (Goerge et al., 1995). With an increasing proportion of the foster care population residing in kinship homes, and with a growing number of kinship homes receiving AFDC-FC payments (Berrick, Needell, & Barth, 1995), more children are likely to remain in the system for longer periods of time, thus depressing the overall number of discharges and inflating the foster care caseload.

One solution to this dilemma is to develop new policies that allow a wider array of exit alternatives for kin. In some cases, however, states are constrained by federal policy in order to be reimbursed for their innovations. In other instances, state fiscal considerations may weigh heavily in their decisions to expand exit opportunities for kin.

Adoption

Although the evidence in this chapter may suggest a payment effect in the foster care system, with higher payments resulting in longer stays in care, the Adoption Assistance Payment (AAP) that would be available to non-eligible kin does not appear to have a powerful effect on family decisions. Currently, both kin and non-kin may adopt the children in their care. This option is generally considered the best alternative for promoting legal permanence among children who otherwise cannot be reunited with their birth parents. Although some kin will adopt their relative children, others are reluctant to do so when the parental rights of family members must be terminated (usually the case involves the grandmother providing care for the children of her own daughter). Some have suggested that adoption appears to be especially problematic for communities of color (Thornton, 1991); adoption may also be more difficult for families with economic concerns or lack of confidence in subsidies.

States interested in expanding the definition of adoption to encourage greater kinship participation may do so, but the implementation of these policies may be compromised by their fiscal implications. For example, new innovations in "kinship adoption" (Takas, 1993) may be pursued, where parental rights are either partially terminated or "set aside," but under current federal law states could not maintain federal participation and would therefore bear the full cost of the subsidies alone.

Legal guardianship

When adoption is not feasible, legal guardianship is often viewed as a practical alternative for ensuring a permanent, legal relationship for children. The primary obstacle to legal guardianship for kin, however, is funding. In California, non-kin may continue to receive the AFDC-FC payment upon assuming guardianship, but relatives in this state (and most others) do not receive guardianship subsidies.[4] AFDC-eligible kinship foster parents who take guardianship, therefore, often face a significant reduction in their monthly payment, as many revert to receiving regular AFDC payments. Other obstacles exist as well, including the fact that in California, legal guardianships can be overturned upon petition of a biological parent and are not necessarily recognized in other states if kin wish to move. Several states are experimenting with subsidies for kin who take guardianship through the Child Welfare IV-E Waiver Demonstration projects. Research in this area should help to clarify the effects of subsidies on exits for children.

Reunification

Reunification is the preferred outcome for children in foster care. More so than other exits from care, however, reunification appears to be strongly negatively associated with federal eligibility for children in kinship care. More children might exit the foster care system to reunification if foster care payments to kin were reduced somewhat. States considering this option, however, should do so very methodically, with a clear philosophical framework about the purpose of foster care subsidies guiding such a policy change.

Clarifying Government's Purpose in Funding Substitute Care for Children

For decades, foster parents in the United States have been offered subsidies to care for others' children—not as payment for services but as reimbursement to cover the cost of expenses incurred. Generally, these rates have been set relatively low in order to symbolically convey the importance of fostering as an act of altruism and humanity rather than a commercial exchange (Tucker & Hurl, 1992; Zelizer, 1985). The number of foster parents in the country is low in comparison to the total adult population and provides some indication of the sacrifice and commitment required in order to rear a stranger's child. In order to ensure that children who cannot be raised by their own parents will have an opportunity to live with substitute parents, the state has an interest in supporting these alternative caregivers. The foster care subsidy provides a modest yet tangible gesture of the state's gratitude to strangers who step forward to care for these children.

The sacrifice of relatives who offer to care for their kin may be significant as well (Minkler & Roe, 1992). Nevertheless, family ties exert a sentiment of moral obligation on relatives that is not otherwise present among non-kin caregivers. Kin may feel compelled to extend themselves to their relative children, but they are not legally required to do so. In order to support kin's natural inclination to care for relative children, it seems appropriate that the state also offer a subsidy to these caregivers as a token of indebtedness for their actions, especially since kinship care tends to bring about positive outcomes for children. Indeed, history reminds us that families who cannot afford to care for their relative children may release these children to the state to be raised by strangers (Costin, Karger, & Stoesz, 1996). States should attempt to guard against this scenario.

Although kinship caregivers should indeed receive some remuneration from the government for extending themselves to family members, it does not necessarily follow that kin should receive the same payment as foster parents. Of course, under the spirit of the *Miller v. Youakim* decision, it seems fitting that kin who become licensed foster parents receive the full rate. Among kin caregivers who do not meet the full licensing commitments, however, it might be appropriate to establish a separate payment structure. Such a payment should exceed the AFDC rate, because kin, although related to the child, have no absolute obligation to the child. The rate could be somewhat lower than conventional foster care rates, however, to acknowledge the non-equivalence of the personal circumstances and relationship between caregiver and child.

Unlike kin, birth parents have an absolute responsibility for the support of their children. When they are unable to exercise this responsibility— usually due to circumstances outside of their control, such as unemployment or disability—the state has an interest in providing temporary financial assistance to their families for the protection of the children. When kinship caregivers step in to rear children, the state has an interest not only in providing temporary financial assistance—similar to AFDC—but also in supporting those alternative caregivers for extending themselves to the families. Kin caregivers who exercise their personal sentiments toward such children, particularly when they are not obliged to do so, should be compensated by the state at a rate higher than the conventional family rate. Because of their special relationship to the children, these caregivers should also be fully exempt from welfare reform initiatives that might limit benefits or that require activities or behaviors of caregivers not directly related to the support and supervision of dependent children.

Due to the unique circumstances of kinship foster care, policymakers may also wish to consider developing special services and supports for kin caregivers. Research on the characteristics of kin indicates that, on average, the caregivers are older, less educated, less financially stable, and in poorer health than foster parents (Berrick et al., 1994; Dubowitz et al., 1994; Mayor's Commission for the Foster Care of Children, 1993; Thornton, 1987). These compromised conditions may point to an elevated need for additional aid in the form of support groups, assistance in accessing medical, dental, mental health, and educational supports for children, respite care, and legal services. Many of these caregivers have come to their newly appointed role with little preparation (LeProhn, 1993); services that are designed to encourage kin caregivers' continued commitments to children may be especially important.

Raising payments to kin who currently receive welfare or providing enriched services to kin caregivers that are not available to birth parents may have indirect effects on the foster care caseload and, potentially, on income maintenance programs. If the payment is considerably higher than the welfare rate, families may see the financial benefits of foster care outweighing the benefits of AFDC, thus reducing the incentive toward family reunification and depressing the overall exit rate from care. Reentry rates may be affected slightly as well, although the magnitude of these differences would be difficult to predict. The effects on income maintenance programs such as AFDC would likely be small but nevertheless may occur. In light of significant changes in welfare policy, public leaders should guard against developing financial rewards and services in kinship foster care that heavily outweigh the financial benefits afforded through welfare. Highly imbalanced systems may create unintentional draws away from income maintenance programs and toward child welfare systems that, ultimately, may be perceived as further testing family integrity.

Given the above considerations, where should the payment rate for kinship caregivers be set? Unfortunately, such a decision cannot be determined by research alone. Unless subjected to a strict experimental design, research cannot currently inform public policymakers about the financial break-even point that might hinder or promote specific child welfare and family outcomes. Payment levels are also political decisions based, in part, upon public values and the availability of resources.

Determining payment levels, services, supervision, and supports for kinship foster care will be the next great challenge for the child welfare system. Kinship foster care is a new type of caregiving within the child welfare system, bringing with it benefits for children and families, positive features for child welfare workers, but challenges, nevertheless, for child welfare practice and policy. The direction in which kinship foster care moves within the next decade will profoundly affect child welfare services into the next century. With roughly half of the foster care caseload now being cared for by kin in many large states, it is unlikely that kinship care will escape public view; instead, it will become more heavily scrutinized by the public, policymakers, and child welfare professionals alike (Nelson, 1990; Sheindlin, 1994). With this greater public visibility, the implications of payments for kin will likely loom large in future public debates. Clarifying the role of government in the lives of caregiving families and understanding the dimensions of kinship care practice for child welfare outcomes will help policymakers promote families while protecting and serving children.

Notes

1. The variable that indicates exits to guardianship somewhat depresses the actual rate of guardianship among non-kin foster parents because some caregivers remain in the foster care system in order to collect guardianship subsidies. Actual exits to guardianship are slightly higher than indicated in the graph and table.

2. Eligibility status may change during children's stay in care. In some instances, children may be initially AFDC eligible but may later change to non-AFDC eligible when the children's placement status changes to preadoption and the families become eligible to collect Adoption Assistance Payments (AAP) or other public funds (e.g., SSI or mental health). These changes may result in somewhat inaccurate effects when examining AFDC eligibility on outcomes, particularly adoption for non-kin.

Children in non-kin foster family care who are AFDC eligible receive half of their monthly board payments from the federal government and the remainder from state (20%) and local sources (30%). Those foster parents caring for non-AFDC-eligible children receive the same monthly payment, but the source of these funds is born fully by the state and county governments. Kinship caregivers who are serving AFDC-eligible children receive the same monthly board payments as non-kin foster parents. Kin who are caring for non-AFDC-eligible children receive the lower monthly welfare rate (as described in the text). The cost-sharing ratios for payments to kin caregivers receiving AFDC in California is 50% federal dollars, 47.5% state dollars, and 2.5% local county dollars.

Because all children in non-kin care receive some kind of subsidy equal to or greater than the foster care rate, all analyses compare three groups: (a) AFDC-eligible children with kin, (b) non-eligible children with kin, and (c) all children in non-kin foster homes.

3. We cannot be certain that all caregivers with these designations are actually receiving these payments. In particular, families who are non-AFDC eligible may be receiving welfare or may not be receiving any payments from the government at all, should they elect to do so.

4. The cost of guardianship subsidies in California is born by state and county funds, with a disproportionate share of costs (60%) paid by the county. In Septem-

ber 1998, Governor Wilson signed SB 1901, which now provides guardianship subsidies to relatives using state and county funds.

References

Benedict, M. I., & White, R. B. (1991). Factors associated with foster care length of stay. *Child Welfare, 70*(1), 45–57.

Benedict, M. I., Zuravin, S., & Stallings, R. (1996, September/October). Adult functioning of children who lived in kin versus nonkin family foster homes. *Child Welfare, 75*(5), 529–549.

Berrick, J. D. (1996). *Assessing quality of care in kinship and foster family care*. Berkeley: University of California, Berkeley, School of Social Welfare, Center for Social Services Research.

Berrick, J. D., Barth, R. P., & Needell, B. (1994). A comparison of kinship foster homes and foster family homes: Implications for kinship foster care as family preservation. *Children and Youth Services Review, 16*(1–2), 33–63.

Berrick, J. D., Needell, B., & Barth, R. P. (1995). *Kinship care in California: An empirically-based curriculum* (Unpublished report). Berkeley: University of California, Berkeley, Child Welfare Research Center.

Berrick, J. D., Needell, B., & Barth, R. P. (1998). Kin as a family and child welfare resource: The child welfare worker's perspective. In R. L. Hegar & M. Scannapieco (Eds.), *Kinship foster care: Practice, policy and research*. New York: Oxford University Press.

Berrick, J. D., Needell, B., Barth, R. P., & Jonson-Reid, M. (1998). *The tender years: Toward developmentally-sensitive child welfare services for very young children*. New York: Oxford University Press.

Child Welfare League of America. (1994). *Kinship care: A natural bridge*. Washington DC: Author.

Costin, L., Karger, H., & Stoesz, D. (1996). *The politics of child abuse in America*. New York: Oxford University Press.

Courtney, M. E. (1994). Factors associated with the reunification of foster children with their families. *Social Service Review, 68*(1), 82–108.

Courtney, M. E. (1995). Reentry to foster care of children returned to their families. *Social Service Review, 69*(2), 226–241.

Courtney, M. E., & Needell, B. (1997). Outcomes of kinship care: Lessons from California. In J. D. Berrick, R. P. Barth, & N. Gilbert (Eds.), *Child welfare research review* (Vol. 2). New York: Columbia University Press.

Dubowitz, H., Feigelman, S., Harrington, D., Starr, R., Zuravin, S., & Sawyer, R. (1994). Children in kinship care: How do they fare? *Children and Youth Services Review, 16*(1–2), 85–106.

Fanshel, D., & Shin, E. (1978). *Children in foster care: A longitudinal investigation.* New York: Columbia University Press.

Gleeson, J. P., & Craig, L. C. (1994). Kinship care in child welfare: An analysis of states' policies. *Children and Youth Services Review, 16*(1–2), 17–31.

Goerge, R. M., Harden, A. W., & Lee, B. J. (1993). *The physical movement of children placed with relatives: A report to the Illinois Department of Children and Family Services.* Chicago: University of Chicago, Chapin Hall Center for Children,.

Goerge, R. M., Wulczyn, F. H., & Harden, A. W. (1995). *Foster care dynamics, 1983–1993: An update on the Multistate Foster Care Data Archive.* Chicago: University of Chicago, Chapin Hall Center for Children.

Hornby, H., Zeller, D., & Karraker, D. (1996, September/October). Kinship care in America: What outcomes should policy seek? *Child Welfare, 75*(5), 397–418.

Iglehart, A. P. (1994). Kinship foster care: Placement, service, and outcome issues. *Children and Youth Services Review, 16*(1–2), 107–122.

LeProhn, N. S. (1993). *Relative foster parents: Role perceptions, motivation, and agency satisfaction.* Unpublished doctoral dissertation, University of Washington.

Mayor's Commission for the Foster Care of Children. (1993). *Family assets: Kinship foster care in New York City.* New York: Author.

Meezan, W., & Shireman, J. F. (1985). *Care and commitment: Foster parent adoption decisions.* Albany: State University of New York Press.

Meyer, B. S., & Link, M. K. (1990). *Kinship foster care: The double edged dilemma.* Rochester NY: Task Force on Permanency Planning for Foster Children.

Miller v. Youakim, 1979, 440 U.S. 125.

Minkler, M., Berrick, J. D., & Needell, B. (1998). *The impact of welfare reform on California grandparents raising grandchildren.* Berkeley: University of California, Berkeley, School of Social Welfare, Center for Social Services Research.

Minkler, M., & Roe, K. M. (1992). *Grandmothers as caregivers: Raising children of the crack-cocaine epidemic.* Newbury Park CA: Sage.

Mullen, F. (1996, spring). Public benefits: Grandparents, grandchildren, and welfare reform. *Generations: Journal of the American Society on Aging, 20*(1), 61–64.

Needell, B. (1996). *Placement stability and permanence for children entering foster care as infants.* Unpublished doctoral dissertation, University of California, Berkeley, School of Social Welfare.

Needell, B., Webster, D., Barth, R. P., Armijo, M., & Fox, A. (1997). *Performance indicators for child welfare services in California: 1996.* Berkeley: University of California, Berkeley, Child Welfare Research Center.

Nelson, D. (1990, 7 January). State rapped on foster care. *Chicago Sun,* 3, 28.

Piliavin, I., & Courtney, M. E. (1996, 11 July). *Analysis of incentive and selection effects on foster care case outcomes: The impact of kinship foster care.* Paper presented at National Association of Welfare Research and Statistics conference, San Francisco.

Rowe, J., Cain, H., Hundleby, M., & Keane, A. (1984). *Long-term foster care.* New York: St. Martin's Press.

Rzepnicki, T. L. (1987). Recidivism of foster children returned to their own homes: A review and new directions for research. *Social Service Review, 61*(1), 56–70.

Sheindlin, J. B. (1994, 29 August). Paying grandmas to keep kids in limbo. *New York Times,* Op-Ed, A15, Col. 1.

Takas, M. (1993). Kinship care: Developing a safe and effective framework for protective placement of children with relatives. *Zero to Three, 13*(3), 12–17.

Testa, M. (1997). Kinship foster care in Illinois. In J. D. Berrick, R. P. Barth, & N. Gilbert (Eds.), *Child welfare research review* (Vol. 2). New York: Columbia University Press.

Thorton, J. L. (1987). *An investigation into the nature of the kinship foster home.* Unpublished doctoral dissertation, Yeshiva University, Wurzweiler School of Social Work, New York.

Thornton, J. L. (1991). Permanency planning for children in kinship foster homes. *Child Welfare, 70*(5), 593–601.

Tucker, D. J., & Hurl, L. F. (1992, December). An ecological study of the dynamics of foster home entries. *Social Service Review, 66*(4), 617–641.

Wulczyn, F. (1991). Caseload dynamics and foster care reentry. *Social Service Review, 65,* 133–156.

Wulczyn, F., & Goerge, R. M. (1992). Foster care in New York and Illinois: The challenge of rapid change. *Social Service Review, 66,* 278–294.

Zelizer, V. A. (1985). *Pricing the priceless child: The changing social value of children.* New York: Basic Books.

8

A Proposal for Universal Medical and Mental Health Screenings for Children Entering Foster Care

Grady Dale Jr., Joshua C. Kendall, and Janet Stein Schultz

Beginning with Fanshel and Shinn's landmark study (1978), the literature has consistently shown evidence of high rates of medical and psychological problems among children entering foster care. The circumstances leading to removal from the home typically jeopardize children's overall health. In many cases, sexual or physical abuse by their caregivers causes long-term distress. In cases where neglect precipitates out-of-home placement, children have often failed to receive appropriate medical care. Thus, by the time children enter foster care, they often suffer from a wide range of acute and chronic medical illnesses in addition to the psychological impairment resulting from abuse and dislocation from the home.

Unfortunately, despite these considerable risks to their health status, children entering foster care have rarely received adequate care. Historically, the local departments of social services, under whose jurisdictions foster children fall, have simply not had the resources to provide for the diagnosis and treatment of their various ailments. Over the past decade, class action suits brought against cities, states, and counties have been successful in bringing about changes in the child welfare system (Halfon and Klee, 1991). Nevertheless, improvement in delivery of health services to these at-risk children has proceeded very slowly. As Simms and Halfon (1994) report, as of 1993, roughly 10 small localized programs were experimenting with innovative ways of delivering health services to foster children. In general, children must still wait long periods of time even though their

We would like to thank Neal Halfon, M.D., M.P.H., for his thoughtful comments on our proposal.

problems are acute, or they simply do not receive any care at all. For example, Schor (1982) found 12% of his sample population had not received any medical care despite active outreach.

This chapter is both descriptive and prescriptive. We begin by offering a brief overview of the literature on the psychological and medical problems of children entering foster care. Given the gravity of these problems, we propose that all children entering care nationwide receive *immediate* medical and mental health screenings. In our view, the failure to provide timely care for foster children compromises their long-term physical and emotional health, with the attendant social and economic consequences.

We offer a specific policy recommendation geared to implement these screenings on a universal basis. At present, federal law provides clinicians the opportunity to conduct health screenings for all Medicaid-eligible children under the age of 21 through the Early and Periodic Screening, Diagnosis and Treatment (EPSDT) program. In some states, such as Maryland, the law already mandates that children entering foster care, who constitute a distinct subset of this Medicaid-eligible group, receive their EPSDT assessment within 60 days of their removal from home. We suggest that all children entering care be required to receive the EPSDT within two weeks after removal from home. This initial health screening would identify medical and mental health problems for all children and refer the most severely delayed and troubled children for follow-up evaluations. Currently, the EPSDT can include a mental health component, but in most cases practitioners, due to a variety of extenuating factors, do not address mental health concerns. By providing distinct and workable guidelines, our proposal is designed to put into place policies and practices assuring early screenings for both medical and mental health problems.

Mental Health and Medical Problems
of Children Entering Foster Care

For over two decades, researchers have identified the high prevalence of mental health problems among foster care children. In their pioneering longitudinal study, Fanshel and Shinn (1978) concluded that "whether we report the judgments of social workers, examining psychologists, parents or teachers it would seem that 25–33 percent of our subjects show signs of emotional impairment" (p. 493).

Figure 1. Performance on the DDST II for children in foster care.

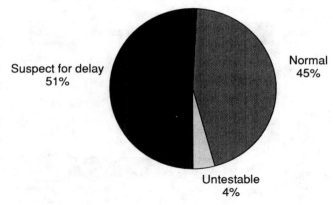

Suspect for delay
51%

Normal
45%

Untestable
4%

Note: N = 100 children aged 2 months to 5 years. DDST II = Denver Developmental Screening Test (version 2).

Kavaler & Swire (1983) reported substantially higher rates of mental health problems, finding some degree of psychiatric impairment in 96% of their sample of 179 foster children. Psychiatric interviews pointed to mild impairment among 26%, moderate impairment among 35%, marked impairment among 25%, and severe levels of impairment among 10%. McIntyre & Kessler (1986) found evidence of psychological disorders in roughly half of their sample. They concluded that the relative risks associated with foster status were almost 2 to 32 times greater than for home-reared children.

In recent studies conducted by our group at the Health Clinic in Baltimore (Kendall, Dale, & Plakitsis, 1995; Dale, Kendall, & Stein-Schultz, 1996), we identified rates of cognitive and emotional impairment among foster children based on their performance on standard screening instruments. Among 100 children aged 2 months to 5 years, 51% were identified on the Denver Developmental Screening Test (Version 2) as "suspect for delay" compared with 10% in normative samples (see Figure 1). Based on scores on the Reynolds Depression Scales (RCDS and RACS), 11% of the 8- to 12-year-olds and 30% of the 13- to 19-year-olds showed evidence of significant depressive symptomatology (see Figure 2). Furthermore, on the Peabody Picture Vocabulary Test–Revised (PPVT-R-L), 53% of 8- to 12-year-olds and 64% of 13- to 19-year-olds showed evidence of severe receptive language difficulties (see Figure 3). Finally, on the Developmental Test of Visual–Motor Integration (VMI), 37% of children aged 13 to 19 years

Figure 2. Percentage of children evidencing depressive symptomatology on the Reynolds Depression Scales (RCDS and RADS).

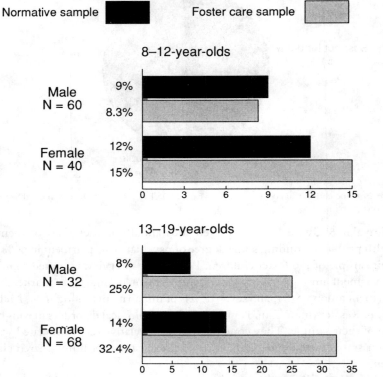

Note: N = 200 case records. RCDS = Reynolds Child Depression Scale; RADS = Reynolds Adolescent Depression Scale.
Source: Kendall, J., Dale, G., & Plakitsis, S. (1995). "The Mental Health Needs of Children Entering the Child Welfare System: A Guide for Caseworkers." *APSAC Advisor 8*, 10–13.

showed evidence of severe deficits in visual–motor skills compared with 10% in normative samples (see Figure 3). In a similar study, Halfon, Mendonca, and Berkowitz (1995) found developmental, emotional, and behavioral problems in over 80% of foster children, based on a chart review of 213 children who received mental health assessments.

With regard to medical problems, the literature also documents a significantly higher incidence of acute and chronic illnesses among foster children than among cohorts living with their families of origin. For example, Hochstadt, Jaudes, Zino, and Schachter (1987) reported that only 13% of

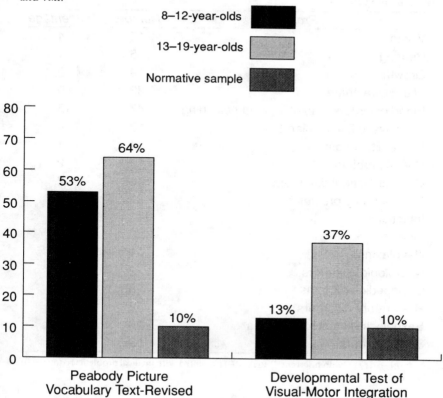

Note: N = 100 case records for each age group. PPVT-R-L = Peabody Picture Vocabulary Test–Revised.

children screened had entirely normal physical exams, and half had multiple physical abnormalities.

Halfon, Mendonca, and Berkowitz (1995) found that over 82% of the children in their sample had at least one chronic condition such as asthma, congenital infections, gastroesophageal reflux, and mild neurological disorders. Infants had an average of 2.6 conditions; toddlers (1 to 3 years of age), 1.5 conditions; preschoolers (3 to 5 years of age), 1.3 conditions; and school-aged children, 1.3 conditions.

We recently performed a chart review of 1,177 children aged 0 to 21 years who were screened at the Health Clinic in Baltimore between November

Table 1. Medical Problems of Children and Adolescents Entering Out-of-Home Placement in Baltimore

Problem	Number	Percentage
Vision	15	4
Hearing	5	1
Growth	9	2
Allergies/asthma	32	9
Blood disorders—anemia, lead poisoning	47	13
Cardiovascular problems	13	4
Congenital anomalies	4	1
Dental problems	7	2
Gastrointestinal disorders	6	2
Genitourinary problems	22	6
Infections	113	31
Injuries	8	2
Neoplasms	1	<1
Neurologic disorders	2	1
Orthopedic problems	8	2
Respiratory disorders	2	<1
Sexually transmitted diseases	16	4
Skin disorders	59	16

Note: N = 1,177 children screened. 364 (31%) presented with medical problems requiring follow-up.

1995 and March 1996 (See Table 1). Three hundred sixty-four children (31%) presented with medical problems that were serious enough to require follow-up by the providers. Infectious problems were common among these children and included ear infections, urinary tract infections, conjunctivitis, bronchitis, sinusitis, sepsis, pharyngitis, cellulitis, tuberculosis, and pneumonia.

EPSDT and Other Pathways to Medical and Mental Health Services for Children Entering Care

Early and Periodic Screening, Diagnosis and Treatment (EPSDT) is the child health component of the Medicaid program established in 1965. EPSDT assessments are designed to be both preventive and comprehensive. Some states use names other than EPSDT to describe this program that is available to nearly all Medicaid–eligible children under 21 years of age. According to a recent publication by the Department of Health and Human Services (undated), the term *EPSDT* describes the services provided:

Early: assessing a child's health early in life so that potential diseases and disabilities can be prevented or detected in the early stages, when they are most effectively treated.

Periodic: assessing a child's health at key points in the child's life to assure continued healthy development.

Screening: the use of tests and procedures to determine if children being examined have conditions requiring closer medical (including mental health) or dental attention.

Diagnosis: determination of the nature and cause of conditions identified by screenings and those that require further attention.

Treatment: the provision of services needed to control, correct, or reduce health problems. (p. 7)

At present, under federal law, pediatric health practitioners are already required to conduct a "mental health assessment" (HHS, undated, p. 9) as part of the EPSDT. Unfortunately, the primary care practitioners administering the EPSDT typically give short shrift to the stated goal of attending to mental and emotional problems. Rather than performing standardized tests, screening clinicians conduct informal inquiries. For example, in the case of a school–aged child, a pediatrician may ask about language skills, home and school behavior, and critical development milestones. For an adolescent, this inquiry may also include questions about sexual behavior, illicit drug use, and depression. Nevertheless, clinicians are, in general, not ever formally assessing the child's mental health functioning.

Primary care practitioners tend to subsume mental health concerns under the broad-based category of developmental history. By thus marginalizing mental health concerns, they rarely identify the serious developmental deficits that may impair up to 80% of children entering foster care (Halfon, Mendonca, & Berkowitz, 1995). The extent of this underidentification of mental health problems is dramatic. In examining EPSDT administrative data in California (unpublished), author Neal Halfon found that primary care practitioners identified developmental problems (requiring referral) in only 1.4% of children in foster care who received EPSDT exams!

Practitioners may not adhere to this legally mandated mental health assessment for a variety of reasons. To begin, many clinicians lack adequate training in detecting and understanding the sequelae of child abuse and neglect. Furthermore, given the meager insurance reimbursement under the Medicaid program for EPSDT services, physicians simply do not have the time or the staff to explore mental health issues to any appreciable degree. Financial pressures also steer clinicians away from diagnosing psychological symptoms because they then would be responsible for arranging for treatment. As we move toward capitated financing arrangements where these kinds of services are likely to be undervalued, this underidentification of mental health problems could become worse. Thus, tragically, although children entering care present with numerous mental health problems, and the law mandates that clinicians conduct mental health assessments under the EPSDT program, in actuality, these at-risk children by and large are not receiving these much needed services. As a result, children entering out-of-home placement who receive the mandated EPSDT also often do not receive appropriate referrals for mental health treatment.

Rather than adding new stipulations to the law, our policy proposal simply aims to provide at-risk children their legally mandated mental health services. Under Title XXI of the Social Security Act passed as part of the 1997 Balanced Budget Amendment, new funds are potentially available to states that want to improve their services to these needy children. Under our proposal, states could institute mandatory screenings by providing adequate reimbursement to medical providers. Alternatively, under a capitated payment mechanism, the costs of the screening could be factored into the rates. Legislators also might want to consider enforcement planks penalizing child welfare agencies that fail to provide this service.

In short, the EPSDT by itself does not ensure that children entering care receive the mental health services that they urgently need. Current screening practice focuses on children's medical needs to the exclusion of their mental health needs. In general, under current practice, as the research demonstrates, level of need does not always dictate whether a particular child receives mental health treatment. As John Landsverk and Ann Garland report in chapter 9, type of maltreatment may, in some cases, be a more significant factor in determining whether a child receives services. For instance, in a San Diego County study, Garland, Landsverk, Hough, and Ellis-MacLeod (1996), controlling for severity of symptomatic distress, found that sexually abused foster children were four and a half times more likely to receive mental health services than those placed for other reasons.

Figure 4. Foster care placement system for the Baltimore program.

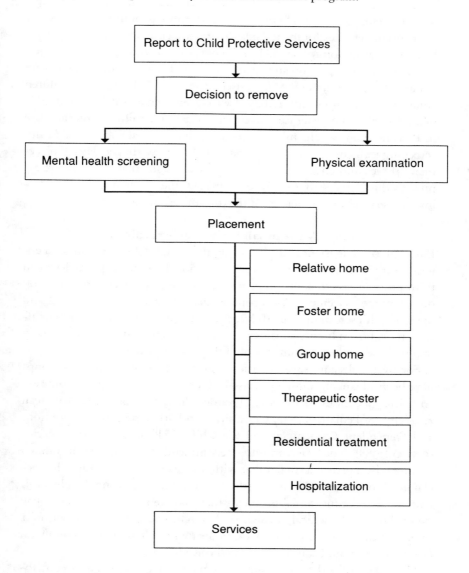

In contrast, children placed for reasons of neglect or abandonment were only half as likely to receive services when compared with children placed for other reasons.

At present, except for children in selected jurisdictions who do receive appropriate referrals for mental health services, cities and states are paying little or no attention to mental health concerns. Baltimore is an exception by virtue of a class action suit filed in 1984 on behalf of children entering foster care. As a result of the "LJ consent decree" issued in 1988, all children entering care are now required by law to receive a medical screening. Figure 4 describes the foster care placement system for children entering care in Baltimore, in which children receive both a medical and mental health screening immediately upon removal from home. Within 60 days of placement, these children also receive the mandated EPSDT that essentially reduplicates this initial step. Finally, once placed, the children receive the follow-up services recommended at the time of screening.

Policy Proposal: Universal Screenings

Based on our experience administering the Health Clinic for children entering care in Baltimore,[1] we advocate a national policy proposal designed to improve access to appropriate mental health care for children entering out-of-home placement. We propose mandating universal medical and mental health screenings for all children entering care within two weeks after removal from home. This new protocol aims to ensure that the legally required mental health component of the EPSDT be carried out.

For over a decade, several national professional and advocacy groups have been advancing similar proposals. Our proposal mirrors, to some extent, the guidelines issued roughly a decade ago by both the American Academy of Pediatrics (AAP) Committee on Early Childhood, Adoption, and Dependent Care (1987) and the Child Welfare League of America (CWLA) (1988). The AAP committee recommended a "complete health assessment by a pediatrician familiar with the foster care system and the special needs of foster children . . . {that} should extend beyond the physical, emotional and educational problems that may be present" (p. 644).[2] The CWLA proposed medical, dental, and psychiatric assessments within 1 month of the foster care placement. In the CWLA proposal, local child welfare agencies would coordinate these services.

The setting of perhaps unattainable standards may, in part, have contributed to the failure to implement these earlier proposals. For example, though ideally only pediatricians with links to the foster care system should assess children entering care, this stipulation seems unrealistic.

Figure 5. Mental health screening model for the Baltimore program.

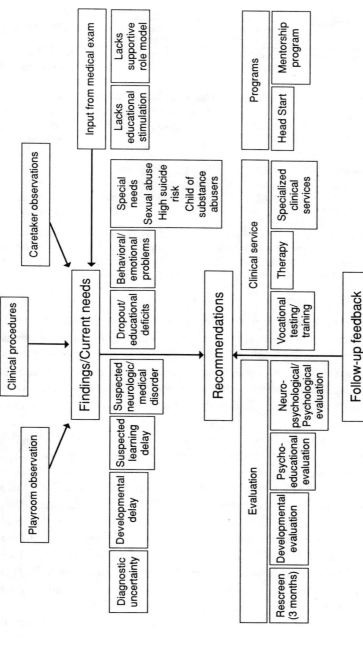

Source: Dale, G., Cargo, A., Ennis, M., Hayes, L., Hessenauer, L., & Kendall, J. (1993, August). *A mental health screening model for children entering foster care.* Poster presented at the 101st annual convention of the American Psychological Association, Toronto, Canada.

Table 2. Screening Protocol for the Baltimore Program

	Assessment Instruments	Domains Assessed	Assessment Criteria
2 months–5 years	DDST II	Developmental skills	Normal vs suspect for delay
6–12 years*	PVT	Receptive language skils	Normal vs suspect for delay
	VMI	Visual-motor integration	
	RCDS	Depressive symptoms	Likely to be depressed
13–19 years	PBT	Receptive language skills	Normal vs suspect for delay
	VMI	Visual-motor integration	
	RADS	Depressive symptoms	Likely to be depressed

Note: DDST II = Denver Developmental Screening Test (version 2), PVT = Beery Picture Vocabulary Screening Protocol, VMI = Developmental Test of Visual-Motor Integration, RCDS = Reynolds Child Depression Scale, RADS = Reynolds Adolescent Depression Scale.
*6- and 7-year-olds are too young to receive the RCDS.

First, unfortunately, all too few pediatricians possess this expertise. Second, other personnel such as nurse practitioners and physician assistants could conceivably perform the same tasks more cost-effectively. Finally, both the AAP and CWLA proposals recommend assessments that require much more time to complete than screenings and cost several fold as much. We thus set forth a proposal that shares the goals of earlier ones but that offers a more practical means to allocate scarce resources.

Our vision of the "enhanced EPSDT" is based on the mental health and medical screening models that have been developed at the Health Clinic. The mental health screening (see Figure 5) lasts about an hour. The screening clinician first gathers information about the child from the social service worker and caretaker before conducting a brief clinical interview. Depending on the child's age, various screening instruments are administered (see Table 2).[3] For example, children aged 6 to 12 years receive the Beery Developmental Test of Visual-Motor Integration (VMI), the Beery Picture Vocabulary Test (PVT), and the Reynold's Child Depression Scale (RCDS). In most cases, these instruments, combined with caretaker and playroom observations, give a detailed snapshot of the children's cognitive, emotional, and behavioral functioning. Through the years, more extensive di-

186

Figure 6. Medical screening model for the Baltimore program.

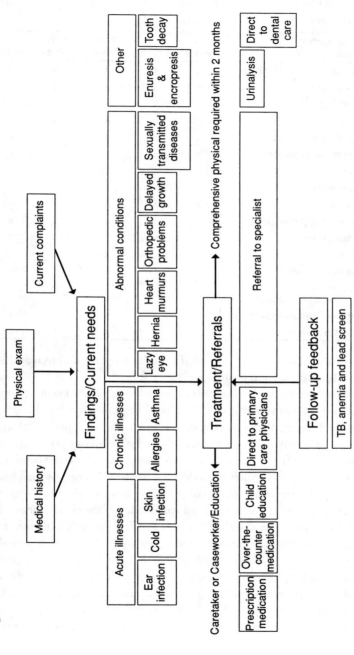

Source: Dale, G., Hessenauer, L., Kendall, J., Lance, M., & Holmes, D. (1993, November). *The Baltimore screening program for children entering foster care: A model for forging a new partnership between Head Start and the foster care system.* Poster presented at the 2nd annual Head Start Research Conference, Washington DC.

Table 3. Initial Health Screening for Children and Adolescents Entering Out-of-Home Placements

Screening components	0–2 years	2–3 years	3–5 years	5–10 years	11–21 years
Health and development history	x	x	x	x	x
Height and weight	x	x	x	x	x
Head circumference		x			
Blood pressure		x	x	x	x
Physical exam (unclothed)	x	x	x	x	x
Developmental assessment	x	x	x	x	x
Vision screening			x	x	x
Hearing screening			x	x	x
Blood lead test	x	x	x		
Anemia screening (Hct/Hgb)	x	x	x	x	x
Immunization history	x	x	x	x	x
Dental referral			x	x	
Substance abuse history					x
Sexual history (include contraceptive efforts)					x
Sexually transmitted deseases hx					x
HIV/Hepatitis B status	x	x	x	x	x

agnostic testing has rarely been needed in order to place children and arrange for follow-up mental health care.

Figure 6 depicts the medical screening model in use at the Health Clinic. This screening essentially follows the guidelines provided by the EPSDT program (see Table 3). Performed by either a pediatrician, a pediatric nurse practitioner, or a physician's assistant, the screening consists of an unclothed medical exam and also lasts about an hour. The clinician spends the greater part of the hour gathering a detailed medical history of the child. Because most children have been subjected to years of medical neglect, special attention is placed on the overall appearance of the child. For example, the clinician measures the child's height and weight with percentiles in order to assess growth abnormalities associated with a failure-to-thrive diagnosis. Furthermore, the thorough physical exam, including a genital exam, is used to help determine whether the child has been physically or sexually abused.[4] In addition to the physical exam, routine blood tests are performed in order to screen for lead poisoning and anemia.

We maintain that a *screening*, rather than an *evaluation*, is the most appropriate and cost-effective means to assess mental health problems for children entering care. As defined by Cicchetti and Wagner (1990), "assessment is the measurement of the relative position of an individual in a larger defined population with respect to some psychological construct." For such at-risk children, screenings can serve to identify the principal mental health problems of most children. A screening is a simple uncovering or discovery that leads to the identification of symptoms. In contrast, an evaluation attends to all domains of development and interpersonal functioning. We ground the use of screenings on both clinical and logistical considerations. In particular, screenings function on the principle of an "economy of scale." Given the massive influx of children entering the foster care system each year nationwide (Tatara, 1994), screenings provide an optimal means of gathering essential information in a brief period of time. Even in rural areas, where only a handful of children enter care at any one time, screenings still constitute the most viable mechanism for identifying significant mental health problems. Comprehensive evaluations would be reserved specifically for the most severely impaired children for whom screenings are not sufficient to assess their overall mental health functioning.

Though we recommend screenings for all children, we acknowledge some logistical problems. Lack of background information often complicates any type of assessment with such at-risk children. As Halfon et al. (1995) note, foster parents and social workers recognized only one-third to one-half of the conditions found during careful assessments. Furthermore, particularly for young children aged 6 months to 10 years, questions arise concerning the predictive validity of screenings. Upon removal from the home, children's mental health status may fluctuate widely. As a rule, clinicians need to interpret the results with caution. Some children may require rescreening within 30 to 60 days. Finally, we also advocate an evaluation component for any particular screening protocol. The screening procedures themselves need to be assessed from time to time in order to improve their efficacy—if needed. For example, research should determine that the levels of "false negatives" (i.e., children whose problems are not properly identified) and "false positives" (i.e., children who are incorrectly identified as having mental health problems) are not too high.

What to Screen For? Some Basic Guidelines

With regard to medical screenings, our proposal follows the guidelines already in place under the EPSDT program. At present, primary care practitioners tend to cover the essential domains. We do recommend, however, that physicians and nurse practitioners enhance their knowledge regarding the medical sequelae of abuse and neglect.

In the case of mental health screenings, however, we advocate improving the delivery of services so that both the "letter and the spirit" of the current law regarding the EPSDT be carried out. The question then arises regarding what particular cognitive and emotional domains the screenings should cover. As stated above, we believe that no matter how many domains are covered, children should be examined first within the context of a screening. Evaluations, which by definition would be comprehensive, constitute a second step for the minority of children who require them.

Based on their experience with the Foster Care Program at the Center for the Vulnerable Child in Oakland, California, Halfon et al. (1995) recommend assessing children on 10 distinct domains: gross motor, fine motor, expressive language, cognition, self-help, emotional function, relational capacity, coping ability, and behavior problems. For the purposes of screening, all of these domains would not need to be covered. A screening should cover a minimum of 6 to 8 basic areas including language development, fine and gross motor skills, social skills, self-help, and behavior problems. Though Halfon et al. point to how relational and emotional functioning tend to determine performance on speech and cognitive measures, full-fledged assessment of these more subtle domains falls outside the purview of a screening. However, follow-up evaluations, when necessary, would cover all domains of development and pay particular attention to children's relationships with their caregivers (Cicchetti and Wagner, 1990).

Although a pediatric practitioner with proper training may cover these domains, it is recommended that an allied health professional conduct the mental health screening and issue appropriate mental health referrals. Allied health professionals encompass mental health practitioners with at least a master's level training in psychology, nurse practitioners, and physician assistants. Those professionals without an advanced psychology degree require specific training in order to administer screening instruments. In general, but particularly when nonpsychologists conduct screenings, a psychologist should interpret the overall results and assist in shaping the mental health recommendations. Halfon has emerged as a particularly strong national advocate for multidisciplinary teams. Such teams may not be practical in rural or semirural areas but are becoming more prevalent in cities across the country.

Conclusion

Given the literature documenting the health problems among children entering care, all children entering foster care need both *immediate* medical and mental health screenings upon removal from home. Our proposal for universal screenings does not, in fact, alter public policy. In essence, we are simply recommending that practitioners carry out the guidelines already in place under the EPSDT program.

We contend that ensuring appropriate care for these at-risk children is vital for their long-term welfare. Furthermore, early intervention constitutes the most cost-efficient means to protect the health of these at-risk and vulnerable citizens.

Notes

1. A unique public-private partnership, the Health Clinic has administered this program since July 1992 and has performed nearly 10,000 medical and mental health screenings on children entering care.

2. The AAP (1994) has since published a revised policy paper on the health care of children in out-of-home placement.

3. We do not mean to prescribe the use of any particular screening instruments. We merely aim to describe how we have chosen to implement our general model. For the purpose of our clinical discussion, the central issue revolves not around particular instruments but, rather, around which domains to assess in the screening. We cover this topic in the next section.

4. As noted above, primary care practitioners rarely have had adequate training in detecting the medical sequelae of abuse. For some overall practice guidelines, see the review article by Bays and Chadwick (1993).

References

American Academy of Pediatrics, Committee on Early Childhood Adoption and Dependent Care. (1987). Health care of foster children. *Pediatrics, 79,* 644–646.

American Academy of Pediatrics, Committee on Early Childhood Adoption and Dependent Care. (1994). Health care of children in foster care. *Pediatrics, 93,* 335–338.

Bays, J., & Chadwick, D. (1993). Medical diagnosis of the sexually abused child. *Child Abuse and Neglect, 17,* 91–110.

Child Welfare League of America. (1988). *Standards for health care services for children in out-of-home care.* Washington DC: Author.

Cicchetti, D., & Wagner, S. (1990). Alternative assessment strategies for the evaluation of infants and toddlers: An organizational perspective. In S. Meisels & J. Shonkoff (Eds.), *Handbook of early childhood intervention* (pp. 246–277). Cambridge: Cambridge University Press.

Dale, G., Kendall, J., & Stein-Schultz, J. (1996, June). Refining screening protocols for "at-risk" children entering foster care. Poster presented at the fourth annual colloquium of the American Professional Society on the Abuse of Children, Chicago.

Fanshel, D., & Shinn, E. (1978). *Children in foster care: A longitudinal investigation.* New York: Columbia University Press.

Garland, A. F., Landsverk, J. L., Hough, R. L., & Ellis-MacLeod, E. (1996, August). Type of maltreatment as a predictor of mental health service use for children in foster care. *Child Abuse and Neglect 20*(8), 675–688.

Halfon, N., & Klee, L. (1991). Health and development services for children with multiple needs: The child in foster care. *Yale Law and Policy Review, 9,* 71–76.

Halfon, N., Mendonca, A., & Berkowitz, G. (1995). Health status of children in foster care: The experience of the Center for the Vulnerable Child. *Archives of Pediatric Adolescent Medicine, 149,* 386–392.

Hochstadt, N., Jaudes, P., Zino, D., & Schachter, J. (1987). The medical and psychosocial needs of children entering foster care. *Child Abuse and Neglect, 2,* 53–62.

Kavaler, F., & Swire, M. (1983). *Foster-child health care.* Lexington MA: D. C. Heath.

Kendall, J., Dale, G., & Plakitsis, S. (1995). The mental health needs of children entering the child welfare system: A guide for caseworkers. *APSAC Advisor, 8,* 10–13.

McIntyre, A., & Kessler, T. (1986). Psychological disorders among foster children. *Journal of Child Clinical Psychology, 15,* 297–303.

Schor, E. (1982). The foster care system and health status of foster children. *Pediatrics, 69,* 521–528.

Simms, M., & Halfon, N. (1994). Research agenda: Health needs of children in foster care. *Child Welfare, 73,* 505–524.

Tatara, T. (1994). Some additional explanations for the recent rise in the U.S. child substitute care population: An analysis of national child substitute care flow data and future research questions. In R. Barth, J. Berrick, & N. Gilbert (Eds.), *Child welfare research review* (Vol. 1). New York: Columbia University Press.

U.S. Department of Health and Human Services. (undated). *EPSDT: A guide for Head Start programs.* Washington DC: Author.

9

Foster Care and Pathways to Mental Health Services

John Landsverk and Ann F. Garland

Research studies over the past two decades have firmly established what practitioners have known for considerably longer, namely, that children in foster care represent a high-risk population for maladaptive outcomes, including socioemotional, behavioral, and psychiatric problems warranting mental health treatments. The major risk factors for maladaptive outcomes include the maltreatment experiences that lead to foster care placement and the stress of removal from home. Given this increased risk for maladaptive outcomes, one would assume that most children in foster care are referred for mental health services. However, although studies document the urgent need for treatment, only recently have researchers begun to describe the patterns of mental health service use by children in foster care. This chapter describes the new research and addresses its policy and practice implications.

The chapter addresses the following three topics: (a) the type of needs shown by children in foster care that warrant mental health services; (b) the overall use of mental health services by children in foster care; and (c) the factors that predict mental health referral and service utilization patterns. In this third section, the study of predictive factors illustrates the pathways into mental health service use by children in foster care. Each section includes a discussion of specific policy and practice implications suggested by the empirical findings.

Need for Mental Health Services
Costello and her colleagues (Costello, Burns, Angold, & Leaf, 1993) have outlined four ways to estimate need for mental health services: "need as

service use," "need as diagnosis," "need as functional impairment," and "need as exposure to risk." The first definition fails to distinguish between need for services and use of services. For children in foster care, the fourth type, "need as exposure to risk," would require universal mental health treatment because almost all these children have experienced maltreatment. For the purpose of this chapter, we define need for mental health services according to the second and third types; namely, as need derived from either diagnosis or functional impairment, especially as established by standardized measures.

Estimates of the need for mental health services for children and adolescents as indicated by standardized measures range widely for both community and special populations. In community studies, estimates of this need range from 10 to 22% (Costello et al., 1988; Gould, Wunsch-Hitzig, & Dohrenwend, 1981; Offord et al., 1987; Zahner, Pawelkiewicz, DeFrancesco, & Adnopoz, 1992).

Most studies of children living in foster care have shown that they exhibit problems requiring mental health assessment and intervention at a considerably higher rate than what would be expected from either normative data or from community studies. Pilowsky's recent review of studies published from 1974 through 1994 (1995) supports this conclusion, noting that externalizing disorders in particular may be more prevalent than internalizing in the foster care population.

Nine more recent studies not included in the Pilowsky review also confirm this widely accepted conclusion. In the state of Washington, Trupin and colleagues (Trupin, Tarico, Benson, Jemelka, & McClellan, 1993) compared children receiving protective services from child welfare with a criterion group of children in the state's most intensive mental health treatment programs and found that 72% of the children in child welfare exhibited profiles of severe emotional disturbance indistinguishable from the criterion group. In a study of children residing in kinship care in Baltimore, Starr, Dubowitz, Harrington, and Feigelman (1994) found that 32% were in the clinical range on behavior problems as reported by the caretaker on the Achenbach Child Behavior Checklist. This study is especially important because of the increasing proportion of foster care children living in this type of placement and the paucity of studies of their psychosocial functioning. In a Tennessee study of children over the age of 4 years entering state custody, of whom 64% were under the supervision of child welfare,

Glisson (1994, 1996) found that 52% were in the clinical range of the Child Behavior Checklist, as determined by both the parent and teacher informant, with 82% scoring in the clinical range of at least one of the three scales of internalizing, externalizing, and total behavior problems. In a study of 272 children entering foster care in Connecticut before the age of 8, Horwitz, Simms, and Farrington (1994) found that 53% showed developmental delays as determined by either the Connecticut Infant/Toddler Developmental Assessment or the Battelle Developmental Inventory. Five of the nine recent studies were conducted with children entering foster care in California. Urquiza, Wirtz, Peterson, and Singer (1994) conducted a comprehensive screening and evaluation of 167 children between the ages of 1 and 10 who were made dependents of the juvenile court in Sacramento for reasons of child abuse and neglect. They found that 68% of the children displayed significant problems in one of four psychosocial domains as operationalized by a score one and a half standard deviations below national norms on one or more of four standardized assessment instruments.

Halfon, Mendonca, and Berkowitz (1995) reported on 213 young children with a mean age of 3 years who were referred to a comprehensive health clinic after entering foster care in Oakland and found that over 80% had developmental, emotional, or behavior problems. They also found that children who were placed after 2 years of age exhibited a higher rate of these problems than children placed at an earlier age.

Clausen, Landsverk, Ganger, Chadwick, and Litrownik (1998) examined 140 children between the ages of 4 and 16 entering foster care in three California counties and found that 54.4% met clinical or borderline criteria on one or more of the narrow, broad band, or total behavior problem scales of the Achenbach Child Behavior Checklist, Parent Report Form, and that 62.6% met clinical or borderline criteria on one or more of the narrow band and social competency scales as well. Only 23.0% were determined to fall in the nonclinical or borderline range on both the behavior problem and social competency dimensions.

Landsverk, Litrownik, Newton, Ganger, and Remmer (1996) conducted a study in San Diego County comparing children entering kinship care with children entering nonrelative foster care through the Parent Report Form of the Achenbach Child Behavior Checklist. For children between the ages of 4 and 16, the investigators determined that 32.9% in the kinship group and 39.8% in the nonrelative foster care group were in the clinical range on total behavior problems. Using the borderline cutoff point, the respective percentages were 43.2% and 51.9%. In the same study, the authors found that 60% of the children under the age of six and a half and residing in kinship care were in the questionable or abnormal range on the Denver Developmental Screening Test–Version Two, as compared to 72% of the same age children residing in nonrelative foster placements. Finally, Madsen (1992) used the Diagnostic Interview Schedule for Children (DISC) with 59 children between the ages of 11 and 16 in the early months of foster care and found that 60% met criteria for one or more *DSM-III-R* diagnoses as determined by either reports from the parent or the youth.

Two of the studies reported findings suggesting that decisions about reunification may be affected by the psychosocial functioning of the child in foster care. Horwitz, Simms, and Farrington (1994) found that children with developmental problems were almost two times more likely to remain in foster care than be reunified. Landsverk, Davis, Ganger, Newton, and Johnson (1996) found that children with significant behavior problems, especially externalizing problems, were one-half as likely to be reunified with their birth parents within 18 months of foster care entry as were those without significant behavior problems.

In summary, the research literature based on studies across several states suggests that between one-half and two-thirds of the children entering foster care exhibit behavior or social competency problems warranting mental health services. The rate of problems is significantly higher than what would be expected in community populations. Furthermore, these maladaptive outcomes range across a number of domains, rather than being concentrated in only broad behavior problems. An especially noteworthy finding includes developmental problems in the large number of children entering foster care prior to the ages of 7 and 8. In addition, evidence suggests that the rate of problems may be somewhat less in children who end up in kinship care as compared to children who are placed in nonrelative foster care, although this relationship remains open to further, more definitive research. Finally, psychosocial functioning of the children in foster care may affect not only the long-term functioning outcomes but also basic decisions regarding their continuity or exit from living in foster care.

POLICY AND PRACTICE IMPLICATIONS

First, the high rate of need for mental health services in the foster care population indicates that full assessment protocols rather than screening protocols may constitute the most appropriate strategy for identifying children with maladaptive problems and linking them to specific interventions. Screening programs are only appropriate when low base rates prevail. The data from a number of studies in diverse states and foster care systems suggest a very high base rate for children and adolescents entering foster care. Therefore, assessment for a wide range of problems in psychosocial functioning should be taken as a routine first step in determining appropriate interventions for specific problems.

Second, the data from recent studies suggest that assessment protocols need to be comprehensive in scope and specific in a wide range of developmentally appropriate domains in order to facilitate better treatment planning. This policy recommendation implies that broad-based behavioral problem checklists such as the Achenbach Child Behavior Checklist may not be sufficient for developing the detailed clinical profiles critical for good treatment planning. Examples of a comprehensive assessment strategy for children entering foster care have been published by Simms (1989) and Halfon, Mendonca, and Berkowitz (1995). These protocols cover a wide range of domains relevant to psychosocial functioning and constitute an excellent foundation for future work. Nevertheless, there is a need for assessment referral practice guidelines with wide support from experienced clinicians and clinical settings that can be implemented by most foster care systems. The development of these guidelines will require extensive collaboration between the child welfare system, the mental health system (Knitzer & Yelton, 1990), and the medical care system.

Third, findings from both the California and Connecticut studies underscore the importance of developmental assessment for all children entering foster care prior to the age of seven. Furthermore, assessment rather than screening protocols would be most appropriate, given the high base rate of developmental problems found in this population. These findings suggest that routine use of standardized assessment measures for developmental delays across multiple areas be considered rather than broad screening instruments such as the Denver Developmental Screening Test or the Battelle Developmental Inventory.

Finally, one study in California and one study in Connecticut have shown the possible impact of a foster child's psychosocial functioning on case decision making. These preliminary investigations suggest that the policy imperatives undergirding reunification and family preservation may be undercut by case workers' perceptions regarding the psychosocial functioning of the children. More research needs to be conducted to understand how caseworkers and courts are using information about psychosocial problems to affect their decisions about exits from foster care. Practice guidelines need to be developed in order to provide direction for caseworkers on the most appropriate use of information about children's psychosocial functioning in making recommendations to dependency courts regarding reunification.

Use of Mental Health Services

In contrast to the psychosocial functioning of children in foster care, fewer studies have examined the use of mental health services for this special population. While studies of psychosocial functioning have been published for over two decades, studies of mental health service use have been conducted only since 1988. This section discusses findings from four studies that provide estimates of service use for three states: California, Tennessee, and Washington. These rates are compared to rates found in community samples.

Estimates regarding rates of mental health service use are difficult to ascertain given the variations in definitions of mental health services, ranging from the traditional outpatient and inpatient modalities to the less traditional services such as case management and therapeutic group homes. Despite these definitional variations, a number of community studies have estimated that between 4 and 12% of children in community samples have received mental health services (Koot & Verhulst, 1992; Offord et al., 1987; Zahner et al., 1992). The national epidemiological studies of need for mental health services and use of mental health services commissioned by the National Institute of Mental Health will provide better estimates for community populations over the next 5 years.

Two studies of mental health service use by the specialized population of children in foster care have used Medicaid program claims data, one in California (Halfon, Berkowitz, & Klee, 1992a, 1992b) and one in Washington State (Takayama, Bergman, & Connell, 1994). The Medicaid data from these two states are especially relevant because Washington and California both have made all children in foster care categorically eligible for the Medicaid program, regardless of the eligibility status of their biological parents.

In the California study conducted by Halfon, Berkowitz, and Klee, Medi-

Cal data (the name for the Medicaid program in California) were examined for all paid claims involving children under 18 years of age in the fee-for-service program in 1988. Rates of health care utilization and associated costs were compared between the 50,634 children identified in foster care and the 1,291,814 children eligible for the total program. Although the children in foster care represented less than 4% of the population of Medi-Cal–eligible users, they represented 41% of the users of reimbursed mental health services and incurred 43% of all mental health expenditures. This overrepresentation among mental health service users held for all age groups within the foster care population, ranging from rates of 31% for children under the age of 6 and 32% for children between the ages of 6 and 11, to 49% for all users between the ages of 12 and 17. The investigators further determined that children in foster care had an age-adjusted rate of mental health service utilization that was 15 times the overall Medi-Cal population that served as the reference group. The investigators found that this pattern of greater utilization was also true across many different types of mental health services, with children in foster care accounting for 53% of all psychology visits, 47% of psychiatry visits, 43% of public hospital inpatient hospitalizations, and 27% of psychiatric inpatient hospitalizations.

The second study using Medicaid claims form data compared the health care utilization rates of 1,631 children in foster care with those of a sample of 5,316 children from the population of children who were AFDC recipients but not in foster care in 1990 (Takayama, Bergman, & Connell, 1994). This research focused on children under the age of 8 in Washington State, making it less inclusive than the California study. Despite the younger age cohort studied, the findings were comparable to those reported by Halfon and colleagues for California, with 25% of the children in Washington foster care using mental health services as compared to only 3% of the AFDC comparison group children. When the diagnoses were examined for high-cost children whose 1990 health care expenditures exceeded $10,000 (8% of foster children and 0.4% of AFDC children), the prominent diagnoses for the children in foster care were mental disorders and neurological conditions.

Further insight into the use of mental health services by children in foster care is provided by two additional studies that shared important design features. The foster care investigations in San Diego County (Landsverk, Litrownik, et al., 1996; Garland, Landsverk, Hough, & Ellis-Macleod, 1996) and in Tennessee (Glisson, 1994, 1996) both studied children entering foster care and both used the Achenbach Child Behavior Checklist to determine the need for mental health services.

The San Diego County study examined need for mental health services in a cohort of 662 children between the ages of 2 and 17 at the first out-of-home interview (approximately 5 to 8 months after entry into foster care) and found that 56% of the children had used mental health services within the period between entry into foster care and the first interview. Need for services was determined by a behavior problems score above the borderline cutoff point on the Parent Report Form of the Child Behavior Checklist. Mental health service utilization was based on reports by the substitute parent regarding any service use for help with behavioral, social, school, or other adjustment problems. In addition, the type of provider and frequency of visits were elicited from the same informant. The percentage of children in foster care using mental health services was 21% of the children aged 2 to 3, 41% of the children aged 4 to 5, 61% of the children aged 6 to 7, and more than 70% of children and adolescents over the age of 7. These rates contrast sharply with the less than 10% of the same foster children for whom there was evidence of mental health care utilization prior to entry into out-of-home placement (Blumberg, Landsverk, Ellis-Macleod, Ganger, & Culver, 1996). By far the largest proportion (60%) were being seen by a clinical psychologist. The frequency of outpatient visits for all subjects receiving services (except those in residential care) was relatively high, with an estimated mean of 15.4 visits in 6 months. This suggests that the majority of subjects who received outpatient services were in some type of ongoing treatment as opposed to an initial evaluation.

The Tennessee study followed a cohort of 600 children between the ages of 5 and 18 who were randomly selected from approximately 2,000 children entering state custody in 24 Tennessee counties over the course of 1 year. Two-thirds of the sample children were placed in the custody of the child welfare system. The social workers for all of the 600 sample children reported that 14% had been referred for mental health treatment after being placed in custody. No information was included on the actual utilization of services.

In summary, two California studies and a Washington State study demonstrate a very high rate of use of mental health services across all age groups, with the highest rate of 70% occurring in children over the age of 7. The studies using Medicaid data confirmed this much higher rate for children in foster care in contrast to the much lower rates seen in AFDC children. The Tennessee studies showed a considerably lower rate of mental health referral, a surprising finding given the older age of the study cohort and the very high rate of behavior problems reported in the Tennessee special population. This lower rate may result in part from the predominantly rural counties in the Tennessee studies compared to the urban counties in the California and Washington State studies.

POLICY AND PRACTICE IMPLICATIONS

First, the high rate of mental health service use observed for children in foster care suggests that the child welfare system and the mental health system may be more strongly linked than commonly thought. In California and Washington State, there is consistent evidence that the foster care system may serve as a large gateway into the mental health service system for children who have been abused or neglected. Since these two systems share many child and adolescent clients, more explicit collaborative ties need to be forged, directed at improving the efficiency of service delivery.

Second, it would appear that the Medicaid program, as categorically applied to children in foster care, provides a powerful impetus to the provision of mental health services to this specialized population. Medicaid is currently undergoing a major transition to a managed care form of service delivery. We do not know how this shift in the organization and financing of mental health care will affect the mental health treatment of children in foster care. The policy implication is that leaders of the child welfare system and foster care systems need to be proactive in developing managed care contracting within the Medicaid program in collaboration with the managers of public mental health systems. Third, there is little information available about the impact of exits from foster care on the continuity of mental health care for these high-risk children. Further study is necessary to determine whether children are only receiving mental health services when they are within the foster care system or whether these treatment services continue across the major permanency plans of reunification and adoption as well as exit at majority. The potential negative impact of developmental problems and behavior problems on exits from foster care would suggest the continued need for mental health services when exits are considered or completed.

Fourth, the widespread use of mental health services for this specialized population is not accompanied by systematic monitoring of service outcomes for the foster children who are receiving these services. No studies have been published to date that examined either the quality of care being provided through mental health services or the outcomes of those services. We do not know whether the services are effective in ameliorating the mental health and developmental problems observed in children entering the foster care system. There is a clear need for efficient monitoring of developmental, behavioral, social, and adaptive functioning for children in foster care who are receiving mental health services. In short, systems of accountability need to be developed in order to determine the course of treatment at the level of the individual foster child.

Finally, collaborators across the child welfare and mental health systems need to develop and test best practice models for the delivery of mental health treatment services. The San Diego County study found that almost all mental health services were being delivered in one-hour office visits, with little evidence of the use of group services, family therapy, or other modalities of treatment. No specialized models exist for determining what services to provide for what children within the context of what types of maladaptive functioning. An excellent example of the type of discussion needed for the development of service delivery models for high-risk children and adolescents has been provided by Halfon, Inkelas, and Wood (1995). The authors hark back to the Anderson and Aday model of health care utilization (Aday & Andersen, 1974) that describes financial and nonfinancial barriers to care for children. Case studies of immunization delivery, children with chronic illness, and mobile populations of children are used to argue for integrated service models for high-risk populations of children that coordinate the delivery of medical, developmental, educational, and social services.

Pathways Into Mental Health Services

This final section considers what is known about the pathways into mental health services for children who experience an episode of placement in foster care. Rogler and Cortes (1993) introduced the concept of pathways to assist in the description of ways in which people seek help for mental health problems and how these help-seeking strategies interact with responses from help-giving organizations. They defined *pathways* as "a sequence of contacts with individuals and organizations prompted by the distressed person's efforts, and those of his or her significant others, to seek help as well as the help that is applied in response to such efforts." In the context of the children in foster care, this definition is translated into a question: How do children and adolescents who need help with mental health problems come to the attention of service providers and receive treatment? Mental health services research generally addresses this question with studies of factors that predict either referral for mental health care or use of mental health care. These studies distinguish between those factors that concern the clinical condition of the help seeker, such as the presence of behavior problems or psychiatric diagnoses, and nonclinical aspects of the help seeker or the organizations that structure the help seeking, such as the demographic status (i.e., age, gender, race, or ethnicity) and the availability of treatment services. An explicit assumption in this discussion is that a rational system of mental health service delivery would emphasize clinical factors rather than nonclinical factors as the major predictors of referral and utilization.

The problem with epidemiologic research that simply reports rates of need for service (section one) and rates of service utilization (section two) is that there is no analysis of the relationship between need and use and the factors that may confound the relationship. Research with community and clinical samples indicates that there is a relationship between need and use of children's mental health services, but that the relationship may not be as strong as expected. A range of factors, other than severity of emotional or behavioral problems, is likely to predict service use patterns, including demographic, behavioral, attitudinal, family, service system (service availability and financing), and policy-level factors (Bui & Takeuchi, 1992; Cohen & Hesselbart, 1993; Costello & Janiszewski, 1990; Koot & Verhulst, 1992; Zahner et al., 1992). Only two studies have reported on the relationship between need, referral, and use of mental health services for children in foster care. In his studies of children entering state custody in Tennessee, Glisson (1994, 1996) found no relationship between the child's mental health status as measured by the Achenbach Child Behavior Checklist and the decision to refer for mental health services. No information about actual use of mental health services was provided in the published reports.

In the San Diego County study (Landsverk, Litrownik, et al., 1996; Garland et al., 1996), investigators found that there was a significant relationship between need for services, as defined by clinically significant total behavior problems on the Achenbach Child Behavior Checklist, and the child's use of services as reported by the foster parent. Even with the effects of other variables controlled, subjects with clinically significant total behavior problem scores were three times as likely to receive services as those without clinically significant scores. These findings for the children in the San Diego foster care system are consistent with community studies that indicate that children and adolescents with clinically significant problems are significantly more likely to receive services (e.g., Koot & Verhulst, 1992).

However, community research on children not in the foster care system also shows that factors other than need for services can be significant predictors of use, including child, family, and service delivery system characteristics (Bui & Takeuchi, 1992; Cohen & Hesselbart, 1993; Costello & Janiszewski, 1990; Koot & Verhulst, 1992; Zahner et al., 1992). An especially pertinent factor for studies of mental health service delivery in the child welfare system is the type of maltreatment for which the child has been placed in foster care. This factor was the special focus of Garland and colleagues in their analysis of data from the San Diego County study (Garland et al, 1996). The investigators found that the subjects' type of maltreatment was a significant predictor of use of mental health services, even when the effects of severity of total behavior problems, gender, and age were controlled. Logistic regression analysis revealed that children who were in foster care due to sexual abuse were almost four and a half times more likely to receive mental health services as were children who were not placed for this reason, whereas children who were in placement due to neglect or caretaker absence were only half as likely to receive mental health services as compared with children not placed for reason of neglect. Type of maltreatment was also observed to affect intensity of services, as measured by the number of outpatient visits in the previous 6 months. The frequency of visits for sexually abused children was significantly higher than the frequency for children placed because of neglect or caretaker absence.

A possible explanation for the increased rates of service use among sexually and physically abused youth may include a general perception by case workers, judges, and caretakers that these types of "active" maltreatment have a more negative effect on a child's psychosocial adjustment than do the more "passive" types of maltreatment, such as neglect. However, there is very little research to support or refute these perceptions. In one study of the impact of various types and dimensions of maltreatment on children's psychosocial functioning, Manly, Cicchetti, and Barnett (1994) found that dimensions of maltreatment, such as severity and chronicity, were more significant predictors of the global severity of behavior problems than was the type of maltreatment. There is nothing in their results to suggest that sexually or physically abused children have increased need for mental health services compared to children who were neglected.

The observed differences in service utilization rates may also reflect the availability of specific types of mental health services. In San Diego, there are established treatment programs for sexually abused children, and the programs receive referrals directly from the county's Child Protective Service. This linkage may help explain why children who were sexually abused were very likely to have received mental health services, regardless of the severity of behavior problems observed by the caretaker. There is no identified treatment program for neglected children. However, this differential in availability of mental health services may also reflect the underlying perception by system managers that sexually and physically abused children are in greater need of services than neglected children. In addition to detecting the effect of maltreatment on mental health service use, the San Diego County study also examined the effects of age and gender on service use. Increased age was associated with a significantly greater likelihood of service use, whereas gender did not exert a significant effect when the effect of other variables was controlled. The age effect for children in foster care was also reported by Halfon, Berkowitz, and Klee (1992b) in their study of Medi-Cal data from California. Studies with community samples do not report an increase in service use associated with age; however, the samples were generally older, with a more restricted age range (Costello & Janiszewski, 1990; Koot & Verhulst, 1992; Offord et al., 1987; Zahner et al., 1992). The lack of a significant effect of gender on service use is consistent with some community studies (Koot & Verhulst, 1992; Zahner et al., 1992). The San Diego County study also found that there were no significant interaction effects of age or gender by type of maltreatment, suggesting that the effects of type of maltreatment on service use operate regardless of the age or gender of the child.

Hough, Garland, and Reynolds (1995) have examined the impact of racial and ethnic background of children in the San Diego County foster care system on their use of mental health services. Even after controlling for age, gender, and total behavior problems, African-American and Latino children in foster care were significantly less likely to receive mental health services. In addition, the frequency of outpatient visits was also significantly predicted by race and ethnic background. This finding is consistent with a recent review of research on race and child welfare services that found that minority families and children were likely to experience fewer services than their majority counterparts involved with the child welfare system (Courtney et al., 1996).

Finally, Garland and Besinger (1997) examined the court records for 142 children between the ages of 2 and 16 who entered foster care in San Diego County, and found significant differences by race and ethnicity for mental health service use both prior to foster care entry and after entry. White youth were more likely to receive court orders for psychotherapy than were African-American and Hispanic youth, even when the potential confounding effects of age and type of maltreatment were controlled.

In summary, there is limited recent evidence that both clinical and nonclinical factors affect mental health referral and utilization patterns for children in foster care. The nonclinical factors implicated in one California study are type of maltreatment, racial or ethnic background, and age.

POLICY AND PRACTICE IMPLICATIONS

First, further research is clearly needed to examine the available service systems for maltreated children and to address implicit and explicit policies that may result in inequitable distribution of service resources based on factors other than need. This work cannot be conducted without parallel lines of research investigating the effectiveness of services for children with different types of maltreatment so that greater specificity in the delivery of appropriate services can be achieved. Specific pathways into services and the barriers to service use must be identified, including an examination of the roles of various gatekeepers and decision makers, such as case managers, judges, and caretakers. Concurrently, advances in developmental psychopathological studies of the sequelae of maltreatment may inform us more specifically about the mental health service needs of children who have been maltreated.

Second, there is a practical need for the development of explicit guidelines to be used in systematically linking children who show need with clinically effective and appropriate services. In particular, these guidelines need to address the issue of nonclinical factors affecting service use in terms such as access to services, acceptability of services, and perception of need for services by gatekeepers. The guidelines also need to address the type and severity of maladaptive behaviors warranting referral for mental health services. Eventually, models need to be developed that both recommend specific treatment services based on specific emotional and behavioral problems and allow for some flexibility and creativity in treatment choices for children in foster care.

Finally, there is a need to develop models for family participation in mental health treatment for children in foster care within the context of dual families. Both biological families in the process of negotiating with child protective services regarding the issues of risk for maltreatment, family functioning, and reunification, and foster care and kinship families who are standing in for the biological parents need to be included in models of family participation. This will be necessary so that the policy impetus of family preservation and family empowerment will be better served while children are receiving mental health services to ameliorate their emotional, behavioral, and social problems.

References

Aday, L. A., & Andersen, R. M. (1974). A framework for the study of access to medical care. *Health Services Research, 9*, 208–220.

Blumberg, E., Landsverk, J., Ellis-Macleod, E., Ganger, W., & Culver, S. (1996). Use of the public mental health system by children in foster care: Client characteristics and service use patterns. *Journal of Mental Health Administration 23*, 389–405.

Bui, K. T., & Takeuchi, D. T. (1992). Ethnic minority adolescents and the use of community mental health care services. *American Journal of Community Psychology, 20*, 403–417.

Clausen, J. M., Landsverk, J., Ganger, W., Chadwick, D., & Litrownik, A. (1998). Mental health problems of children in foster care. *Journal of Child and Family Studies, 7*, 283–296.

Cohen, P., & Hesselbart, C. S. (1993). Demographic factors in the use of children's mental health services. *American Journal of Public Health, 83*, 49–52.

Costello, E. J., Burns, B. J., Angold, A., & Leaf, P. J. (1993). How can epidemiology improve mental health services for children and adolescents? *Journal of the American Academy of Child and Adolescent Psychiatry, 32*, 1106–1113.

Costello, E. J., Costello, A. J., Edelbrock, C., Burns, B. J., Dulcan, M. K., Brent, D., & Janiszewski, S. (1988). Psychiatric disorders in pediatric primary care. *Archives of General Psychiatry, 45,* 1107–1116.

Costello, E. J., & Janiszewski, S. (1990). Who gets treated? Factors associated with referral in children with psychiatric disorders. *Acta Psychiatrica Scandanavica, 81,* 523–529.

Courtney, M. E., Barth, R. P., Berrick, J. D., Brooks, D., Needell, B., & Park, L. (1996). Race and child welfare services: Past research and future directions. *Child Welfare, 75,* 99–137.

Garland, A. F., & Besinger, B. A. (1997). Ethnic differences in court referred pathways to mental health services for children in foster care. *Children and Youth Services Review, 19,* 1–16.

Garland, A. F., Landsverk, J. A., Hough, R. L., & Ellis-Macleod, E. (1996). Type of maltreatment as a predictor of mental health service use in foster care. *Child Abuse and Neglect, 20,* 675–688.

Glisson, C. (1994). The effects of services coordination teams on outcomes for children in state custody. *Administration in Social Work, 18,* 1–23.

Glisson, C. (1996, June). Judicial and service decisions for children entering state custody: The limited role of mental health. *Social Service Review, 70,* 257–281.

Gould, M. S., Wunsch-Hitzig, R., & Dohrenwend, B. (1981). Estimating the prevalence of childhood psychopathology. *Journal of the American Academy of Child and Adolescent Psychiatry, 20,* 462–476.

Halfon, N., Berkowitz, G., & Klee, L. (1992a). Children in foster care in California: An examination of Medicaid reimbursed health services utilization. *Pediatrics, 89,* 1230–1237.

Halfon, N., Berkowitz, G., & Klee, L. (1992b). Mental health service utilization by children in foster care in California. *Pediatrics, 89,* 1238–1244.

Halfon, N., Inkelas, M., & Wood, D. (1995). Nonfinancial barriers to care for children and youth. *Annual Review of Public Health, 16,* 447–472.

Halfon, N., Mendonca, A., & Berkowitz, G. (1955). Health status of children in foster care: The experience of the Center for the Vulnerable Child. *Archives of Pediatric and Adolescent Medicine, 149,* 386–392.

Horwitz, S. M., Simms, M. D., & Farrington, R. (1994). Impact of developmental problems on young children's exits from foster care. *Journal of Developmental and Behavioral Pediatrics, 15,* 105–110.

Hough, R., Garland, A. F., & Reynolds, B. (1995, September). Race/ethnic differences in the use of mental health services among children in foster care. Paper presented at the Mental Health Services Research conference, NIMH, Bethesda MD.

Knitzer, J., & Yelton, S. (1990). Collaborations between child welfare and mental health: Both systems must exploit the program possibilities. *Public Welfare, 48,* 24–33.

Koot, H. M., & Verhulst, F. C. (1992). Prediction of children's referral to mental health and special education services from earlier adjustment. *Journal of Child Psychology and Psychiatry, 33,* 717–729.

Landsverk, J., Davis, I., Ganger, W., Newton, R., & Johnson, I. (1996). Impact of child psychosocial functioning on reunification from out-of-home care. *Children and Youth Services Review, 18,* 447–462.

Landsverk, J., Litrownik, A., Newton, R., Ganger, W., & Remmer, J. (1996). *Psychological impact of child maltreatment* (Final Report to National Center on Child Abuse and Neglect).

Madsen, J. (1992). *Mental health assessment of children in foster care.* Unpublished doctoral dissertation, University of California, San Diego, and San Diego State University.

Manly, J. T., Cicchetti, D., & Barnett, D. (1994). The impact of subtype, frequency, chronicity, and severity of child maltreatment on social competence and behavior problems. *Development and Psychopathology, 6,* 121–143.

Offord, D. R., Boyle, M. H., Szatmari, P., Rae-Grant, N. I., Links, P. S., Cadman, D. T., Byles, J. A., Crawford, J. W., Blum, H. M., Byrne, C., Thomas, H., & Woodword, C. A. (1987). Ontario child health study: Part 2. Six-month prevalence of disorder and rates of service utilization. *Archives of General Psychiatry, 44,* 832–836.

Pilowsky, D. (1995). Psychopathology among children placed in family foster care. *Psychiatric Services, 46,* 906–910.

Rogler, L. H., & Cortes, D. E. (1993). Help-seeking pathways: A unifying concept in mental health care. *American Journal of Psychiatry, 150,* 554–561.

Simms, M. D. (1989). The foster care clinic: A community program to identify treatment needs of children in foster care. *Journal of Developmental and Behavioral Pediatrics, 10,* 121–128.

Starr, R. H., Dubowitz, H., Harrington, D., & Feigelman, S. (1994). *Behavior problems of teens in kinship care: Cross-informant reports.* Unpublished manuscript.

Takayama, J. I., Bergman, A. B., & Connell, F. A. (1994). Children in foster care in the state of Washington: Health care utilization and expenditures. *Journal of the American Medical Association, 271,* 1850–1855.

Trupin, E. W., Tarico, V. S., Benson, P. L., Jemelka, R., & McClellan, J. (1993). Children on child protective service caseloads: Prevalence and nature of serious emotional disturbance. *Child Abuse and Neglect, 17*, 345–355.

Urquiza, A. J., Wirtz, S. J., Peterson, M. S., & Singer, V. A. (1994). Screening and evaluating abused and neglected children entering protective custody. *Child Welfare, 123*, 155–171.

Zahner, G. E. P., Pawelkiewicz, W., DeFrancesco, J. J., & Adnopoz, J. (1992). Children's mental health service needs and utilization patterns in an urban community: An epidemiological assessment. *Journal of the American Academy of Child and Adolescent Psychiatry, 31*, 951–960.

Foster Care and Family Reunification

Anthony N. Maluccio

Reunification of children and youths in out-of-home care with their families of origin is becoming increasingly controversial. Some policymakers who take a punitive stance toward parents of children in foster care are calling for a return to the "old days" of the orphanage. In addition, tragic events such as severe maltreatment and even death of children who return to their own homes from placement are not uncommon. Although some authors advocate a balance between preserving families and protecting children (Lindsey, 1994; Maluccio, Pine, & Warsh, 1994), others condemn family preservation as an approach that ignores child safety and costs some children their lives (Berliner, 1993; Gelles, 1996). The emotions that are thus aroused further complicate agency efforts to plan and provide effective services for children and youths in foster care and their families.

Within this controversial context, how can research be of help to practitioners, administrators, and policymakers in the field of foster care? In this chapter, we examine recent research on family reunification in order to delineate policy and practice recommendations whose ultimate effect would be to diminish the number of children in foster care.

Family reunification is addressed in much of the research on foster care, family preservation, permanency planning, and decision making in child welfare. This chapter, however, focuses on recent studies regarding patterns of exit from foster care, follow-up services and supports, parent-child visiting, recidivism and reentry of children into care following episodes of

The author appreciates Edith Fein's thoughtful review of an earlier version of this chapter.

reunification, and the relationship between the child's psychosocial functioning and reunification outcomes. These areas were chosen primarily because of the number of carefully implemented studies containing recommendations for reducing the numbers of children in care.

Background

Before we review pertinent research, it is useful to consider the concept of family reunification as well as the challenge of doing research in this area of child welfare. Family reunification of children in out-of-home care has been defined as: "the planned process of reconnecting children in out-of-home care with their families by means of a variety of services and supports to the children, their families, and their foster parents or other service providers. It aims to help each child and family to achieve and maintain, at any given time, their optimal level of reconnection—from full reentry of the child into the family system to other forms of contact, such as visiting, that affirm the child's membership in the family" (Maluccio, Warsh, & Pine, 1993, p. 6).

This definition goes beyond the traditional view of reunification as essentially the *physical* reunion of children with their birth families. In particular, it "recognizes that not every parent can be a daily caregiver and that some families, though not able to live together, can still maintain kinship bonds" and be meaningfully reconnected though they may be living apart (Maluccio et al., 1993, p. 6). Although such a flexible definition is increasingly influencing the decisions of child welfare workers in individual cases, the legal and policy framework is still guided largely by the traditional concept noted above.

RESEARCH ON FAMILY REUNIFICATION

The concept of family reunification tends to be oversimplified and poorly understood. In addition, the results of some studies on the outcome of reunification services are inconclusive or discrepant. A recent review of available outcome studies, for example, revealed "a wide range of reunification rates (from 13% to 70%) and of rates of reentry into out-of-home care (from 10% to 33%)" (Maluccio, Fein, & Davis, 1994, p. 494). The main reason for such an inconsistent picture seems to be "the inappropriateness of comparing and aggregating findings of diverse studies in regard to operational definitions of crucial study variables, study samples, timing of the studies, geographic locations, length of placement and follow-up periods, and service factors as well as child and family characteristics" (Maluccio, Fein, & Davis, 1994, p. 494).

Because human interactions are so complex, it is not surprising that research in the human services reflects that complexity, often producing insufficient and sometimes contradictory information. The same problem is now being encountered in the biological sciences, "where the new biology of complexity that genetics is revealing is beginning to strike a cautionary note in planning of many scientists" (Golub, 1994, p. 222). Nevertheless, without expecting panaceas or simplistic answers, some order can be created out of the apparent chaos. The findings that emerge from the studies on family reunification reviewed in this chapter can be applied with insight—albeit with caution—to policy and practice planning. While they may have methodological flaws, these studies represent some of the most sophisticated recent efforts to explore the phenomenon of family reunification and, therefore, make noteworthy contributions that can help guide the decisions and actions of practitioners as well as policymakers.

Exit From Foster Care

Children exit from foster care in a number of ways that are qualitatively distinct. In an analysis of longitudinal data from a cohort study of 8,625 children in foster care, Courtney and Wong (1996) examined the factors that affect discharge to their original families or guardians, placement in adoptive families, or running away. This methodologically rigorous study shows the complexities and subtleties of the exit process in foster care. The authors found that a large number of children returned to their homes or to the homes of guardians in the first few months after placement. Later, however, fewer children returned home, and an increasing number were adopted, while others ran away.

It is not clear from the above study or related research by Davis, Landsverk, Newton, and Ganger (1996) whether some children return home earlier because they and their families are functioning at a higher level and thus make better use of services than is the case with other families. Nevertheless, these studies call attention to the importance of providing comprehensive and easily accessible supportive services to children and their families in both the preplacement phase and early in the placement period in order to promote family reunification.

Child welfare workers have long recognized the need to address the traumatic impact of separation and placement on children, their parents, and other family members as a means of helping them move toward reunification (Kadushin & Martin, 1988). As the above studies suggest, equally vital is involving both children and parents actively in the helping process by providing not only therapeutic services but also concrete assistance with their everyday needs (Staff & Fein, 1994). Traditionally, the emphasis in child welfare practice has been on services to the children, in response to their immediate need for care and protection. While this is appropriate, parents also need special attention; help to them should be provided on an intensive basis, so as to enhance their rehabilitation and increase the likelihood that they will be able to take their children back home, keep them there, and function as competent parents.

In this regard, successful outcomes depend on treating parents as individuals with problems and needs of their own, rather than solely as caregivers with responsibility for their children. In addition, parents and other family members need to be involved as partners in the change process and as active agents in preparing for reunification, "including having an understanding of the reasons for placement, participating in developing goals, sharing in determining visiting plans and purposes, and evaluating their own progress" (Warsh, Pine, & Maluccio, 1996, p. 125).

After-Care Services

RESEARCH FINDINGS

The value of providing supportive services to parents and children following reunification is demonstrated in a number of studies. For example, Walton, Fraser, Lewis, Pecora, and Walton (1993) and Fraser, Walton, Lewis, Pecora, and Walton (1996) report on an experimental evaluation of a state program established to reunify children in foster care with their biological families. This carefully conceived study employed a posttest-only experimental design, extensive multivariate analyses, and a "hazard model" designed to examine the impact of multiple variables on reunification outcomes. The researchers randomly assigned the cases of foster children to (a) a control group of 53 children whose families received routine agency services as a component of an overall foster care plan and (b) an experimental group of 57 children whose families received intensive family reunification services, with the goal of family preservation.

Walton et al. (1993) and Fraser et al. (1996) found that children in the experimental group receiving intensive services were more likely to be reunited successfully with their families than those in the control group receiving routine services. These differences proved to be statistically significant at the conclusion of treatment as well as during the follow-up period. In particular, relatively brief but intensive in-home family-based services positively affected reunification rates and outcomes. These services primarily involved building strong worker alliances with family members, providing skills training to parents, and meeting the concrete needs of the children and other family members. The findings suggested "that reunification and permanence are promoted by the skillful delivery of in-vivo family-strengthening services" (Walton et al., 1993, p. 485).

A series of descriptive follow-up studies of children and adolescents discharged from foster care was also conducted in Great Britain, with emphasis on reunification issues (Biehal & Wade, 1996; Farmer, 1996). Despite certain limitations to be noted below, these investigations are quite informative in regard to the after-care period.

In the Farmer (1996) study, the sample consisted of 321 children reunited with their families after a period of court-ordered out-of-home placement. The researcher employed qualitative methodology, specifically intensive review of the children's case records, and in-depth interviews with a small number of birth parents and social workers. She found that there were two distinctly different groups of children: the "disaffected" adolescents who had been removed due to juvenile offenses or truancy and the "protected" younger children who had been removed for abuse, neglect, or family breakdown. The research revealed that the most successful reunifications in both groups were first attempts; later reunifications had higher failure rates.

Biehal and Wade (1996), on the other hand, conducted a longitudinal study of adolescents leaving care in several public child welfare agencies. Their project involved both an initial survey of 183 youths during their first 3 to 9 months of independent living and semistructured interviews with 74 of the adolescents, conducted soon after leaving care and on two later occasions during a 2-year period. In addition, the young people's social workers were interviewed on each occasion. In each phase, the researchers focused on the varied patterns of family contact and the quality of the children's and youths' relationships with their families.

Since the Farmer and the Biehal and Wade studies employed qualitative methodology, their findings and conclusions should be viewed with caution. For example, as with other such investigations, there are questions about the reliability and validity of the data and the extent to which one can generalize to other populations. Nevertheless, these studies are useful for policy and practice, as they shed light on the supports required by children and adolescents as well as their families. In particular, it should be noted that supportive services such as special education contributed to the success of reunification efforts. Also prominent in the young people's postdischarge functioning were ongoing connections with one or more family members and a sense of belonging to and identification with a family unit; that is, their original family or a foster family with whom they maintained contact.

POLICY AND PRACTICE IMPLICATIONS

Emphasis on the provision of follow-up services after reunification is clearly the most common theme in the findings of the studies on the aftercare period. The results point to a number of policy and practice strategies. Most notable are providing brief, time-limited but intensive services (Fraser et al., 1996); offering a range of social supports to the families, including concrete services in areas such as health, housing, and income, as well as counseling services in areas such as parent-child conflicts and the challenges presented by the children's behavioral difficulties (Fraser et al., 1996; Festinger, 1996); and facilitating ongoing supports to children and youths in regard to special education, treatment of emotional/behavioral and developmental/learning problems, and other special needs (Biehal & Wade, 1996; Farmer, 1996; and Landsverk, Davis, Ganger, Newton, & Johnson, 1996).

As various studies indicate, the services provided to children and their families in the post-reunification phase can be critical in helping to keep them together. Furthermore, it has been found that in most child welfare agencies post-reunification services are at first intensive but then taper off to a less frequent contact. "A few families, however, may need some level of services indefinitely to maintain their children at home" (Warsh, Pine, & Maluccio, 1996, p. 137). In addition, research has shown that strategies such as the following can be useful in maintaining the reunification (Warsh et al., 1996, pp. 136–137):

helping the child to cope with feelings of fear, guilt, grief, and anger that may be reactivated as separation from the foster home or residential placement approaches;

developing a post-reunification safety plan for protection of a child who was originally placed because of harm in the biological home;

assisting the child and other members of the biological and foster families to clarify—and plan for—their continuing relationship following reunification;

helping the child and his or her parents and other family members to anticipate and deal with conflicts that are likely to develop once the child returns home; and, above all,

ensuring the family's access to services following reunification and eventual termination of their case.

Parental Visiting

During the placement period it is also crucial to sustain and enhance connections between children and their families, particularly parents or other caregivers. Parent-child visiting in foster care has been described as a crucial determinant of the outcome of foster care services (Hess & Proch, 1988) and as the "heart of family reunification" (Warsh, Maluccio, & Pine, 1994, p. 49).

RESEARCH FINDINGS

In an extensive follow-up investigation of permanency planning for children in foster care, Davis et al. (1996) examined the relationship between parental visiting and reunification. In this descriptive study, the sample consisted of 925 children, 12 years or younger, placed in foster care for more than 72 hours through the auspices of a large California public agency. The sample of children and parents was ethnically and racially diverse. Data were gathered primarily from agency case files. The cases were followed for up to 18 months, and information was collected on such variables as child and family characteristics, reasons for placement, placement experiences, permanency planning, and outcomes.

Although the study contained limitations common to descriptive research, including the use of archival data that may not have been sufficiently reliable, it had a number of strengths. In particular, it utilized a cohort rather than a cross-sectional sample, thus reducing possible bias from overrepresentation of children in foster care for long periods. Also, "because all children in the cohort who met study criteria were studied, sampling errors were of no concern" (Davis et al., 1996, p. 366). It was found that the majority of children who had visited with their parents at the level recommended by the courts were reunified with their families. However, there was no significant relationship between parent–child visiting and whether the child remained in the biological home at a follow-up point a year after the reunification.

POLICY AND PRACTICE IMPLICATIONS

The findings of the study by Davis et al. (1996) suggest that explicit policies and practices should be instituted to facilitate parent–child visiting throughout the placement process and to use visiting deliberately as a therapeutic vehicle in preparation for reunification. Visiting helps maintain family ties and provides opportunities for family members to learn and practice new behaviors and patterns of communicating with each other, with the assistance of social workers and foster parents.

In line with the above findings, such authors as Hess and Proch (1988) and Warsh et al. (1994 and 1996) offer guidelines for employing parent–child visiting as a strategy for reuniting children in out-of-home care with their families of origin. These authors emphasize that visiting should be carefully planned and implemented, with attention to its different purposes during each phase of the foster care placement. These purposes include providing reassurance to the child and the family that the agency is concerned with reuniting them, if at all possible; assessing the children's and parents' capacity for reunification; offering opportunities for staff members to help parents and children to reconnect with each other and learn or relearn skills for being together; and documenting the progress of children and parents in becoming reunited.

To accomplish the above purposes, child welfare agencies "should provide and support quality visiting services that promote a child's timely return home or make possible a determination that he/she cannot return to full-time care in the family. Whether or not children are able to return home, visiting maintains family ties that are essential to a child's healthy development" (Warsh et al., 1996, p. 133).

Researchers have identified a number of pertinent policies and strategies for facilitating visitation and promoting connectedness between children in placement and their families (Hess & Proch, 1988; Warsh et al., 1996):

placing children near their parents and other significant kin;

placing siblings together, unless otherwise indicated;

encouraging foster parents to allow family visits in the foster home, unless contraindicated;

requiring written visiting plans that specify such aspects as the purposes, frequency, length, and location of each visit;

selecting visiting activities that provide children and parents with opportunities to learn more effective patterns of interaction; and

preparing children, families, and foster parents for visits and giving them opportunities to work through their reactions before and after each visit.

ISSUES FOR FURTHER CONSIDERATION

The research findings reviewed above attest to the complexity of the reunification phenomenon and the factors that affect its outcome. The studies highlight a number of issues for further consideration, including the role of foster parents in facilitating parent–child visiting, the parents' need for support in connection with visiting, and the provision of services to parents as well as children following reunification. Moreover, research on child development has demonstrated the significance of the family in the child's identity formation, psychosocial functioning, sense of competence, and preparation for adulthood. When children are placed in out-of-home care, child welfare policies and services should, therefore, aim to preserve ties between them and their families as much as possible (Pine, Warsh, & Maluccio, 1993). Indeed, the natural bonds between children in care and their parents continue to be prominent for parents as well as children long after they are physically separated (Pecora, Whittaker, Maluccio, & Barth, in press).

Recidivism Following Reunification

As noted earlier, recidivism is a common problem in foster care, as substantial numbers of children discharged to their families return to one form or another of out-of-home placement. In an elaborate and rigorous study involving a random sample of nearly 1,200 children placed in foster care in Illinois, Goerge (1990) analyzed whether the probability of reunification changes with duration of the placement. The findings confirmed the central hypothesis that the probability of reunification decreases with time in placement. More specifically, the study showed that "there is a great decline in the probability of reunification after the first few weeks in placement," and that "the greatest decrease in the probability of reunification occurs for abused and neglected children" (p. 422). The study thus demonstrated the importance of prompt and efficient decision making and also the need for planned long-term care, especially for children involved in situations of child abuse or neglect. Although this study did not focus on the dimensions of race and ethnicity, other researchers have demonstrated that there are differential rates of out-of-home placement and reentry into foster care for children of color. In particular, it has been found that there is a higher rate of reentry among minority adolescents (Fein, Maluccio, & Kluger, 1990; Wulczyn, 1991).

In a more recent descriptive study conducted in New York City, Festinger (1996) investigated recidivism in a sample of 210 children from 20 agencies returning to their families from foster homes and group care settings. The study explored whether there were any differences between children who reentered care within 2 years of discharge and those who did not reenter, taking into account the characteristics of the children, their caregivers, and their social situations.

As the author points out, there were several limitations in the above research. "All data came from one large city at a particular point in time. Also, the 20 agencies were not selected on a random basis but were included to provide a range of agency types of varying size, sectarian and non-sectarian auspices, levels of care, and child populations served" (Festinger, 1996, p. 397). In addition, since it was not possible to gather data directly through the children and their families, the researcher relied primarily on the social workers' perceptions and observations and on data obtained from computerized files of the state agency. Although these subjective and typically unreliable data sources weakened the study, some noteworthy findings did emerge. In particular, the strongest predictors of reentry into foster care within 1 year of discharge were lower ratings of parenting skills by social workers and few social supports available to the families. The strongest predictors of reentry within 2 years were the number and the severity of problems experienced by the biological parents or substitute caregivers.

Child Psychosocial Functioning

RESEARCH FINDINGS

A recurring question in the field of child welfare concerns the potential impact of children's psychosocial functioning on the outcome of their placement in out-of-home care. Landsverk et al. (1996) explored this theme in a descriptive, longitudinal study of 669 children who had been removed from their families and placed in either foster care or kinship care at a large county agency in California. The study was enriched by the use of standardized measures to assess the children's psychosocial functioning. The researchers examined emotional or behavioral difficulties, developmental or learning problems, and physical handicaps or acute medical problems.

The findings indicated that children with behavioral or emotional difficulties were half as likely to be reunified with their families as children without problems, regardless of their type of maltreatment, family circumstances, and other background characteristics. Developmental and medical problems did not have an effect on reunification. The authors stress the importance of assisting parents in coping with the behavioral problem challenges presented by children following reunification, underlining the role of after-care services discussed earlier in this chapter.

The findings of the study by Landsverk et al. (1996) are consistent with the results of an earlier research and demonstration project conducted at the Florida Mental Health Institute, which examined the efficacy of intensive, individualized services in improving the functioning of foster children with emotional and behavioral problems (Clark et al., 1994). The latter study involved a controlled experiment, with children assigned randomly to an experimental group receiving specialized services and a control group of children receiving standard agency services. In this carefully implemented study it was found that the outcomes, in terms of the children's adjustment as well as the stability of permanency plans, were significantly more positive for subjects in the experimental group than those in the control group. In light of the findings, these researchers emphasized the importance of providing intensive services and supports as well as individualized permanency plans for children with, or at risk for, emotional and behavioral disorders.

POLICY AND PRACTICE IMPLICATIONS

The studies reviewed in this section pertain to the developmental needs, multiple problems, and disruptive behaviors of the children. The results point to various implications for practice and policy, especially in regard to the timely provision of mental health and other services to the children. By the same token, it should be emphasized that the problems faced by the families of these children, especially the birth parents, must be acknowledged and confronted through adequate services and supports in each case as well as through societal reforms. As concluded in an earlier article recommending a range of family reunification services, a focus on the child is not enough: "Service delivery must take into account the competing interests of adults and children. In particular, the treatment of substance abusing adults needs to be reconciled with their role as parents. On a larger scale, the social and economic conditions that produce our addicted adults and our children in need of permanency planning must be addressed for families to survive" (Fein & Staff, 1991, p. 342).

Conclusion

Reducing the increasing number of children and youths in out-of-home care should be the paramount strategy in any efforts to alleviate the foster care crisis. The strategy should include stronger efforts to increase the number of children in foster care who are reunited with their families of origin, to facilitate their remaining reunited, and to promote their growth and development. The studies reviewed in this chapter highlight a number of implications for policy and practice that can contribute to these purposes. As previously indicated, these implications pertain to serving children and parents during the out-of-home placement episode, maintaining connections between children and their parents, and providing supports following reunification.

The challenge of helping children in out-of-home care and their families requires supportive as well as flexible agencies and staff members, since the needs in most case situations are not only multiple and complex but also increasing. As the research presented in this chapter suggests, many families with children in foster care can be helped to move toward reunification through a range of policies and practice strategies that have been empirically documented. As practitioners and researchers continue to examine the experiences of these families, changes in policy and practice should lead to more effective programs and models of intervention before and during placement as well as following reunification.

References

Berliner, L. (1993). Is family preservation in the best interest of children? *Journal of Interpersonal Violence, 8,* 556–557.

Biehal, N., & Wade, J. (1996). Looking back, looking forward: Care leavers, families and change. *Children and Youth Services Review, 18*, 425–446.

Clark, H. B., Prange, M. E., Lee, B., Boyd, L. A., McDonald, B. A., & Stewart, E. S. (1994). Improving adjustment outcomes for foster children with emotional and behavioral disorders: Early findings from a controlled study on individualized services. *Journal of Emotional and Behavioral Disorders, 2*, 207–218.

Courtney, M. E., & Wong, Y.-L. I. (1996). Comparing the timing of exits from substitute care. *Children and Youth Services Review, 18*, 307–334.

Davis, I. P., Landsverk, J., Newton, R., & Ganger, W. (1996). Parental visiting and foster care reunification. *Children and Youth Services Review, 18*, 363–382.

Farmer, E. (1996). Family reunification with high-risk children: Lessons from research. *Children and Youth Services Review, 18*, 403–424.

Fein, E., Maluccio, A. N., & Kluger, M. (1990). *No more partings: An examination of long-term foster family care.* Washington DC: Child Welfare League of America.

Fein, E., & Staff, I. (1991). Implementing reunification services. *Families in Society: Journal of Contemporary Human Services, 72*, 335–343.

Festinger, T. (1996). Going home and returning to foster care. *Children and Youth Services Review, 18*, 383–402.

Fraser, M. W., Walton, E., Lewis, R. E., Pecora, P. J., & Walton, W. K. (1996). An experiment in family reunification: Correlates of outcomes at one-year follow-up. *Children and Youth Services Review, 18*, 335–362.

Gelles, R. J. (1996). *The book of David: How preserving families can cost children's lives.* New York: Basic Books.

Goerge, R. M. (1990). The reunification process in substitute care. *Social Service Review, 64*, 422–457.

Golub, E. S. (1994). *The limits of medicine.* New York: Times Books–Random House.

Hess, P. M., & Proch, K. O. (1988). *Family visiting in out-of-home care: A guide to practice.* Washington DC: Child Welfare League of America.

Kadushin, A., & Martin, J. K. (1988). *Child welfare services* (4th ed.). New York: Macmillan.

Landsverk, J., Davis, I., Ganger, W., Newton, R., & Johnson, I. (1996). Impact of child psychosocial functioning on reunification from out-of-home placement. *Children and Youth Services Review, 18*, 447–462.

Lindsey, D. (1994). Family preservation and child protection: Striking a balance. *Children and Youth Services Review, 16*, 279–294.

Maluccio, A. N., Fein, E., & Davis, I. (1994). Family reunification: Research findings, issues, and directions. *Child Welfare, 73*, 489–504.

Maluccio, A. N., Pine, B. A., & Warsh, R. (1994). Protecting children by preserving their families. *Children and Youth Services Review, 16*, 295–307.

Maluccio, A. N., Warsh, R., & Pine, B. A. (1993). Family reunification: An overview. In B. A. Pine, R. Warsh, & A. N. Maluccio (Eds.), *Together again: Family reunification in foster care* (pp. 3–19). Washington DC: Child Welfare League of America.

Pecora, P. J., Whittaker, J. K., Maluccio, A. N., & Barth, R. P. (in press). *The child welfare challenge: Policy, practice, and research* (Rev. ed.). New York: Aldine de Gruyter.

Pine, B. A., Warsh, R., & Maluccio, A. N. (1993). *Together again: Family reunification in foster care.* Washington DC: Child Welfare League of America.

Staff, E., & Fein, E. (1994). Inside the black box: An exploration of service delivery in a family reunification program. *Child Welfare, 73*, 195–211.

Walton, E., Fraser, M. W., Lewis, R. E., Pecora, P. J., & Walton, W. K. (1993). In-home family-focused reunification: An experimental study. *Child Welfare, 72*, 473–487.

Warsh, R., Maluccio, A. N., & Pine, B. A. (1994). *Teaching family reunification: A sourcebook.* Washington DC: Child Welfare League of America.

Warsh, R., Pine, B. A., & Maluccio, A. N. (1996). *Reconnecting families: A guide to strengthening family reunification services.* Washington DC: Child Welfare League of America.

Wulczyn, F. (1991). Caseload dynamics and foster care reentry. *Social Service Review, 65*, 133–156.

11

The Rationalization of Foster Care in the Twenty-First Century

Mark E. Courtney and Anthony N. Maluccio

Prophesizing about the future of public institutions is always a hazardous pursuit. With the winds of change blowing hard regarding the proper role of government in people's lives, long-term predictions about an intervention as costly and potentially intrusive in family life as foster care are almost impossible to make with any degree of certainty. On the one hand, calls for a return to the use of orphanages for the children of indigent parents summon an image of a foster care system radically different from the one that has existed for the past several decades. On the other hand, we are reminded of the observation of Wolins and Piliavin (1964) that a century of sometimes furious debate over the relative merits of foster family care versus institutional care resulted in no consensus within the child welfare field and relatively little change in the overall use of these two forms of foster care. One thing is certain, however: the need for foster care may wax and wane over time, but it will not go away anytime soon.

The face of foster care may be altered by many factors over the next few decades. Some of these factors, such as changes in federal and state child welfare policies, have historically received considerable attention from scholars and practitioners in discussions of how foster care has developed into what it is today. Indeed, chapters in this volume describe how developments in policy have contributed to changes in child protective services, foster care caseload dynamics, the growth of kinship care, and the creation of administrative databases with which to better understand the pathways of children through the system. In contrast, other factors, such as developments in public assistance programs and labor market trends, have received relatively little attention in analyses of the foster care system, even though it could be argued that they have had as much if not more of an effect on the system as a whole.

Our task in this chapter is to speculate about the future of foster care, both where it might go and where we believe that it should go. Our colleagues' contributions to this volume provide a thorough description of many of the challenges facing the foster care system today and include a number of sound policy and practice recommendations. Therefore, we have chosen not to attempt to provide a comprehensive description of the many potential contributors to the development of foster care or a detailed list of remedies for the system's ills. Instead, we identify a few forces, largely external to the foster care system per se, that we believe will condition to some extent how foster care evolves over time, and that warrant the attention of scholars, policymakers, and administrators. In some cases we suggest ways in which these forces might be responded to by the child welfare community. In addition, we take up the issue of the increasing rationalization of child welfare services, including foster care. By this we mean the evolving efforts to base child welfare practice on a firm theoretical and empirical foundation oriented toward producing measurable outcomes for children and families. We believe that this is a desirable and long-overdue process, but that it involves many risks as well. We conclude that only thoughtful and patient evolution of service delivery in foster care will realize the full potential of the new era of accountability in child welfare.

External Forces

There are a number of factors external to the foster care system that may, nevertheless, have a significant impact on the system. Some of these are undoubtedly more important than others; moreover, members of the child welfare services community may be in a better position to respond to or plan for some developments than others. At any rate, we need to move beyond the tendency of scholars and policymakers in the past to view foster care in a vacuum, failing to consider how it is powerfully affected by larger social forces. Over the next few decades an external focus could, more than ever, lead to an expanded view of the constraints on, and opportunities for, foster care reform.

WHITE ELDERS, CHILDREN OF COLOR

Demographers have projected that the American demographic profile will change dramatically by the middle of the next century (Day, 1996). The growth of a large elderly population, already noted by the media and the public, drives much of the concern over the future of the Social Security program. The overwhelming majority of these elders, at least over the next few decades, will be white. In contrast, the fact that children of color will grow substantially as a proportion of all children over the next few decades, becoming a majority of all children by the year 2030, has received less attention (Day, 1996).

This demographic shift may contribute to undermining the support of the white middle class for services and supports for low-income children, who will overwhelmingly be children of color. For similar reasons, this trend raises serious questions about the ability of child advocates to garner the political support necessary to maintain a national commitment to funding foster care and related services. In the past decade, children of color have come to be the majority of children in foster care. Given the strong association between race and family poverty and entry into foster care (Brown & Bailey-Etta, 1997; Courtney et al., 1996; Goerge, Wulczyn, & Harden, 1995; Lindsey, 1994), it appears quite possible that children of color early in the next century will come to dominate the ranks of foster children even more than at present. If this occurs, child advocates may have a hard time maintaining support for foster care funding since white taxpayers and their elected representatives may no longer see foster children as "their" children.

To be sure, one could argue that the foster care system has never received sufficient governmental financial support to guarantee quality care for children removed from their homes. Still, the federal foster care entitlement has provided a crucial part of the social safety net for children who need out-of-home care due to abuse or neglect. Elimination of the federal entitlement could jeopardize the safety of children removed from their homes or lead child welfare agencies to leave children in unsafe homes. Those who find it hard to believe that the foster care entitlement could be ended need look no further than the original welfare reform legislation passed by the House of Representatives in 1996 (H.R. 4). This legislation would have eliminated the foster care entitlement and significantly decreased federal protections for maltreated children.

The demographic shift described above need not lead to a worsening of the foster care crisis. The next century *could* see a new political alignment and the renegotiation of the social contract in a way that provides better support for children and families across the life span, especially if government and other leaders can appreciate the urgency and value of interdependence across racial, social class, and generational dimensions. In particular, the largely white elderly population may see the growing diversity of the country as something to be supported and may see children, regardless of their color, as worthy of investment since they represent the future of the country.

How the nation manages the monumental demographic shift noted above is likely to have significant consequences for the foster care system. At a minimum, persons running the system as well as those who provide direct services will need to become increasingly culturally competent and be committed to ethnic-sensitive practice (Cohen, 1992; Iglehart & Becerra, 1995). As Pinderhughes (1997, p. 18) has observed, "In tomorrow's world, multicultural transactions will be commonplace. . . . Strengthening and enhancing families, which must become an imperative in the work to be done, will require strong commitment to training helpers who are highly skilled in the application of knowledge about power, diversity, and human systems." Furthermore, if the system is to look like those it serves, more people of color will have to be included as foster parents, group care providers, social workers, administrators, and researchers. Perhaps most important, the child welfare community will need to become more directly involved in societal debates about how to achieve social justice in the context of an increasingly diverse nation.

THE CHANGING NATURE OF THE FAMILY

The growth in the number of single-parent families, their predominance among low-income households, and the strong reliance of many of these families on extended kin networks are well known. At the same time, the general public and political leaders have, at best, an ambivalent attitude toward single-parent families. Regardless of public attitudes, the changing nature of the family has already had an enormous impact on the foster care system. The vast majority of children in care come from single-parent families, and about one-third of children in court-ordered foster care now live with kin. Nevertheless, as Berrick and Needell point out in chapter 7, foster care policy regarding the role of extended family in caring for maltreated children remains problematic. Even the explicit encouragement of placement with kin found in the Adoption and Safe Families Act of 1997 (Public Law 105-89) does not address the issue of how to move children from long-term kinship foster care out of the system without threatening kinship caregivers with the loss of financial assistance as well as other supports.

Given the uncertain policy environment for kinship care, it is not surprising that several of the recent waivers granted to the states by the federal government of Title IV-E provisions involve kinship guardianship. Specifically, the waivers allow the use of federal foster care funds to subsidize kinship guardianship arrangements for children who have been in long-term kinship foster care. This is a promising policy development since subsidized guardianship offers a more permanent arrangement for children and their kin than long-term foster care, minimizes the need for unnecessary court and caseworker supervision of the family, and maintains the availability of financial support for kin who otherwise would be unable to provide ongoing care.

Yet, such policies may not fare well in the long run if societal attitudes toward poor *extended* families become as negative as they have become over the past several decades toward poor single-parent families. Already some states are moving away from supporting kinship foster care on a par with foster family care. Some of these new programs offer relatives less reimbursement than that formerly provided to kin caregivers under Aid to Families with Dependent Children (AFDC), and all offer considerably less than that provided to foster parents. It does not seem completely out of the realm of possibility that subsidized kinship care could come to be seen in the minds of some critics as the new "welfare" if the number of children in kinship care continues to grow.

This could have serious implications for the foster care system if it results in limitations on the ability of child welfare authorities to identify and support kinship caregivers, especially in light of the multiple problems and developmental needs of children in kinship care (Scannapieco, Hegar, & McAlpine, 1997). This is crucial, as research has demonstrated the complexity of practice in kinship care. In particular, the rapidly expanding use of this resource will require further examination, as kinship caregivers are frequently single women—often grandmothers—from families of color who receive limited training or support in their roles despite already being burdened by family demands and having limited resources (Brown & Bailey-Etta, 1997).

INCREASING COMPETITION FOR CHILD CAREGIVERS

It is no mystery that child welfare agencies have had an increasingly diffi-cult time over the past decade finding and licensing an adequate supply of foster family homes. Two developments, the first more obvious than the second, could contribute to a further decline in the availability of family foster care providers. First, all else being equal, the continuing movement of women into the paid workforce could reduce the number of women staying at home who are able and willing to become foster parents. This factor has been commonly cited as a reason for the decline in the number of foster homes over the past decade (Pasztor, 1989). Although various coun-tervailing factors (e.g., a "family values" movement to return women to the home, the desire of an increasing number of men to care for children, and the recruitment of professional foster parents) may counteract this to some extent, at least in the short run it seems fair to say that the trend will continue.

Second, the growing push to increase the role of government in subsi-dizing child care (to some extent spurred on by welfare reform) should help expand an employment option for women that competes in important ways with foster parenting. This phenomenon may have already played a large role in decreasing the ranks of foster parents, but the research base in this area is so inadequate that there is no way to know for sure. As family day care becomes more commonly subsidized by government, there will be an opportunity for a growing number of people to choose to care for children 40 hours per week at $400 and up per child per month as family day-care providers. This competes very favorably with 24-hour-a-day li-censed family foster care, given current foster care reimbursement rates, the fact that it is much easier to be licensed to care for several children in day care than a similar number in foster care, and the likelihood that chil-dren requiring foster home placement have more extensive and severe problems and needs than most children in the general day-care population.

These market forces need not lead to a critical shortage of foster parents. Better recruitment and retention efforts, including higher payments, can help to make foster parenting a more attractive option for parents who con-template providing care for abused and neglected children. Still, given the growing availability of other more financially rewarding options for persons who might in the past have become foster parents, politicians and child welfare administrators must come to terms with the need to better compensate foster parents. Competition for child caregivers from outside of the child welfare system may contribute as much as any other factor to the growing "professionalization" of family foster care through payment of much higher foster care boarding rates to attract foster parents and commensurate demands for enhanced training of foster parents.

FERTILITY TECHNOLOGY

Although "preferential" adopters will always be with us and have accounted for a sizable proportion of all adoptions of foster children (Rosenthal & Groze, 1994; MacKenzie, 1993), the inability of would-be parents to conceive and bear their own children has always been a crucial element in the overall demand for children to adopt (Bachrach, London, & Maza, 1991). The rapid growth of fertility treatments, surrogate parenting, and now the brave new world of genetic engineering are likely to put downward pressure on the demand for adoption by couples and individuals who in the past would have had no other option.

The magnitude of the effect of fertility technology on adoption of foster children, particularly children with special needs, is impossible to anticipate but should not be ignored. Even with the recent push for increasing adoption manifest in President Clinton's Adoptions 2000 program and the Adoption and Safe Families Act of 1997, public and private adoption agencies may have an uphill struggle to increase significantly the adoption of children in foster care. More than ever, child welfare agencies may need to recognize the crucial resource that foster parents have become in special needs adoptions by enhancing development of foster parent adoption programs through fiscal and other supports to the foster families (Meezan & Shireman, 1985). Similarly, adoption agencies may need to become more creative in recruiting potential adoptive parents who are not able to take advantage of fertility technology due to its expense, such as working-class couples and would-be single parents.

WELFARE REFORM

It is difficult to overemphasize the impact that welfare reform *could* have on the foster care system. At a minimum, it has already sparked a discussion among policymakers, administrators, and child welfare practitioners about how best to cope with drastic changes in the economic safety net for families and children. Welfare reform also poses at least a potential threat of a substantial increase in demand for foster care (see chapter 6). Still, early experience suggests that there will be a variety of state and local approaches to work-based public assistance, making it reasonable to expect that reform will lead to a wide range of impacts on the foster care system. It is still far too early to obtain any empirical evidence regarding which new workfare programs will have the greatest implications for foster care. Nevertheless, now is a good time to contemplate how work-based public assistance and child welfare services can best be coordinated, or even integrated, so as to maximize the opportunities for low-income parents and children to thrive. Failure to explicitly plan for this relationship is foolhardy in light of what such a laissez-faire attitude could mean for children and families in the foster care system.

Consideration of two closely related visions of how the child welfare system could function in the new era illustrates the perils of poorly informed thinking about the future of foster care. One vision paints the child welfare system as a sort of benign, last "safety net" for poor families. In this scenario, if parents cannot cope with the new demands imposed by welfare reform and end up unable to house, feed, or otherwise care for their children, foster care will always be there as a last resort. Unfortunately, this view does not take into account that many parents, regardless of their economic circumstances, will not choose to give up their children. Only coercive intervention of some sort is likely to protect the children in such families from the consequences of extreme poverty.

Moreover, advocates of this view have yet to provide, or even suggest, a realistic plan for where to house any significant number of children removed from the care of their families for reasons of poverty. We have already pointed out the shortage of foster homes and related factors that could make this shortage worse. Aside from its questionable relevance for children and youths needing out-of-home care today, a "return to the orphanage" is unlikely to have much appeal to state legislatures or county governments, especially given the high cost of such out-of-home care. It is telling, and troubling, that orphanage advocates have now begun to attack community care licensing and child labor laws as unnecessary bureaucratic obstacles to implementing economical group care (McKenzie, 1998). Of course, child advocates will continue to oppose large-scale expansion of institutional care, given the magnitude of evidence generated over the years pointing to the negative developmental consequences of long-term institutional care for children, particularly younger children. For example, in their examination of research on the long-term effects of placement in out-of-home care, McDonald, Allen, Westerfelt, and Piliavin (1996, p. 140) observe that "most of the findings are consistent with practice and practice knowledge supporting the use of foster family placement over group or institutional placement."

Another vision of a post-welfare-reform child welfare system seems even more sinister. The rhetoric of some state and local welfare program managers suggests that they intend to use the child welfare system as a sort of inquisition against bad parents (i.e., those who appear not to be able to hold down a family-supporting job). From this perspective, the mere fact that a parent is denied financial assistance due to failure to comply with work program requirements constitutes de facto evidence of child maltreatment and warrants child protective services investigation. Anecdotal evidence also indicates that some child welfare jurisdictions are planning to treat compliance problems in workfare programs as triggers for intervention by child protective services. Ironically, this view does explicitly call for coordination of public assistance and child welfare services programs. It also recognizes that some parents in dire economic circumstances will try to care for their children even when they can no longer safely do so. Nevertheless, if child welfare agencies uncritically acquiesce in removing children from homes rendered unsafe mainly for reasons of poverty, they will have largely abandoned the strengths-based, family-centered perspective that child and family advocates have fought so long to bring into child welfare agencies (Maluccio, Pine, & Warsh, 1994; Pelton, 1989).

There is an alternative view of how work-based public assistance programs and child welfare services can be made to complement each other. In this view, welfare reform serves as an impetus to create a comprehensive, integrated system of supports for families, particularly low-income families. Managers of public assistance programs recognize that as caseloads have declined, an increasing proportion of the remaining parents face major obstacles to successful participation in the labor force. Some of the most formidable include parental substance abuse, domestic violence, mental illness, problems associated with parenting children with physical, cognitive, and behavioral disabilities, and the inability to obtain adequate and affordable child care. Interestingly, most of the families that ultimately have children placed in foster care face one or more of these challenges, and historically the overwhelming majority of these families are either public assistance recipients or the working poor.

If welfare reform is to be successful, program managers will need to find ways to help parents build upon their strengths while dealing with the challenges mentioned above. If efforts to move public assistance recipients successfully into the work force ultimately fail due to a lack of attention to these challenges, there will undoubtedly be unwanted and costly consequences for the foster care system. Efforts to provide a comprehensive web of community-based family support services have been gaining ground in recent years and are supported, at least in principle, by federal policy. Inadequate coordination with economic assistance programs is an important missing link in these efforts. Work-based welfare reform should be nested within an overall effort to provide working families with what they need to support themselves and parent their children, including a living wage, quality child care, health care, and social services when appropriate. If child and family advocates are able to turn welfare reform to this purpose, then Aid to Families with Dependent Children will truly have been rendered an unhappy memory. If not, then the foster care system may take on a much larger role in raising America's children.

Rationalization and Professionalization of Child Welfare Services

The "age of accountability" has come late to the foster care system. While other service realms have seen rapid growth in the development of outcome-focused management strategies and methods of tracking improvement in service provision, child welfare services are still primarily provided according to "practice wisdom" that has been subject to relatively little empirical verification over the years. Throughout the history of child welfare, policy choices and preferred programs have been determined primarily "by prevailing values and biases more than validated theories and empirically-based knowledge" (Maluccio and Whittaker, 1997, pp. 5–6). The next decade, however, is likely to see, and arguably should see, an increasing rationalization and professionalization of foster care. This process is being driven, and will continue to be driven, by a number of factors that are described below.

234

THE DEVELOPMENT OF INCREASINGLY SOPHISTICATED
MANAGEMENT INFORMATION SYSTEMS

The past decade has seen the proliferation of management information systems (MIS) in child welfare, particularly systems capable of tracking the movement of children through the foster care system (see chapter 2). Although many of these systems have fairly limited capacities, the inability of child welfare managers to make use of data generated by their MIS has been at least as great a barrier to using foster care data to guide policy and practice as the deficits of the systems themselves. In recent years, however, statisticians, social work scholars, and child advocacy organizations have been working with child welfare administrators to make sense of MIS data and to draw implications for policy and practice (Barth, Courtney, Berrick, & Albert, 1994; Goerge et al., 1995; Petit & Curtis, 1997; Usher, Gibbs, & Wildfire, 1995).

To be sure, those responsible for the foster care system have had an interest in child and family outcomes for many years. Any perusal of the child welfare literature of the past three decades will find numerous references to what the system ought to have been achieving for its clients. However, in the absence of concrete evidence regarding the functioning of the system, it was difficult for managers to know how their services were performing. Moreover, critics of the system, including child advocates, did not have access to aggregate-level data that could confirm their observations concerning the system's failures.

As MIS data become more available, the broad outlines of children's pathways through the foster care system are becoming more apparent, and expectations for improvement of outcomes are growing. Two recent publications are particularly timely. The first, by Pecora, Seelig, Zirps, and Davis (1996), provides a coherent set of principles and guidelines as well as practical tools for conducting quality improvement and evaluation in family and children's services. The second is a report of the proceedings of the Fifth National Roundtable on Outcome Measures in Child Welfare Services sponsored by the American Humane Association (McDaniel & Alsop, 1998). The proceedings provide examples of emerging trends in child welfare outcome measurement.

In many places it is now also possible to compare child welfare jurisdictions in terms of the growth of foster care caseloads, the timing of various child exits from foster care, and the likelihood that children will return to care after being reunited with their families. Although it is far too early in the process to establish outcome benchmarks for most foster care agencies, the mere discussion of performance standards requires the kind of data only now being made available through MIS. Many Statewide Automated Child Welfare Information Systems (SACWIS) developed with the help of enhanced federal funding will include increasingly rich data on risk and safety assessment, service needs and provision, and child and family functioning. Not only will such data make it easier to hold child welfare agencies accountable for the outcomes experienced by children in foster care, but the data will also be much more useful to the child welfare workers who generate them.

Lawsuits by child advocates in federal and state courts against the failures of the child welfare system have also played a major role in system reform over the past decade, including the heightened focus on outcomes (Pear, 1996). The consent decrees and less formal agreements that have emerged from these lawsuits have, in many cases, resulted in substantial increases in resource availability, hiring of needed child welfare workers, and improved training of workers. At the same time, such legal intervention has contributed to an increased focus on measuring the outcomes of child welfare services intervention, including the creation of MIS capable of tracking outcomes over time.

MANAGED CARE

There can be no doubt that managed care will transform foster care in many ways, though the ultimate legacy of the implementation of managed care principles in foster care will not be known for quite some time. Now is a good time for interested parties to contemplate ways in which managed care can benefit children and families who come into contact with the foster care system, and potential pitfalls that should be avoided along the way. Although a detailed examination of managed care and child welfare services is beyond the scope of this discussion and has been taken up elsewhere (e.g., Drissel & Brach, undated; Emenhiser, Barker, & DeWoody, 1995; Feild, 1996), certain issues are worthy of mention.

The outcome-focused management information systems that will be developed by managed care companies over the next decade should greatly increase our knowledge of some crucial foster care processes and outcomes. For example, better assessment data will be needed at every major transition point in out-of-home care (e.g., initial risk and safety assessment, level-of-care assessment for children entering care, returning children home, and case closing) in order for public child welfare authorities to draft and monitor managed care contracts. Meaningful and cost-effective contracts between public agencies and private managed care entities will also require a much greater knowledge of the relationship between family and child needs, service provision, and outcomes than the field currently has at its disposal.

Some areas of child welfare practice that have been subject to relatively little systematic empirical investigation over the years might be subject to considerable attention under managed care. For example, managed care could lead over the next few years to a much greater scrutiny of the proper role of group care in the overall continuum of care. This will occur simply because group care accounts for a large proportion of total child welfare expenditures in most states (R. Geen, Urban Institute, personal communication, February 1998), and managed care entities will therefore seek to realize cost savings by minimizing the use of group care and developing community-based alternatives. Similarly, public agencies are already contemplating how to write managed care contracts that will hold providers accountable for postdischarge outcomes of children returned home to their families. This should encourage the thoughtful development and evaluation of after-care services.

At the same time, however, variations of the many horror stories associated with managed health care will no doubt be heard with respect to managed foster care. In particular, the federal welfare reform law, in making federal Title IV-E funding available to for-profit providers of institutional care, raises troubling issues in the context of managed care. For-profit managed care entities could reap a windfall, at least in the short term, by moving into the multibillion-dollar group care business and extracting "cost savings" at the expense of children in care and their families. Public child welfare administrators may look like lambs going to the slaughter in negotiations with large for-profit managed care entities, given the almost nonexistent relationship between performance and funding that has heretofore been typical of child welfare services and the consequent inexperience of public child welfare authorities in managing performance-based contracts. Moreover, given the sordid history of corruption in government contracting with for-profit entities in other areas (e.g., national defense), public officials will be wise to think carefully about the implications of opening up the foster care system to the profit motive.

The almost total lack of attention by many managed care advocates to the proper qualifications and training of child welfare workers is also troubling. In some discussions of the promise of managed care, there appears to be an unspoken assumption, if not promise, that the assessment tools and service protocols typical of managed care will render professional judgment unnecessary. This may be an important part of the cost-saving allure of managed care. Child welfare services is already an area that has seen more than its share of de-professionalization, and child welfare workers have little empirical support for the superiority of their work to that of paraprofessionals. This makes child welfare workers particularly vulnerable to the power of managed care to undermine professional standards. It would be a shame if managed care ended up lowering the qualifications of child welfare workers precisely at a time when many large public child welfare jurisdictions are in a state of crisis, court orders are calling for better training of workers, and the federal government is increasing child welfare training funds.

Last but certainly not least, those interested in the future of foster care must remember that the tension that inevitably arises in child welfare practice between child protection and family preservation will not magically be resolved by managed care. The fact remains that a radical focus on child protection will result in an increase in the demand for foster care. Similarly, pushing the envelope with respect to family preservation inevitably runs the risk of exposing children to further maltreatment at the hands of their parents. The balance that must be struck in child welfare practice between these sometimes competing goals should reflect *community and professional values* regarding their relative importance. In other words, this should ultimately be a political decision, rather than a business decision. In the absence of careful thought by public officials and child welfare administrators about which child welfare services outcomes reflect the public will and how they should be measured, managed care could lead to a foster care system driven largely by an emphasis on saving money.

GROWING RECOGNITION OF THE SPECIAL NEEDS
OF CHILDREN IN FOSTER CARE

As our coauthors have pointed out in some detail (chapters 8 and 9), a substantial and arguably growing proportion of the foster care population has extensive health and mental health problems. Current evidence indicates that a child entering foster care more likely than not exhibits at least one significant health or mental health problem (see, for example, Schneiderman, Connors, Fribourg, & Gonzales, 1998; Simms & Halfon, 1994). This population requires both more timely and comprehensive assessment of their needs and more comprehensive services than are currently available. Nevertheless, the studies that have identified these problems appear to have been largely neglected by many foster care agencies. As MIS improve the capacity of the system to keep track of these children, it may become more common to pay attention to their needs. Another group of foster children with special needs are those affected, or whose parents are affected, by HIV/AIDS (see, for example, Anderson, Ryan, Taylor-Brown, & White-Gray, 1998; Merkel-Holguin, 1996). Agencies will increasingly be faced with the need to provide specialized foster care services for these children and their families.

The recognition of the special needs of foster children also supports an argument for increasing the "professionalization" of foster care. This should take the form of increased access of foster children to professional health, mental health, and substance abuse treatment services either provided by child welfare agencies or through arrangements with other service systems. In addition, the foster care system itself must be professionalized through better training for child welfare workers and foster care providers (both kin and non-kin) in order to adequately meet the unique challenges of children in care. As has already been mentioned, an added impetus for enhancing the role of nonrelative foster parents comes from the need to increase financial incentives for adults to become foster parents. The rapid growth of treatment foster care in recent years (Hudson, Nutter, & Galaway, 1994; Meadowcroft & Trout, 1990; Meadowcroft, Thomlison, & Chamberlain, 1994) may largely reflect the need to better reimburse, train, and support foster parents, given the nature of the children in foster care today. Professionalization of family foster care may be the only real hope for the field to realize the ideal of regarding foster parents as the crucial element in a treatment team approach to caring for abused and neglected children in out-of-home care.

In summary, the next few decades should see a rapid growth in knowledge of the processes and outcomes of the foster care system. This *should* lead to an improvement in foster care and a professionalization of child welfare practice in general, rather than to an undermining of basic practice standards and a managed care "race to the bottom" in the care of foster children.

Conclusion

Foster care is likely to be around as long as society sees fit to provide homes for children whose families are unable or should not be allowed to do so. The next century will see vast changes in the social context of the foster care system. Policymakers, administrators, scholars, and advocates interested in the foster care system will do well to monitor these changes in order to maximize the possibility that the families and children involved with it benefit, rather than suffer, from the impact of societal and institutional changes on the system. At the same time, interested parties must take an active role in ensuring that the rationalization of foster care that will almost certainly take place over the next few decades results in better services and outcomes for children and families.

References

Anderson, G., Ryan, C., Taylor-Brown, S., & White-Gray, M. (Eds.) (1998, March/April). HIV/AIDS and children, youths, and families: Lessons learned [Special issue]. *Child Welfare, 77.*

Bachrach, C. A., London, K. A., & Maza, P. L. (1991). On the path to adoption: Adoption seeking in the United States, 1988. *Journal of Marriage and the Family, 53,* 705–18.

Barth, R. P., Courtney, M. E., Berrick, J. D., & Albert, V. (1994). *From child abuse to permanency planning: Child welfare services, pathways, and placements.* New York: Aldine de Gruyter.

Brown, A. W., & Bailey-Etta, B. (1997). An out-of-home care system in crisis: Implications for African American children in the foster care system. *Child Welfare, 76,* 65–83.

Cohen, N. A. (Ed.) (1992). *Child welfare: A multicultural focus.* Boston: Allyn & Bacon.

Courtney, M. E., Barth, R. P., Berrick, J. D., Brooks, D., Needell, B., & Park, L. (1996). Race and child welfare services: Past research and future directions. *Child Welfare, 76,* 99–137.

Day, J. C. (1996). *Population projections of the United States by age, sex, race, and Hispanic origin: 1995 to 2050* (U.S. Bureau of the Census, Current Population Reports, P25–1130). Washington DC: U.S. Government Printing Office.

Drissel, A. B., & Brach, C. (Eds.). (undated). *Managed care and children and family services.* Baltimore: Annie E. Casey Foundation.

Emenhiser, R. B., Barker, R., & DeWoody, M. (1995). *Managed care: An agency guide to surviving and thriving.* Washington DC: Child Welfare League of America.

Feild, T. (1996). Managed care and child welfare: Will it work? *Public Welfare, 54,* 4–10.

Goerge, R. M., Wulczyn, F. H., & Harden, A. W. (1995). *Foster care dynamics, 1983–1993: California, Illinois, Michigan, New York, and Texas: An update from the Multistate Foster Care Data Archive.* Chicago: University of Chicago, Chapin Hall Center for Children.

Hudson, J., Nutter, R. W., & Galaway, B. (1994). Treatment foster family care: Development and current status. *Community Alternatives: International Journal of Family Care, 6,* 1–24.

Iglehart, A. P., & Becerra, R. M. (1995). *Social services in the ethnic community.* Boston: Allyn & Bacon.

Lindsey, D. (1994). *The welfare of children.* New York: Oxford University Press.

MacKenzie, J. K. (1993). Adoption of children with special needs. *Future of Children, 3*(1), 62–76.

Maluccio, A. N., Pine, B. A., & Warsh, R. (1994). Protecting children by preserving their families. *Children and Youth Services Review, 16,* 295–307.

Maluccio, A. N., & Whittaker, J. K. (1997). Learning from the "family preservation" initiative. *Children and Youth Services Review, 19,* 5–16.

McDaniel, N. C., & Alsop, R. (1998). *Fifth National Roundtable on Outcomes Measures in Child Welfare Services: Summary of proceedings.* Englewood CO: American Humane Association.

McDonald, T. P., Allen, R. I., Westerfelt, A., & Piliavin, I. (1996). *Assessing the long-term effects of foster care: A research synthesis.* Washington DC: Child Welfare League of America.

McKenzie, R. B. (Ed.). (1998). *Rethinking orphanages for the 21st century.* Thousand Oaks CA: Sage.

Meadowcroft, P., Thomlison, B., & Chamberlain, P. (1994). Treatment foster care services: A research agenda for child welfare. *Child Welfare, 73,* 565–582.

Meadowcroft, P., & Trout, B. A. (Eds.). (1990). *Troubled youth in treatment homes: A handbook of therapeutic foster care.* Washington DC: Child Welfare League of America.

Meezan, W. J., & Shireman, J. S. (1985). *Care and commitment: Foster parent adoption decisions.* Albany: State University of New York Press.

Merkel-Holguin, L. (1996). *Children who lose their parents to HIV/AIDS: Agency guidelines for adoptive and kinship placement*. Washington DC: Child Welfare League of America.

Pasztor, E. M. (1989). *The influence of foster parent ownership of permanency planning tasks on role retention and permanent placements*. Doctoral dissertation, Catholic University of America, National Catholic School of Social Service, Washington DC.

Pear, R. (1996, 17 March). Many states fail to meet mandates on child welfare. *New York Times*, pp. 1, 14.

Pecora, P. J., Seelig, W. R., Zirps, F. A., & Davis, S. M. (1996). *Quality improvement and evaluation in child and family services: Managing into the next century*. Washington DC: Child Welfare League of America.

Pelton, L. H. (1989). *For reasons of poverty: A critical analysis of the public child welfare system in the United States*. New York: Praeger.

Petit, M. R., & Curtis, P. A. (1997). *Child abuse and neglect: A look at the states: The CWLA stat book*. Washington DC: Child Welfare League of America.

Pinderhughes, E. (1997). Developing diversity competence in child welfare and permanency planning. In G. W. Anderson, A. S. Ryan, & B. R. Leashore (Eds.), *The challenge of permanency planning in a multicultural society* (pp. 19–38). New York: Haworth Press.

Rosenthal, J. A., & Groze, V. K. (1994). A longitudinal study of special-needs adoptive families. *Child Welfare, 73*, 689–706.

Scannapieco, M., Hegar, R. L., & McAlpine, C. (1997). Kinship care and foster care: A comparison of characteristics and outcomes. *Families in Society: Journal of Contemporary Human Services, 78*, 480–488.

Schneiderman, M., Connors, M. M., Fribourg, L. G., & Gonzales, M. (1998). Mental health services for children in out-of-home care. *Child Welfare, 77*, 5–27.

Simms, M. D., & Halfon, N. (1994). The health care needs of children in foster care: A research agenda. *Child Welfare, 73*, 505–524.

Usher, C. L., Gibbs, D. A., & Wildfire, J. B. (1995). A framework for planning, implementing and evaluating child welfare reforms. *Child Welfare, 74*, 859–876.

Wolins, M., & Piliavin, I. (1964). *Institution or foster family: A century of debate*. New York: Child Welfare League of America.

Contributors

Jill Duerr Berrick, Ph.D., is director, Center for Social Services Research, and associate adjunct professor at the School of Social Welfare, University of California, Berkeley. She currently teaches social policy and research and conducts research on various topics concerning poor children and families. She has authored or coauthored seven books on child abuse, foster care, and family poverty and has written extensively for academic journals. Her most recent book, *The Tender Years*, was published by Oxford University Press.

Joaquin Borrego Jr. is a graduate student in the doctoral (Ph.D.) program in clinical psychology at the University of Nevada. His research interests include ethnic minority issues in clinical psychology and examining physically abusive parent-child relationships. He is especially interested in examining the role culture plays in different parenting and potentially physically abusive behaviors among ethnic minority groups. He is also interested in the generalizability and applicability of empirical treatments with Spanish-speaking populations.

Raymond Collins, Ph.D., is president of Collins Management Consulting, Inc., in Vienna, Virginia. He has been involved in the Adoption and Foster Care Analysis and Reporting System (AFCARS) from its inception as executive secretary of the Advisory Committee on Adoption and Foster Care Information. In addition to his involvement with AFCARS, he administers the National Child Care Information Center and the AmeriCorps Early Childhood Technical Assistance Center.

Mark E. Courtney, D.S.W., is assistant professor in the School of Social Work and an affiliate of the Institute for Research on Poverty at the University of Wisconsin–Madison. His research has focused on the factors associated with various pathways of children through the child welfare system. He serves as a consultant on child welfare services programs to state and local governments and private child welfare agencies.

Mary C. Curran, M.S.W., is currently a legal advocate for the Northwest Immigrant Rights Project in Seattle, Washington. She provides legal advocacy to battered immigrant women and their children who are self-petitioning under the Violence Against Women Act or requesting a waiver of the joint filing requirement. She formerly coordinated the support group and child care program for the Domestic Abuse Women's Network and continues to facilitate support groups for survivors of domestic violence.

Patrick A. Curtis, Ph.D., is director of research, Child Welfare League of America, Washington DC. He is principal investigator for a longitudinal, multisite study of residential group care, group homes, and therapeutic foster care. His most recent publications are "The Beginnings of Child Welfare Research in the United States" in *Child and Adolescent Social Work* (in press) and *Child Abuse and Neglect, A View from the States: The CWLA Stat Book* with Michael Petit (1997).

Grady Dale Jr., Ed.D., is the former program director of the Mental Health Screening for children entering out-of-home placement/foster care in Baltimore, Maryland. A clinical and consulting psychologist in private practice, he has concentrated much of his professional and personal time and effort on local, regional, and national advocacy programs for children. As president of the American Institute for Urban Psychological Studies, he has achieved local and regional recognition as an advocate for neglected and abused children.

Diane DePanfilis, M.S.W., Ph.D., is assistant professor at the University of Maryland School of Social Work, where she specializes in teaching child welfare practice and research courses. As president of the American Professional Society on the Abuse of Children, she has achieved national recognition as a child welfare advocate. Currently, she is principal investigator for an NCCAN-funded intervention study on child neglect.

Ann F. Garland, Ph.D., is assistant professor of psychiatry, University of California, San Diego, and the scientific coordinator for the NIMH-funded Center for Research on Child and Adolescent Mental Health Services at Children's Hospital and Health Center, San Diego, California. She is the author of numerous publications, and her research interests include factors that predict the need, use, and outcomes of mental health services for high-risk youth and their families.

Robert M. Goerge, Ph.D., is associate director of the Chapin Hall Center for Children at the University of Chicago. He also codirects the National Foster Care Data Archive funded by the Children's Bureau at the Department of Health and Human Services and leads an NIMH-funded project on the disabilities of foster children. His numerous scholarly publications center on the experiences of children in the child welfare system.

Allen Harden, M.A., is senior research associate at the Chapin Hall Center for Children at the University of Chicago, where his responsibilities include management of the Multistate Foster Care Data Archive project. He is also a primary analyst in Chapin Hall's Integrated Database effort that links administrative records on children in the Illinois child welfare system.

Joshua C. Kendall, M.A., is a freelance writer and editor based in Baltimore. He has published numerous articles and book chapters on subjects ranging from child abuse to contemporary literature. His current work focuses on the relationship between childhood trauma and creativity. He serves as book review editor for *Treating Abuse Today*.

John Landsverk, Ph.D., is currently director of research for the Center for Child Protection at the Children's Hospital in San Diego. He is also professor of social work at San Diego State University and director of the Center for Research on Child and Adolescent Mental Health Services at Children's Hospital, which is funded by NIMH. His current research includes studies of mental health service use by children in foster care and studies on the effectiveness of early intervention programs for families at risk for child abuse and neglect.

Anthony N. Maluccio, D.S.W., is professor of social work at Boston College. A frequent consultant to child welfare agencies and schools of social work, he has published a series of studies and books in the area of child and family welfare. His research has focused on adoption, permanency planning for children and youth, family reunification of children in out-of-home care, family preservation, and preparation for adolescents for life after foster care.

Barbara Needell, M.S.W., Ph.D., is a researcher at the Child Welfare Research Center, University of California, Berkeley. She is coauthor of several articles, chapters, and a curriculum on kinship care as well as *The Tender Years* (Oxford University Press, 1998). As project director of the Performance Indicators for Child Welfare Services in California project and senior research analyst for the California Children's Services Archive, she has worked extensively with statewide administrative data.

Peter J. Pecora, Ph.D., is manager of research, Casey Family Program, and associate professor of social work, University of Washington. The author of a number of books and articles on child welfare, he serves on the Quality Improvement and Evaluation Committee of the National Research Council in Child Welfare and is cochair of the Center for Mental Health Services Outcomes Roundtable for Children and Adolescents.

Janet Stein Schultz, M.A., R.N., C.P.N.P., is a pediatric nurse practitioner who has cared for at-risk children and their families for over 20 years. As a pediatric clinician, she has served as a consultant to state and federal child health agencies on practice and policy issues affecting at-risk children and youth. Most recently she was the program manager and part-time clinician for the Health Clinic, an agency serving children entering foster care in Baltimore, Maryland.

Anthony J. Urquiza, Ph.D., is assistant professor of psychology and a child psychologist at the Child Protection Center, Department of Pediatrics, University of California Medical Center, Davis. His primary clinical and research interests center on family violence, with specific focus on ethnic minorities, abused and neglected children in foster care, and the clinical assessment of maltreated children. He is the author of a treatment manual for sexually abused children, published by the National Center on Child Abuse and Neglect, and a member of the Board of Directors of the American Professional Society on the Abuse of Children.

Jane Wu, M.S.W., has been a program manager for the Washington State Division of Children and Family Services for eight years. Prior to that, she was a community educator, mental health advocate, and child and family therapist. Although her program management spans a broad spectrum of services ranging from mental health to child welfare, cultural diversity has been the consistent thread throughout her professional career.

Fred Wulczyn, Ph.D., is director of managed care, Division of Family and Children's Services, New York State Department of Social Services. He also teaches at the Columbia University School of Social Work. In addition, he is codirector of the National Foster Care Data Archive funded by the Children's Bureau at the Department of Health and Human Services.

Susan Zuravin, M.S.W., Ph.D., is associate professor of social work at the University of Maryland at Baltimore. She has authored or coauthored papers on topics such as kinship care, child maltreatment by family foster care providers, and factors that drive foster care decision making by child welfare professionals. At present, she is studying the functioning of young adults who spent time in foster care as children.

Author Index

247

Subject Index

Page numbers set in italics refer to figures or tables.

Achenbach Child Behavior Checklist (CBCL), 197, 86, 194; Parent Report Form, 195–196

Administration for Children and Families (ACF), 50

admissions and discharges, effect on caseloads, 36, 36–37

Adoption and Foster Care Analysis and Reporting System (AFCARS), 45; benefits and limitations of, 55–56; data made available by, 50–55; description and purpose of, 45–46; genesis of, 47–48; policy and program implications of, 56; state options for using, 49

Adoption and Safe Families Act (1997), ix–x, 229, 231

Adoption Assistance and Child Welfare Act (1980), 5, 133

Adoptions 2000 program, 231

adoption strategy, 12–13

Advisory Committee on Adoption and Foster Care, 47–48

African American children: duration in care, 39; entry rates, 34–35, 35; mental health services use by, 206; percentage in foster care, 54, 136–138; in poverty, 7–8. See also ethnic/racial minority children

age: duration in care and, 39–40; entry into care and, 32–34, 33, 34, 136; at time of discharge, 55

Aid to Families with Dependent Children (AFDC): federal spending on, AFDC vs. Title IV-E, 130, 130–131, 131, 154, 155; foster care program (Title IV-E) of, 129–132, 133

Alaskan native children in foster care, 54

alcohol and other drugs: costs associated with, 136; foster care crisis and, 8–9

Aldgate, Stein, and Carey study, youth perspectives in, 107–108

American Academy of Pediatrics, Committee on Early Childhood, Adoption, and Dependent Care, 184

American Humane Association, 235

American Indian children in foster care, 54

American Psychological Association, 1

American Public Welfare Association, 17, 23, 47, 132

Asian children in foster care, 54

Baltimore: foster care placement system in, 183, 184; medical screening model in, 187, 188; mental health screening model in, 184–186, 185, 186

Baltimore City Department of Social Services' Division of Child Protective Services, 65

Barth and Berry literature review: limitations of, 116–117; studies of child satis-

In the Child, Youth, and Family Services series

The Foster Care Crisis: Translating Research into Policy and Practice
Edited by Patrick A. Curtis, Grady Dale Jr., and Joshua C. Kendall
Foreword by Senator John D. Rockefeller IV

Big World, Small Screen: The Role of Television in American Society
By Aletha C. Huston, Edward Donnerstein, Halford Fairchild,
Norma D. Feshbach, Phyllis A. Katz, John P. Murray, Eli A. Rubinstein,
Brian L. Wilcox, and Diana M. Zuckerman

Health Issues for Minority Adolescents
Edited by Marjorie Kagawa-Singer, Phyllis A. Katz,
Dalmas A. Taylor, and Judith Vanderryn

Home-Based Services for Troubled Children
Edited by Ira M. Schwartz and Philip AuClaire

Preventing Child Sexual Abuse: Sharing the Responsibility
By Sandy K. Wurtele and Cindy L. Miller-Perrin